SPIRIT POSSESSION, THEOLOGY, AND IDENTITY: A PACIFIC EXPLORATION

Elaine M Wainwright, General Editor
with Philip Culbertson and Susan Smith

2010

An imprint of the ATF Ltd
P O Box 504
Hindmarsh
SA 5007
ABN 90 116 359 963
www.atfpress.com

TABLE OF CONTENTS

SPIRITS THROUGH THE LENS OF THEOLOGY AND HISTORY

Introduction

Elaine M Wainwright

Spirit possession is a way of viewing or describing the world. It finds different expressions in different ages. It is evident in a variety of ways in a wide range of cultures—in their religious stories and secular worldviews, in the arts and in people's lives. For many in the contemporary world, the notion of spirit possession would be seen as anachronistic, belonging to a previous era in which belief in a spirit world helped to explain phenomena which now can be given a more scientific explanation, whether that be medical, psychological, sociological, or anthropological. For others, however, the presence of and possession by spirits remains a significant aspect of their worldview and/or of religious belief.

This has been evident recently in New Zealand society. A young filmmaker in 2000 prepared a documentary named *The Truth about Demons* that explores quite bizarre phenomena that occur in the life of a young man who is researching the world of demons or evil spirits. In 2001, a man was convicted of the manslaughter of a young Korean woman who died as a result of being exorcised of evil or demonic spirits. As recently as 2007, a young Māori woman was drowned in a ritual designed to control a spirit that was believed to have possessed her. Also, New Zealand society is significantly impacted by Māori and Pacific cultures in which the spirit world occupies a significant place. It is not surprising, therefore, that the George Sainsbury Foundation would be set up by George Sainsbury on 10 March, 1989, 'for research into and treatment of spirit possession as it relates to mental illness for the benefit of those persons suffering from such sickness.' We do not know what experiences led to the family's desire for such research. In 2006, however, Anthony Molloy QC, a legal representative for the Foundation, approached the School of Theology at the University of Auckland, asking if the School could conduct research into spirit possession.

Approaches to the study of spirit possession are many and varied. Emma Cohen, in her book *The Mind Possessed: The Cognition of Spirit Possession in an Afro-Brazilian Religious Tradition,* combines careful ethnographic study with theory in contemporary psychology and religious studies.[1] The significance of location for such studies and their interdisciplinary character is similarly demonstrated by

1. Emma Cohen, *The Mind Possessed: The Cognition of Spirit Possession in an Afro-Brazilian Religious Tradition* (New York: Oxford University Press, 2007).

Susan J Rasmussen in *Spirit Possession and Personhood among the Kel Ewey Tuareg*.[2] The research project undertaken by the School of Theology in response to the grant of funds from the George Sainsbury Foundation likewise gives particular attention to context. It is undertaken in Aotearoa New Zealand for the 'benefit of those suffering' from spirit possession in this particular context.

The research project's grounding in experience is indicative of the contextual approach to theology that characterises the School of Theology in the University of Auckland. Initially, it was hoped that this project could be undertaken as an exercise in contextual theology. While this was not possible, the volume does provide some of the raw materials toward such theologising in its structuring and extensive conclusion. The conclusion is not a theology per se but it highlights some of the directions opened up by the research that could contribute to ongoing theological reflection on issues relating to spirit possession. Its authors, Philip Culbertson and Susan Smith, give the sort of description of each essay that one would normally find in an Introduction. I will not repeat those descriptions but simply locate each contribution within the structure of a possible contextual theology.

The first four essays, by Henare Tate, Philip Culbertson and Mary Caygill, Ann Nolan, and Winston Halapua, open some small windows onto aspects of spirit possession in New Zealand and its wider context of Oceania. Two essays draw on the experience of the researchers,

2. Susan J Rasmussen, *Spirit Possession and Personhood among the Kel Ewey Tuareg* (Cambridge: Cambridge University Press, 2006).

namely that of 'Pa' Tate, a Māori Roman Catholic priest who has spent a lifetime doing ministry among his people, and Winston Halapua, a Tongan Anglican priest and bishop who reflects on his own encounter with the spirit world in his native Tonga. Caygill and Culbertson likewise explore located experience, though not their own, but rather, the experiences of a limited number of Samoan and Tongan adults now living in New Zealand. Ann Nolan sheds light on spirit possession in the areas of psychiatry and the health professions, especially mental health, by way of a study of literature, both historical and contemporary, that has had an impact on 'the treatment of spirit possession as it relates to mental illness', in the language of the George Sainsbury Foundation.

Initial analysis of the experience of spirit possession in the context of Aotearoa New Zealand and Oceania in the four opening articles is followed by four articles that engage with aspects of the theological tradition. Keith Stuart, Alice Sinnott, and Elaine Wainwright examine representative texts within the biblical tradition, which is always a significant dialogue partner in doing theology. Stuart and Wainwright both demonstrate that the very language of spirits, especially evil spirits and possession, emerges late in the biblical period. Social scientific and literary approaches to the Book of Tobit and to the story of the Gerasene demoniac in the Gospel of Mark demonstrate the interdisciplinary nature of contemporary biblical studies and the ways it can contribute to the interdisciplinary study of spirit possession within religious studies and the social sciences. Alice Sinnott analyses the way in which the Book of Tobit features in Salley Vickers' novel

Miss Garnet's Angel and the contribution that this contemporary literary work can make to the doing of theology as a response to the articulated experience of spirit possession.

Just as Sinnott's study demonstrated that possession may not necessarily be by an evil spirit, Helen Bergin engages with the Christian tradition of a spirit that is named 'holy', or the Holy Spirit. In keeping with the Foundation's yearning toward what will be of benefit to those suffering from possession of a spirit that is debilitating or causing illness, or what will bring well-being for them, Bergin demonstrates how the Christian tradition of the Holy Spirit is associated with freedom, power, and wholeness. These aspects together with the biblical tradition of casting out of evil spirits provide foundations for developing a theology of well-being in contexts of spirit possession. The Conclusion raises important questions as to how the theological tradition can be brought into dialogue with other disciplines in the social sciences and mental health.

Manifestations named as spirit possession and deliverance ministries emerge in different ways in different historical periods and Christian denominations as well as in other religious traditions. The final two essays in this limited project examine such manifestations and ministries. Laurie Guy, as a historian, opens one small window onto spirit possession and exorcism within New Zealand in the Assembly of God church between 1970 and 1989. Susan Smith takes her readers on a more global journey, introducing them to the challenge being brought to First World 'liberal Christians' by the emerging voices and experiences of indigenous churches in which spirit possession and deliverance are significant phenomena. A number of strands of this volume come together in this essay in which Smith demonstrates the importance of a contextualised and inculturated, as well as an ecumenical, theology if the churches are going to be able to respond to spirit possession in today's world in a way that leads to healing.

This volume represents the first stage of research into spirit possession in the context of Aotearoa New Zealand under the auspices of the George Sainsbury Foundation. Undertaken, as it has been, by staff from the School of Theology at the University of Auckland and their former research students, it is limited to the theological disciplines and to the New Zealand context. Many essays have made clear, however, that New Zealand cannot be understood in isolation from its more immediate context of Oceania and its membership in the global community. It has also become evident that theology is informed by other disciplines, just as it can inform other research. A more interdisciplinary study undertaken with a body of international scholars and across other disciplines would further enhance what has been initiated in this volume. It is proposed, therefore, to extend the research requested under the auspices of the George Sainsbury Foundation to include such interdisciplinary and international studies. This second phase will, it is hoped, be accompanied by an International Conference in Auckland that would bring such studies to the New Zealand context. This is both the hope and dream that this present set of essays has evoked for its writers and we trust for you, its readers.

A Māori Perspective on Spirit Possession

Henare Tate

In this essay, I will draw on my personal experience over a period of forty years as a Catholic Māori priest, beginning by sharing some thoughts on the role of people involved in *mahi whakaora* (healing work). Traditional healers in Māori society were the *tohunga* (skilled person, priest, or wizard). In general, *tohunga* were skilled people involved in various spheres of activity. Here, I am speaking of them with reference to healing, and specifically to spiritual healing. More than the average person, the *tohunga* had specific knowledge concerning *karakia* (prayers, chants), *ritenga* (rituals), and *rongoā* (medicine) for healing. He or she may also have had the gift of *matakite* (foresight, vision) by which they could recognise in affected people the cause of the *mate* (illness). The gift for healing could have been hereditary; that is, it was handed down from generation to generation in particular *whānau* (family) lines.

The *tauira* (aspirants) would have had to learn the *karakia, ritenga,* and *rongoā*. This they would do by sitting at the feet of other practising *tohunga* and by being involved in some of the rituals conducted by them. Through their links with acknowledged *tohunga,* the *tauira* would receive recognition from the *whānau*. However, to be fully acknowledged and approved, they would need to achieve the healing of affected people.

These days, there are some people—men and women—who would be referred to as *tohunga* in the field of healing, though some may not be comfortable with the name. Their gift for healing may also have been handed down from *mātua* (parents) or from *tūpuna* (ancestors). It may have been given to them and fostered by *kaumātua* (male elders) or *kuia* (female elders) who saw in them the inclination to be involved in *mahi whakaora*. I know of one Māori woman who received the training from a *kuia* from outside of the *whānau*. Whoever the source, the *tauira* would have been trained under the close scrutiny of an older and experienced *tohunga* or *kaiako* (teacher). On the passing of the *tohunga* or *kaiako,* the *tauira* would assume the *tūranga* (role) of their *kaiako*. To receive the approval and sanction of their *whānau, hapū* (sub-tribe), and *iwi* (tribe) would require that they be effective in their *mahi whakaora*. If they are effective, their reputation soon spreads. The need for healing is always present.

I certainly do not consider myself a *tohunga,* nor do I allow anyone to refer to me as one. I have become involved with healing because I consider it is the role of the priest to come to the aid of those in need of spiritual healing. It is the role of the priest to pray for the sick. It is the role of the priest to call upon *te mana o te Atua* (the power of God) to assist people in their spiritual needs. Thus, for me, the commissioning and empowerment to heal come from the sacrament of ordination, with the support of the community and *whānau*. Unlike the traditional *tohunga* with pre-Christian *karakia* and *ritenga*, the prayers and rituals I and many others use are Christian-based. Quite often I have recourse to the anointing of the sick. The formulation of some *karakia* has developed by being mindful of concepts and phrases expressed by *kaumātua* and *kuia* over the years.

I have worked in city, town, and country parishes. During this time I have been called on by their *whānau* to minister to those adversely affected by spirit possession.

A story: In 2007, I was phoned by a desperate young Māori woman who wanted a priest to call at their place and pray over two young people who seemed to be possessed. Having known the *tūpuna* and *mātua* of the young woman, it was not *tika* (right, proper) to decline. Conscious of her anxiety, I asked if she had made contact with a *kaumātua* in their area of the city. She had, but when the *kaumātua* had seen the violent reactions of the young people, he was afraid. He prayed from outside the house and then left. When I arrived at the house, I was met by the young woman and other members of the *whānau*. I began the *karakia* and *uwhiuwhi* (sprinkling with holy water) over the *whenua* (land) around the house and shed. After blessings outside, we entered the house. I continued the *karakia* and the *uwhiuwhi* in the house and in each room—living room, bedrooms, bathroom, wash-house, and kitchen. As I approached the young male person sitting on the couch and began the *karakia*, he began to shake, writhe, and cry out with anguish. Two other people in the house, including the young woman who had called for help, rushed to restrain the person's flailing arms and legs, all the while praying that the evil spirit would leave him. After fifteen minutes of prayer and physical struggle, he came out of the attack and calmed down. Everyone was exhausted. Then I turned to the other affected young person, a teenage girl. She also began to shake and writhe. The *whānau* had to use some restraint on her. Again I prayed. She tried to block out the *karakia,* and she rejected the crucifix I attempted to give her. After fifteen minutes of prayer and physical restraint, the person stopped struggling, wept quietly, calmed down, and was able to engage in ordinary conversation. However, the *whānau* warned that it would last for a half hour at the most, and that one or other, or both, would have another attack.

Pono mārika (true indeed)! It happened again. Again the *whānau* struggled to restrain the two sufferers, praying, "In the name of Jesus, come out of him, you evil spirit," to which the writhing and groaning person responded, "Jesus is dead!" After some time, the household seemed at peace again, and I took my leave of the *whānau,* assuring them of my continued prayer for them, particularly for the two young people. As I departed, I felt I had not been effective in helping to free these two from the spiritual illness affecting them.

An Analysis of This Story

In seeking to understand better what lies behind my story, I will consider some approaches taken by people seeking help for a *whānau* member who may be affected by *mate wairua* (spiritual illness). I will analyse the language used in describing the *mate wairua* affecting someone. It is also important to consider the symptoms, and to identify who else can be affected, or indeed 'infected', by a family member's spiritual illness. Possible responses to situation of *mate wairua* will be examined, plus a brief analysis of the symptoms of the affected person as perceived by those responding to the request for help. I will then see if various forms of *mate wairua* can be accurately identified, before reflecting on how Māori understand a spirit world. It is also necessary to consider the possible effects on the affected persons and their *whānau*. *Karakia whakaora i te mate* (prayers of healing) and *ritenga* used warrant attention, as does the evidence that healing has occurred, and finally the place of follow-up care and supervision will be considered.

Approach for Help

What causes a concerned *whānau* member to approach a priest, minister, or *tohunga* for help when a family person appears to be suffering from a spiritual illness, and how is contact made? The initial contact is usually by phone—and in my experience, the call can come from anywhere in the country—but sometimes people simply turn up unannounced on the doorstep. In these times, more Māori are turning to the *tohunga*, priest, or minister for help. I will refer to these three groups of people collectively as 'healers'.

Calls for help come not only from the *whānau*. They may also come from friends, medical and mental health workers, or social workers, who acknowledge that they cannot provide all the help required. Increasingly, Māori mental health workers, aware that modern medical practices are not always effective in helping afflicted people, turn to more traditional Māori practices for help.

Unfortunately, in some cases, affected persons may not seek help. They will not admit that they are unwell. At times, they can be so distressed that they cannot bring themselves to seek help. I often ask if the person affected is asking for me, or is prepared to let me visit. In severe cases, it is not unknown for the affected one to decline or refuse the visit of a certain person or persons.

Language used to Describe the Affected Person

When people phone for help, they often stutter and stammer, are slow to get to the point, or are hesitant in articulating why they are calling. There are at least three reasons for this. First, they may consider themselves unable to provide a diagnosis or cause of illness; second, they may be concerned that the healer will not understand them or appreciate what is happening to their *whānau* member; and third, they are afraid of the *whakahāwea* (despising, belittling attitude and words) of the other person, and of being put down, or being told *kua pōrangi koutou katoa* (you are all mental). More positively, they may say: 'something is wrong with a member of our *whanau*', or 'the doctors don't know what is wrong. There is nothing physically wrong but we know the person is not well.'

Symptoms Presenting in the Affected Person

If people seeking help are not clear about the nature of the illness, the healer should ask: '*He aha nga tohu* (what are the symptoms)?' The *whānau* may not be able to diagnose the illness or determine whether it is *mate Māori* (Māori sickness), *poke kēhua* (haunted by a ghost), *mākutu* (accursed), drug or substance abuse, depression, mental illness, or schizophrenia. Though the above story represents a more extreme example of spiritual illness, some of its characteristics are there in less severe cases.

The healer needs some idea of the symptoms. The affected persons may say they sense a presence of someone other than *whānau*. Children may say that they see things in their room that scare them, and they are afraid to be on their own. Sometimes the affected persons will say there is physical contact from 'someone', usually a deceased person whom they know and whose touch they may experience as a pressure on their shoulders or chest. Usually this sense of the presence of someone occurs during the night, and can last for some time, causing significant distress and fear. This experience is sometimes described as 'chilling', causing the visited persons to freeze, be unable to call out or pray, or even make the sign of the Cross. *Ka mataku te tangata* (the person is afraid). It is frightening, in that people feel a force that is more powerful than their own. They even feel they could die. In other words, they experience a sense of powerlessness, diminishment, and despair.

Sadly, anyone can be affected. I have been called to some *kaumātua* and *kuia*, middle-aged people, young people, children as young as four years of age; even Pākehā people can be affected. For example, a Pākehā woman was affected by wrongful actions of her Pākehā grandfather, who had violated a Māori *wāhi tapu* (sacred or forbidden place), and had taken a *taonga* (artefact, treasured possession) without the knowledge or permission of the local Māori. The Māori partner of the Pākehā woman was from that particular *hapū*, and knew the place and people. The Pākehā woman, in her efforts to free herself, travelled far to find people who could have the issue righted. She kept prompting her Māori partner to help her address the matter and lay it to rest. She persisted until it was eventually addressed.

Normally the people whom I meet in my healing ministry are living in the urban areas of Aotearoa New Zealand, which suggests that Māori affected by spiritual illness are those most alienated from their *tūrangawaewae* (land as 'their standing place').

For some people, spirit possession may be a recurring experience. Others may not have been previously affected. Some people can be severely affected, as in our story; others are mildly affected and, in due time, will almost forget it had happened. A *kuia* came with her vivid story of being visited in the night by a *kēhua* (ghost, evil spirit). She was a woman confident in her Māori culture and strong in her faith. She was able to attend to her own recovery, particularly through her own *karakia*.

Whānau and friends of the affected persons can also be affected, especially in severe cases. They can get exhausted, physically and mentally. They are kept awake at night, and yet must go to work the next day. The affected ones cannot be left on their own, as they could cause harm to themselves and to others. Night time can be particularly bad for the *whānau*, because that is when the affected people are most vulnerable to outbursts that disturb them and the *whānau*. Therefore, *whānau* can be hesitant to get involved in attempts at healing. They are fearful because this kind of illness is in the realm of the spiritual, and therefore can be unknown and unpredictable. People are fearful of a spiritual backlash, or that even the healer can be 'infected'. Because the affected person can have such extraordinary physical strength, *whānau* can fear for their own safety and well-being.

Since the spirit affecting someone can also affect *whānau* members, potential helpers can be hesitant or reluctant to intervene. The tell-tale signs of being affected are seen in the tired and glazed look in the eyes, and an unusually quiet demeanour. These signs were recognisable in a Pākehā man in his early forties, who had not had this kind of experience before. In another case, it was also noticeable in two men who were professional Māori mental health and social workers. They admitted they were so affected that they could not continue to attend to their client.

Response for Help

Whatever the perceptions of the affected person or of the *whānau*, healers and professional people should respond to the cry for help, if not for the sake of the affected one, at least for the *whānau*. On the basis of *pono* (reality and truth), the healer needs to check out the possible causes and reality of the affliction. On the basis of *tika*, the *whānau* should be supported in their difficult situation. Their call for help needs to be taken seriously. On the basis of *aroha* (compassion) for the affected one, and the *whānau*, the healer should respond.

Symptoms Perceived by Those Called to Help

The spiritually ill person can appear to go through a personality change to the extent that the *whānau* says, 'This is not who we have known this person to be'. Some can rant and rave and growl like a dog. Sometimes, those affected *ka aue noaiho i te pō* (cry out in the night), *ka potete* (they speak as if in a delirious state). Some say they can see *kēhua*, or *he hunga mate* (a dead person). Generally, *te mate e kitea ana i nga kanohi* (the illness is seen in the eyes). Their eyes have a glazed and distant look, and may become dilated and red. In severe cases, observers may say they can see hatred in their eyes. Some can have an insolent or contemptuous look on their faces as if to say, 'Who do you think you are? What do you think you can do for me?' As we saw in our opening story, they can exhibit extreme physical strength beyond what they would otherwise show. A forty year old woman put her arms around her ninety kilogram brother and squeezed him until he fell to the floor. She unsuccessfully tried the same thing on a healer. In another case, two young people split apart the arm-rests of the chairs they were sitting on.

Affected persons can be a danger to themselves and to others, hence the need to apply some measure of physical restraint. I have also referred to their aversion to such Catholic sacramentals as holy water or the crucifix, and to prayer. I recall sprinkling holy water over one affected person who did not know this was going to happen. He jumped as if he had had an electric shock. In some cases, a suspicion about holy water means the affected people may not drink water or wash. Again, we have noted that in two or three cases, the affected people would not hold the cross. They flicked their hands as if they were holding red-hot bricks. We have already seen in our story that one person blocked her ears to drown out the prayers, while the other yelled out 'Jesus is dead'. I have also witnessed at least one case of *ruaki* (vomiting and spewing).

Identifying Various Forms of *Mate Wairua* (Spiritual Illness)

The first people to attempt diagnosis or naming of the affliction are usually *whānau* members. They have to describe what the problem is when they go in search of help. Sometimes, they will attribute strange behaviour to *mate Māori* or *poke kēhua* or *mākutu*. A second group of people who would like to know what the affliction might be before venturing forth includes the *tohunga*, priest or minister, and other healers. Sometimes a wise *tohunga* can 'see' the afflicted person, or sense the affliction, before any personal approach is made by the *whānau*. A third group are the mental health and social service workers who need to be called in to offer their particular expertise and services.

To better gauge the situation, the mental health and social workers will ask the *whānau* some initial questions, such as 'Has this happened before? Is the person involved in drugs of any kind? Has the person been under stress of late? Has there been a breakdown in marriage or other relationships?'

A particularly important question today is, 'Is the person involved in drug-taking of any kind?' The reason for this question is that the symptoms of drug-taking or drug-abuse can be similar to those of spiritual afflictions. If the afflicted person is not taking drugs, the *whānau* will immediately say so, or their response might be, 'Not as far as we know'—which may or may not be the truth. The spiritual healers will say they can help with spiritual healing, but cannot deal with the effects of chemical substance abuse. Today, unfortunately, there is a greater possibility that the person suffers from drug and substance abuse, such as 'P' or alcohol abuse, or from the effects of withdrawal.

Some people suffer from spiritual effects of emotional stress, such as the loss of a loved one, a break-down in marriage or other relationships, or from a guilty and restless conscience. Perhaps the affected person has a mental or psychiatric illness. There could be a history of mental illness with the individual or the *whānau*. Spiritual healing has little, if any, effect in a person with schizophrenia.

Whatever the diagnosis or illness, the healer should give the *whānau* the benefit of the doubt and go to them. On arrival, it is important to assess the state of the affected person in accordance with the symptoms that the *whānau* has identified.

The Māori World of Spirit Possession

We return to terms used earlier: *mate wairua, mate Māori, poke kēhua, mākutu*. All four refer to some form of spiritual illness. The term *mate wairua* suggests that the illness is of a spiritual nature. It is not a medical condition. *He mate tēnei ēkore e ora i te rata* (this is an illness that the doctor can not cure) means that there is nothing physically wrong with the person.

Mate Māori means that the illness has links with something specifically Māori, like a violation of *tapu*. The affected persons went somewhere they ought not to have gone, such as to a *wāhi tapu* (a forbidden or sacred place) or an *urupā* (burial place or burial cave). In other cases, someone has taken something *tapu*, like a *taonga pōunamu* (greenstone pendant, club, or artifact). Perhaps there was an act of *whakanoa* (violation) of the *tapu* (being and sacredness) of people, either living or dead.

Poke kēhua describes the illness of one who is being haunted (*poke*) by a ghost or malevolent spirit (*kēhua*). Sometimes, those affected may say it was the spirit of a deceased ancestor or *whānau* member.

When people use the term *mākutu* (accursed), they are saying that the affected persons have been cursed by someone else. They are suffering from the ill-will of another, or of others who are exercising spiritual power to diminish or disempower the afflicted person as a form of punishment and retribution. The *tapu* and *mana* (spiritual power and authority, prestige, and honour) of a person, people, or place may have been violated. It is important to find out whether the illness has really been caused by an act of *mākutu* by another. Any of these states of spiritual illness can be caused by a sense of guilt on the part of the afflicted person regarding an act of *whakanoa* committed, or of right action omitted.

Therefore we ask, 'What is meant by spirit possession?' The English words suggest that a person is 'taken over' by some other spirit, or by the spirit of another person. The 'spirit' takes control of the person, causing the person to act 'out of character.' They become so possessed by a spirit that they lose their free will, and say and do things they would not otherwise say and do. We have noted that there can be some changes in their physical appearance, in their physical strength, and in their usual patterns of behaviour. Occasionally, they speak with a knowledge they did not previously have or was not previously apparent in them, for example, knowledge of *whakapapa* (genealogy) or *te reo* (Māori language). These factors can lead people to say there is present in the person the *wairua a tētahi tangata kē* (spirit of another person). I cannot personally vouch for this. In the situations I dealt with personally, I did not know the extent of knowledge of a person concerned, and was not present when they exhibited this knowledge. However, there was a case of a young Māori man badly affected by some *mate wairua*. While he was in a trance-like state, he responded and conversed totally in Māori. It was a surprise to me to come across a young man who could respond in this way. On the other hand, he may have already been an accomplished speaker of the language. However, it suited me because I conducted all *karakia* and conversation with him in Māori.

When affected persons vehemently reject prayer, the cross, and holy water, which are used as ritual links with

Atua, we can conclude that there is a *wairua kino* (evil spirit) in those affected. At times, the healer is sure that 'we see the devil in their eyes'. When their behaviour is frightening and destructive, and their language is blasphemous and insulting, we can say that the spirit of evil is in them. They have been visited and taken over by a *kēhua.* To that extent, they are said to be possessed by *he wairua kē* (another spirit, a spirit other than their own).

Possible Effects of Spirit Possession on People

An affected person is in a state of negative *noa,* a state of diminishment and disempowerment, even powerlessness. *Te mate wairua* negatively affects the mental, emotional, and physical state of the person. It diminishes *te tapu o te tangata,* the right and enhancing relationship of the person with *Atua,* with *whānau* and with the *whenua* where the person resides. The person is the object of pity and compassion. Not only is the person in the state of *noa* (diminishment and powerlessness), but so also are the members of the *whānau* and friends. Family and friends feel diminished in their powerlessness to bring their *whanaunga* (relative) and friend out of this state. Hence the desperation with which they try to find help and relief from others.

Further questions might be '*He aha te take i pēnei ai*? (Why has this happened?) What may have been the cause? Is there some good purpose behind it all?'

In some cases, the *whānau* may suggest what they think was the cause, for example, a young man had violated the *tapu* of the *wāhi tapu* when he chased a pig through it. In some cases, a healer may discover that it is an issue of *whakaatu* (advising) concerning some matter that needs attention. That may have been the case of a four-year-old boy who was being visited by a spirit over many nights. Fatal car and motorbike accidents had occurred directly outside the front gate of the house where the boy lived with his family. *Karakia* needed to be said to *whakawātea* (set free) the *whenua* and *ara* (roadway) from the spiritual effects of the fatal accidents. Nor do we know why some have visitations and not others. The four year old boy was a twin, but his twin brother was not affected in any way. There was also the story of a seven-year-old boy visited by a frightening *kēhua,* night after night. His father had been painting tombstones in a *wāhi tapu,* and had brought home the remainder of the paint, with which he then painted the kitchen and lounge.

In most cases, however, the causes are not known. The reality is that we know so little of the spiritual world. However, the Māori world-view is that the spiritual is not separate from, but rather that it interpenetrates, the material world of *Te Ao Mārama*.

Spirit possession does not apply to all spiritual visitations. By 'spiritual visitation' I am referring to experiences some people say they have of being visited by a deceased *tūpuna, whānau* member, or friend. Some say it is a real experience, in that the visitor appears as a living person. Others say the visitor came in a dream. Some visitations can be momentarily frightening. Some of the same symptoms can be present, for example, a glassy look of the eyes or a tired appearance. They may say they experienced the 'freeze', when they were not able to call out or to pray. These visitations are generally brief and may be experienced once only. There are other spiritual visitations which people describe as awesome, overwhelming, enhancing but not frightening. Spiritual visitations differ from spirit possession in that they are generally brief, may be experienced only once, can be awesome and enhancing, and need not be frightening, diminishing, or disempowering.

Whakaora i Te Mate: Healing through *Karakia* and *Ritenga*

As mentioned earlier, no matter what the healer thinks about the affected person or the *whānau*, the healer should respond and offer whatever help is possible. A healer's role is to free the affected person from the power of the evil spirit and to remove the spiritual effects of the illness. Though the healers may have their particular *karakia* and *ritenga*, they share common elements and a common intention. Some use the Māori term, *pure* (ceremony of removing the effects of *tapu* violations) for the cleansing rituals. In *karakia*, they will have recourse to *atua kaitiaki* (gods, spiritual guardians). Christian Māori will direct their *karakia* to *Atua* through *Hehu* (or *Īhu*) *Karaiti* (Jesus Christ), to plead for *te mana o te Atua* (the spiritual power and authority of God) to empower the healer and the *whānau* in the work of healing. Their *karakia* will include asking *Atua*

- to lift from the affected one, and from the *whānau*, the effects of any form of *whakanoa* that may have contributed to the illness;
- to free the person from the effects of violating *tapu* restrictions;
- to restore *te tapu i te tangata* (spiritual, psychological or mental, and physical well-being) to those who may have been the victims of *tapu* violation;
- to restore the *mana* to those who have been diminished and disempowered by the affected one.

The *ritenga* may vary from healer to healer, but included would be *uwhiuwhi ki te wai*, *whakawahi* (anointing), and/or *whakapā* (the imposition of hands) on the affected person/persons. At some stage, the *kaupapa o hohou rongo* (principle of reconciliation) may require that the person be accompanied to find reconciliation and peace with other *whānau*, with *tūpuna*, and with *whenua*. In the latter case, there may have been a violation of *wāhi tapu* and the unauthorised taking of *taonga* from those places. As part of the *ritenga* of healing, the *taonga* would need to be returned. Sometimes the person and *whānau* may be required to visit a particular place or building. The death of a friend or member of the *whānau*, by accident or suicide, may have occurred in those places. The *ritenga* of *whakawātea* (setting free) is used to remove from the place, and perhaps from affected persons, the effects of the death or suicide.

The healer will encourage the person and *whānau* to participate in *karakia*, especially if blasphemy and cursing have occurred, and the healer will remind them that the power to heal and be healed comes from *Atua*. Christian Māori have strong faith in the power of *Atua* to bring about healing and goodness, a power they believe is greater than the power of evil.

A number of questions may now arise: 'Can people be freed from spirit possession? Can they be freed permanently? Does spiritual possession return? Will the power of evil forces be stronger or weaker than the power for good? What is meant by "the last fling"?'

In response we say that people can be freed from spirit possession. They can be freed permanently, though some may relapse. There may be other factors, such as the person's emotional state. People may involve themselves in situations that make them vulnerable to relapse. Some may relinquish prayer or faith in *Atua*, resorting instead to seances or fortune-telling. If healing is achieved on the first attempt, the healer may remind the *whānau* of 'the last fling'. This refers to the fact that the evil spirit may not 'go without a fight'. Sometimes, a spirit may return the following night and try to re-enter the person. If the healing has been effective, the influence of the evil spirit will weaken and disappear entirely. It is obvious with many people that they are no longer affected and they hardly remember the incident.

However, there are some cases where healers may admit that they have not been successful in dispelling the evil spirit. The behaviour of the affected person did not change; attacks continued. The *whānau* may then call on other professional and medical people, or on other healers, to come to their assistance.

Some symptoms which indicate that healing has occurred or is occurring include the cessation of the person's ranting and raving, or the subsidence of physical force or physical resistance. The person, though exhausted, is at peace and is no longer averse to *karakia*, or the cross, and can even manage to join in or repeat a *karakia*, will take a drink of water, will speak coherently, and will recognise people around them. Most importantly, the person will express gratitude for healing.

Follow-up Care and Supervision

It is important that spiritual healers be brought in from the beginning of an episode of suspected spirit possession. If they can remove the spiritual effects, then greater will be the efficacy of follow-up services by professional people such as psychologists, psychiatrists, Māori mental health workers, counsellors, and social workers. These other people need to come to the assistance of both the formerly-affected person and the *whānau*. Emotional and physical damage have been done. Patterns of behaviour have been established. The affected person is usually over-tired from lack of sleep, and fatigued from lack of exercise. The person may be starving from having not eaten over many days. Care and supervision need to be in place to ensure that the person does not relapse, *kei hoki te pāpaka ki raro i tōna kōhatu* (lest the crab retreat under its rock). This is a reference to the person returning to earlier patterns of behaviour which provided a comfort zone, but not healing.

In conclusion, *whakawātea* from spirit possession is a great blessing for the person and the *whānau*. It is not just the freedom from evil forces, but it is also the freedom to be fully human. Our opening story has a promising future. The young people concerned have improved, and are now under the care and supervision of a team of professionals.

Glossary of Māori terms

ara - roadway
aroha - compassion
atua kaitiaki - gods, spiritual guardians
hapū - sub-tribe
he aha te take i pēnei ai? - why has this happened?
he hunga mate - a dead person
he mate tēnei ēkore e ora i te rata - an illness the doctor can not cure
he wairua kē - another spirit, a spirit other than their own
Hehu (or *Īhu*) *Karaiti* - Jesus Christ
iwi - tribe
ka aue noaiho i te pō - cry out in the night
ka mataku te tangata - the person is afraid
ka potete - speak as in a delirious state
kaiako - teacher
karakia - prayers, chants
karakia whakaora i te mate - prayers of healing
kaumātua - male elders

kaupapa o hohou rongo - principle of reconciliation
kēhua - ghost, evil spirit
kei hoki te pāpaka ki raro i tōna kōhatu - lest the crab retreat under its rock
kua pōrangi koutou katoa - you are all mental
kuia - female elders
mahi whakaora - healing work
mākutu - accursed
mana o te Atua - the spiritual power and authority of God
matakite - foresight, vision
mate - illness
mate Māori - Māori sickness
mate wairua - spiritual illness
mātua - parents
noa - state of diminishment and powerlessness
poke kēhua - haunted by a ghost
pono - reality, truth
pono mārika - true indeed
pure - ceremony of removing the effects of *tapu* violations
ritenga - rituals
rongoā - medicine
ruaki - vomiting, spewing
taonga - artefact, treasured possession
taonga pōunamu - greenstone pendant, club, or artefact
tapu - being and sacredness
tauira - aspirants
te mate e kitea ana i nga kanohi - the illness seen in the eyes
te reo - Māori language
te tapu i te tangata - spiritual, psychological or mental, and physical well-being of the person
tika - right, proper

tohunga - skilled person, priest, wizard
tūpuna - ancestors
tūrangawaewae - land as 'standing place'
urupā - burial place or cave
uwhiuwhi - sprinkling with holy water
wāhi tapu - sacred, forbidden place
wairua kino - evil spirit
whakaatu - advising
whakahāwea - despising, belittling
whakanoa - violation
whakapā - imposition of hands
whakapapa - genealogy
whakawahi - anointing
whakawātea - set free
whakawātea - setting free
whānau - family, families
whanaunga - relative
whenua - land

Constructing Identity and Theology in the World of Samoan and Tongan Spirits

Mary Caygill and Philip Culbertson

' . . . the dead can open the minds of innocent children to wisdom . . .'[1]

This essay addresses the topic of 'spirit possession' and mental health, arguing that in order for there to be any adequate contextual theological understanding of well-being from a Tongan or Samoan perspective, the continuing centrality of the spirit world must be acknowledged. In our readings of anthropology and contextual Pacific pastoral theologies, as well as our personal experience and a variety of anecdotal evidence, we are not convinced that the spirit world of Tongan and Samoan people should be pathologised in the ways that some western mental health professionals and theologians often do.

1. Albert Wendt, *The Mango's Kiss* (Auckland: Vintage Books, 2003), 64.

Our Research Methodology

According to Schopenhauer, 'Every man takes the limits of his own field of vision for the limits of the world'.[2] In the course of this cross-cultural research, we were at times taken far outside our own fields of vision as Pākehā New Zealanders. Hence we had to define our research methodology carefully, not only to keep ourselves safe as researchers, but more importantly, to respect the worlds of the research participants into which we were generously invited.

Five Samoans and two Tongans, all island-born but now resident in New Zealand and of mature age, were interviewed for this qualitative research project, with the approval of the Ethics Committee of the University of Auckland. Three of the interviewees were ordained clergy, and the others were active in various ways in their churches and local communities. All participants were given the opportunity to choose a pseudonym for use when they would be quoted in this essay. Interviews were taped and transcribed, and the transcriptions were returned to the participants for checking before our analysis of the transcripts began. Our research process and the findings from the analysis were checked for cultural appropriateness by the project's cultural consultant, a Fijian-born Tongan and prominent Pasifika mental health worker. None of the participants are quoted herein without their permission and the consent of the cultural consultant.

2. Arthur Schopenhauer, *Studies in Pessimism* (1851), quoted in *The Yale Book of Quotations*, edited by FR Shapiro (New Haven: Yale University Press, 2006), 672.

One of the challenges of this research was to avoid lumping together the opinions of the research participants. We have attempted to honor the diversity among the participants—not simply the difference between Tongans and Samoans, but each participant's differences from the others. Houston Wood identifies the promotion of diversity within Pasifika as one of the marks of good research practice,[3] for it engages the fluid, multiple, and complex nature of Pasifika cultures.[4] Glossing over the differences of opinion in Oceania and Pasifika dishonors the many peoples in that 'sea of islands', as Hau'ofa calls it.[5] Flattening out the complexities within this vibrant and evolving population ends up dehumanising us all.

The structure of this essay intentionally sets in dialogue the various theories about the world of Samoan and Tongan spirits as they appear in published academic literature, and the 'real-life' experiences of a handful of Samoans and Tongans who are in daily contact with that same world. It is our hope that these two groups each recognise their own voices in what we have written.

---

3. Houston Wood, 'Three Competing Research Perspectives for Oceania', in *The Contemporary Pacific* 18, No 1 (2006): 34.
4. Teresia Teaiwa, 'Militarism, Tourism, and the Native: Articulations in Oceania', (PhD dissertation, University of California, Santa Cruz, 2001), 77.
5. Epeli Hau'ofa, 'Our Sea of Islands', in *A New Oceania: Rediscovering Our Sea of Islands*, edited by E Waddell, V Naidu, and E Hau'ofa (Suva: University of the South Pacific, 1993).

The World of Samoan and Tongan Spirits

Many Samoans and Tongans believe that the affairs of the human community are influenced by supernatural agencies of various kinds.[6] These spirits are ever-present in a shared socioeconomic universe. As Houston Wood writes,

> Ancestors, spirits, gods, animals, fish, waves, winds, plants, stars, even places, as well as many other entities, manifest their own interpretive and non-interpretive practices . . . The natural and human sciences, then, would no longer work separately, nor would researchers need to squirm when Oceania's people point to invisibles as palpable presences.[7]

Tongans and Samoans who live their culture speak to the dead and have contact with other spirits. 'The dialogue between the living and dead is the essence of the [Pasifika] spiritual being. It is this dialogue which provides substance and direction to human life.'[8] These spirits are always watching, just as after the arrival of Christianity in

6. Cluny Macpherson and La'avasa Macpherson, *Samoan Medical Belief and Practice* (Auckland: Auckland University Press, 1990), 197.
7. Wood, 'Three Competing', 50.
8. Tui Atua Tupua Tamasese Efi, 'In Search of Meaning, Nuance, and Metaphor in Social Policy' (keynote address, The Social Policy Research and Evaluation Conference, Ministry of Social Development, Wellington, New Zealand, April 29, 2003), http://www.msd.govt.nz/documents/publications/msd/journal/issue20/20-pages49-63.pdf (accessed September 27, 2007). 4.

the Pacific, people understood that God too was watching.

One Samoan interviewee described her understanding of the spirit world in the following manner:

> We live in the spirit world every moment of our earthly life, then who knows? Those who know with absolute conviction that his or her spirit will continue to live after his body realize that what they do now on earth, now, will determine their status at home in the spirit world. So I see the spirit world *now*. It is all around us and it came from God. (Sui)

Another Samoan participant, who was married to a traditional *fofō*, explained how it was for him when he encountered his wife's spiritual world:

> There are things that I never believed before until now, that there is a different world—we are here—and there is another world, the spiritual world that can affect us, I suppose, according to our behaviour, and also protect us from harm, from other sources like disrespecting our cultural inheritance and also misbehaving and not respecting especially the culture we were brought up with . . . We are living in this world *and* a spiritual world. If we do anything wrong, they will remind us by affecting us by means of a sickness. But they are also there to protect us. (Alec)

Types of Spirits

Some parts of the Samoan and Tongan spirit worlds resemble each other closely, and yet in other instances they are distinctly unique. The generic name for spirits is, in Samoan, *aitu* or *aiku*, and in Tongan, *'aitu* or *'eitu*. Some scholars hold that the *aitu* were originally the gods of families or clans, or what Sigmund Freud called 'totems'.[9] But over centuries, these *aitu* have often become disconnected from specific blood groups, and instead manifest in a variety of forms within relationship groups, villages, or specific localities. Contact with western Christians has also altered the vocabulary, particularly in Tonga, where *'aitu* are sometimes referred to as *tevolo* (devils), a characterisation not apparent in pre-contact Tonga.

There are various kinds of Samoan spirits, but Drozdow-St Christian summarises: '*Aitu* are either spirit beings in their own right, or the spirits of dead ancestors, or the hand servants of dead ancestors.'[10] Samoan *aitu* perform various roles within the human world—protecting, creating mischief, and punishing—but are not generally

9. Sigmund Freud, *Totem and Taboo: Resemblances Between the Psychic Lives of Savages and Neurotics* (1913), in *The Standard Edition of the Complete Psychological Works of Sigmund Freud,* edited by James Strachey (New York: WW Norton, 1950); see also *aiga atua,* in Albert Wendt, 'Afterword: Tatauing the Post-Colonial Body', in *Inside Out: Literature, Cultural Politics, and Identity in the New Pacific,* edited by Vilsoni Hereniko and Rob Wilson (Lanham: Rowman & Littlefield, 1999), 405.

10. Douglass Drozdow-St Christian, *Elusive Fragments: Making Power, Propriety, and Health in Samoa* (Durham: Carolina Academic Press), 126–127.

understood as 'evil'. Their presence can be, however, quite frightening. Of the non-ancestral spirits, the most powerful are Sauma'iafe and Telesā. These two are referred to as the *teine sā,* or 'forbidden women'. According to history, they have two things in common: they were both beautiful young women, and something dramatic happened in their lives. Until today, the *teine sā* abduct young women who are behaving outside of accepted social norms, in order to teach them a lesson.[11]

Lavinia, one of the Samoan women interviewed, whose ancestral village is located in the region where Sauma'iafe and Telesā originated from, speaks of the reality of their ongoing presence:

> In Samoa there is a generally accepted belief and theory that there are two ladies who are half-human and half-spirit. Their names are Sauma'iafe and Telesā, and for the majority of Samoans, it is so real for them and they are petrified of these ladies...Telesā is supposed to be reigning around that region. I have no fear because I feel if they are around me then they are there to protect me. So I never have a problem with it. (Lavinia)

11. Terry Tavita, 'Samoa's women with spirit', in *Samoan Observer Online,* November 9, 2004, http://www.samoaobserver.ws/news/opinion/op1104/0911op001.htm (accessed December 26, 2006).

Alongside Lavinia's clear understanding is the comparable view of Alec and Marie, two further Samoan interviewees:

> . . . and that is the thing with Sauma'iafe and Telesā, they are the girls that have been troubling people because of their [people's] behaviour. To my understanding they are out there because they love us and they look out for us. (Alec)

Alec's wife Marie learned about the *teine sā* from her mum:

> . . . Mum was the one who told me . . . She is the main *fofō* (traditional healer), very very popular in the islands, and she has been taking me around to where Sauma'iafe's family were, and also Telesā's as well, because there were two girls. So therefore I have heard from the mouths from the parents of these girls while I was really very very young, telling about their daughters and what happened to them and how you should be very careful with your tongue when you talk and say things, and that's why I advised Alec to be very careful what you say. (Marie)

This instruction to 'be careful' was said directly in relation to being interviewed for the purposes of this study.

Tongan spirits are generally those of the deceased. According to McGrath:

> After [Tongan] people die, their bodies have a place in the cemetery, their souls are up in heaven (it is hoped), and their spirits remain among the living . . . their interaction with individuals is private, psychological and spiritual.[12]

As is the case with Samoans, for Tongans these beliefs are part of their pre-contact cultural heritage, and no amount of subsequent Christianisation has completely dislodged their belief in the continuing presence of the spirits of the deceased, and the necessity to cherish and nourish a mutual relationship that is close and intimate.

Within both cultures, an attitude of respect is accorded to the spirits, especially those of the dead ancestors, and the relationship between the living and the dead is 'pragmatic, social, and symbolic'.[13] The dailyness of their interaction with human beings is narrated regularly, thus sustaining the sensitivity to their presence. This public discourse of relationships among human beings, and between human beings and 'invisibles', links ideology and

12. Barbara Burns McGrath, 'A View from the Other Side: The Place of Spirits in the Tongan Social Field', in *Culture, Medicine and Psychiatry* 27 (2003): 29.
13. McGrath, 'A View from the Other Side', 29.

social institutions, and creates and maintains cultural identity through reinforcing 'the culturally ideal self'.[14]

In the Presence of Spirits

The function of the spirits' presence is to draw attention to broken relationships; protect gendered boundaries; remind others of the protocols of respect, obedience, and self-sacrifice; and comfort and protect those in trouble or distress. In each case, identification of the purpose for a spirit's presence serves Pasifika people as a form of meaning-making. And yet occasionally, the reasons for spirit presence and punishments are beyond discovery.

Culturally, illness and injury are usually not understood as things that 'just happen'. They require discernment and explanation. The naming of a present spirit and the identification of its message offer a pragmatic solution for events which beset the frailty of the human self, whether physical, mental, relational, or spiritual.

The intervention of the spirits in human affairs is sometimes dramatic, and sometimes not. Drozdow-St Christian explains:

> . . . it involves being tripped or hit and occasionally entered by the *aitu*, each of which can cause injury or illness. It is also not necessarily enacted on the specific offender in a family. As often as not, *aitu* will attack some other,

14. McGrath, 'A View from the Other Side', 32.

> usually weaker, family member, including unborn children.[15]

Pregnant women and foetuses are particularly vulnerable, as are young women who are found 'out of place'—for example, alone in the dark places of the bush or near bodies of water. *Aitu* may pull a woman's hair or kick her, or may attack the foetus by entering the sleeping woman's *fa'aautagata* (womb-place) through the vagina, mouth, or armpit. Drozdow-St Christian claims that among Samoans, *aitu* attack is considered to be the second most-dangerous form of illness, preceded only by diabetes (*ma'i suka*).[16]

Spirits may also affect a person's mental condition, in the form of temporary 'possession' According to Richard Goodman, '[p]reliminary data suggest that women are affected by this sort of affliction far more often than men. It may be that the position of women in Samoan society, far more of a subordinate one to males than that of their middle-class American contemporaries, requires some sort of mechanism for relieving social stress.'[17] This concurs with the work of Mary Keller, who argues that 'possessed women function paradoxically to transgress traditional gender hierarchies *and* to conserve traditional

15. Drozdow-St Christian, *Elusive Fragments*, 127.
16. Drozdow-St Christian, *Elusive Fragments*, 172.
17. Richard A Goodman, 'Some Aitu Beliefs of Modern Samoans', in *Journal of the Polynesian Society* 80 (1971): 478.

order' [18] Keller, like her predecessors Erika Bourguignon[19] and Felicitas Goodman,[20] does not consider possession to be insanity. She values possession as one example of the biologically determined human need and propensity to experience alternate reality.

The stories of our research participants, as well as most of the stories we could locate within a literature search on Pasifika spirits, position the genesis of the spirits' presence within the dailyness of human relationships. As Tamasese and others point out, the Pasifika self is a relational self:

> The idea that a person can be an individual within him/herself is a new concept which was introduced with Christianity. Christianity introduced the notion that one looked to oneself first. The Samoan belief is that in need, we look to each other. You cannot prosper on your own, by yourself . . . [21]

18. Mary Keller, *The Hammer and the Flute: Women, Power, and Spirit Possession* (Baltimore: Johns Hopkins University Press, 2002), 58.
19. Erika Bourguignon, *A World of Women: Anthropological Studies of Women in the Societies of the World* (New York: Praeger, 1980).
20. Felicitas Goodman, *Speaking in Tongues: A Cross-Cultural Study of Glossolalia* (Chicago: University of Chicago Press, 1972).
21. Kiwi Tamasese, Carmel Peteru, Charles Waldegrave, and Allister Bush, '*Ole Taeao Afua*, the New Morning: A Qualitative Investigation into Samoan Perspectives on Mental Health and Culturally Appropriate Services', in *Australian and New Zealand Journal of Psychiatry* 39 (2005): 303.

The Samoan self has meaning only in relationship with other people, not as an individual. The self can not be separated from the *va*, or relational space, that occurs between an individual and parents, siblings, grandparents, aunts, uncles, and other extended family and community members. This same geography holds true for the Tongan self.

One Tongan participant understood this geography as follows:

> There's a Tongan word that comes to mind that is *tauhi va* and this means keeping one's responsibilities and obligations. When I keep that in order then we are always at peace... When harmony is not kept, the relationship between the two individuals or any party becomes cold and leads to disconnection. One may become concerned or worried. One may become offensive and abusive. Other unhelpful negative actions may happen. These are signs of spiritual sickness . . . If the harmony of the relationship is not kept or if obligations are not held to or done, then it can cause illness. Some claim it to be mental illness, but it's something deeper than that. The cause and source of the illness is the spirit. (Sylvia)

This consequence of disconnectedness or disruption in family harmony, either immediate or past, was also commonly recognised by a number of the Samoan participants. One in particular spoke of a family he knew who had been deeply affected:

> The disruption of a family line can be passed down from one generation to the next, whether or not the family is being consciously aware of it. It is something that really bothers and actually disrupts the harmony of the family life and the quality of relationship. For example, members of one particular family were not quite sure what was wrong with their family line and wondered whether continued family conflicts and unidentified illnesses among some of their children and women were manifestations of a disruption from the past. They consulted a *taulāsea* (medicinal doctor) and were told to raise some money and go back to Samoa to exhume the remains of their great-grandad, and re-bury them in their own piece of land. The family went back to Samoa and invited the whole of their side of the extended family. They organised and performed a kind of ceremony, exhuming and reburying the remains. That was the end of their prolonged disconnected experience. The ceremony and the gathering of the family members was a point of reconciliation, not only between the living and the dead (the spirits), but also amongst the generations of the living. (Soa)

Healing Spirits

Before colonial contact with Samoa and Tonga, illness was often thought to be an indication of an *aitu's* displeasure with human behavior.[22] The arrival of western diseases in the island, brought by the sailors and missionaries, soon taught the people to distinguish between an indigenous disease, which necessitated an indigenous solution, and a western disease, which necessitated a western solution. But it also became clear that westerners could neither prevent nor treat diseases that originated in the spirit world. As Tamasese and others state: '. . . where the cause of the unwellness originated from breaches of Tapu and Sa, and where this had a history of being intergenerational, then western treatment was not effective.'[23]

From before the arrival of Christianity, both Tonga and Samoa had a developed network of practitioners who were adept at diagnosing and treating illness related to the world of spirits. Early British ethnographer JB Stair identified four types of *taula-aitu*, or 'anchors of the spirit'.[24] Over the course of time, these ancient distinctions have become blurred, so that today the generic Samoan term of *fofō* is used to nominate those with special skills in treating *ma'i samoa* (Samoan sickness).

22. Cluny Macpherson, 'Samoan Medicine', in *Healing Practices in the South Pacific*, edited by Claire Parsons (Honolulu: Institute for Polynesian Studies, Brigham Young University, 1985), 2.
23. Tamasese and others, '*Ole Taeao Afua*', 305.
24. Macpherson, 'Samoan Medicine', 7–8.

> *Fofō* are people with varying amounts of knowledge and levels of skill. The most useful distinction is between *taulasea* and *taula-aitu*, based on the former's skill in the treatment of *ma'i samoa* 'Samoan illness' and the latter's skill in the treatment of *ma'i aitu* 'ghost illness,' which is believed to involve supernatural agency. These categories are not exclusive and some healers practice both as *taulasea* and as *taula-aitu*.[25]

Some argue that *fofō* treat illness through massage, while *taulasea* treat illness through herbal cures combined with psychological counseling.[26] Macpherson and Macpherson, however, claim that these same terms refer to types of healing practices, and not to distinctions between practitioners themselves.[27] Macpherson claims that many indigenous healers now practice eclectically, rather than observing the ancient distinctions.

Macpherson continues:

> The *taula-aitu* must first establish what *aitu* is involved and the nature of the event giving rise to the *aitu*'s annoyance . . . If the *taula-aitu* decides that none of the major *aitu* is involved, attention will then focus on the family *aitu*. In some cases these family *aitu* are well

25. Macpherson, 'Samoan Medicine', 9.
26. Drozdow-St. Christian, *Elusive Fragments*, 183.
27. Macpherson and Macpherson, *Samoan Medical Belief*, 116–120.

> known through previous manifestations; in other cases it might be that the *aitu* has never been encountered before. The intervention is usually the consequence of misbehavior which the *aitu* has witnessed, and the patient must identify and admit to it before recovery is possible.[28]

With the arrival of Christianity, Christian figures—such as Jesus or God or one of the saints—have been added to the pantheon of spirits which may be offended, though such offense, when committed by a Samoan, is still treated by a *fofō*, or occasionally, a Samoan minister.[29]

Rarely is there a time when a *fofō* is consulted without having other family members in attendance. Walters points out the social benefit of this system of diagnosis and healing as being two-fold: 1) it unites the family in support of the affected individual, with a view toward expiating the offense and breaking the spell of the *aitu* through family prayer and visiting the *taulasea*, and 2) it offers a kind of built-in confessional whereby the guilt associated with mental illness is diffused over the entire family.[30]

---

28. Macpherson, 'Samoan Medicine', 12.
29. Drozdow-St Christian, *Elusive Fragments*, 182; see also Melani Anae, 'Draft of Preliminary Findings on the Mental Health of Pacific Islands People in New Zealand from a Literature Review undertaken by way of HRC Seeding Grant', Auckland: Department of Anthropology, University of Auckland, 1999, 4–5.
30. William Walters, 'Community Psychiatry in Tutuila, American Samoa', in *American Journal of Psychiatry* 134, No 8 (1997): 917.

Participants interviewed spoke freely of the many incidents they had been part of, either from within their extended families, or in their varying professional care-giving roles within local communities, where healing came from a return to traditional Pacific means. One of the Samoan participants described accompanying her mother to a specific Samoan village to find healing:

> . . . we didn't really know where we were going but as we were nearing the village, we asked the question out loud in the bus. And somebody said, 'I know his house, I will tell the driver where to stop to let you off.' . . . We went in and sat down and the man straight away said to us, 'I was expecting you to come.' All he asked was for a glass of water. He put a couple of drops in from pounded leaves . . . And then he looked at the glass and he started to tell my Mum's life story to my Mum, having never met her, because we didn't even know what he looked like; we only had his name and the village. And he said all these things to my mother and all Mum could say was, 'Yes, that's right.' . . . and so I said [to her], 'Okay, I will give you this dose now.' So I made Mum drink this—I'm not sure whether it was the bark of a tree or some leaves concoction. Mum drank it and straight away she said she felt life coming back into her. (Lavinia)

Psychiatry and the Spirit World

Mental illness is a strange concept to Samoans; the disturbed person is seen as troubled rather than sick.[31] Indeed, a great deal of resistance has been expressed by Samoans and Tongans about their inability to find culturally-sensitive treatment, or even to feel understood, by non-Polynesian psychiatrists.[32] Bush and others have also written about the difficulty that non-Polynesian psychiatrists experience in understanding Tongan and Samoan clients. Pasifika people complain that western psychiatrists:

- Do not work holistically, weaving together the body, mind, spirit, and nature;

31. Walters, 'Community Psychiatry in Tutuila', 917.
32. Anae, 'Draft'; Miriam Azaunce, 'Is It Schizophrenia or Spirit Possession?', in *Journal of Social Distress and the Homeless* 4/3 (1995): 255–263; Allister Bush, Sunny Collings, Kiwi Tamasese, and Charles Waldegrave, 'Samoan and Psychiatrists' Perspectives on the Self: Qualitative Comparison', in *Australian and New Zealand Journal of Psychiatry* 39 (2005): 621–626; Ruth DeSouza, 'Sailing in a New Direction: Multicultural Mental Health in New Zealand', in *Australian e-Journal for the Advancement of Mental Health* 5/2 (2006): 1–11; Michael Kenny, 'Multiple Personality and Spirit Possession', in *Psychiatry* 44 (1981): 337–358; David Lui, 'Spiritual Injury: A Samoan Perspective on Spirituality's Impact on Mental Health', in *Penina Uliuli: Contemporary Challenges in Mental Health for Pacific Peoples*, edited by Philip Culbertson, Margaret Nelson Agee, and Cabrini 'Ofa Makasiale (Honolulu: University of Hawai'i Press, 2007), 66–76; Macpherson, 'Samoan Medicine'; Michael Poltorak, 'Nemesis, Speaking, and *Tauhi Vaha'a*: Interdisciplinarity and the Truth of 'Mental Illness' in Vava'u, Tonga', in *The Contemporary Pacific* 19/ 1 (2007): 1–36; and Tamasese and others, *'Ole Taeao Afua'*.

- Do not understand their deep relational identity; and
- Do not understand how thin is the veil that separates human beings from the 'invisibles'.[33]

Some contextual models have been developed in New Zealand in an effort to address the mental health needs of Pasifika persons, though these models have unfortunately not gained significant currency within the practice of psychiatry.[34] But recently, DeSouza reported that the New Zealand Ministry of Health acknowledges that 'there is no national strategy or policy to address the mental health issues of the full range of ethnic groups in New Zealand'.[35] Poltorak, citing Warwick Anderson, correctly points out that 'the language of western medicine, with its claims to universalism and modernity, has always used, as it still does, the vocabulary of empire'.[36] The post-colonial challenge is to seek liberation from western nosological assumptions, thus fostering insight into 'the behaviour and thought processes of both the former colonizers and those people they colonized'.[37]

33. Bush and others, 'Samoan and Psychiatrists' Perspectives', 624.
34. See, for example, the *fonofale* model developed by Fuimaono Karl Pulotu-Endemann, in *Pacific Mental Health Services and the Workforce: Moving on the Blueprint* (Wellington: Ministry of Health, 2001).
35. DeSouza, 'Sailing in a New Direction', 5–6.
36. Poltorak, 'Nemesis', 9.
37. Frederick Hickling and Gerard Hutchison, 'Post-colonialism and Mental Health: Understanding the Roast Breadfruit', in *Psychiatric*

Pacific peoples are among the least likely to use mental health services of any cultural or ethnic groups in New Zealand. Pasifika clients who do present to a European psychiatrist, but fail to act in accordance with the patterns of behaviour acceptable to the clinician, are frequently diagnosed as having a major pathology.[38] These issues are further exacerbated by the almost-non-existence of psychiatric clinicians of Tongan or Samoan descent. The authors know of only one Tongan psychiatrist in Auckland, one Tongan psychiatrist in Tonga, and no Samoan psychiatrist practicing either in Samoa or New Zealand.

One of the Samoan participants interviewed described the reality of working for a community organisation which gives priority to looking after Pacific people with mental health problems:

> . . . the doctors find it all too easy to just prescribe medication and half those people walk around like zombies. They are so drugged up, they are no good for themselves or anyone else . . . We have shared many hours discussing these issues, and I have expressed my concerns about how a lot of our people are written off as mentally unstable, when all perhaps they are going through could be something to do with a so-called family curse,

Bulletin 24 (2000): 94.

38. Azaunce, 'Is It Schizophrenia?', 262; Bush and others, 'Samoan and Psychiatrists' Perspectives', 621.

> or a so-called voodoo breaking, or something like that. (Lavinia)

Another Samoan participant described his understanding of mental illness in relation to the spirit world:

> Whether those people are actually mentally ill or not: to some, they are spirit-possessed, but again to others, there is no clear definition. Everything in human existence is somewhat connected to the past; the world of the past is the spirit world of the present. Whether that connection is like we understand today, a genetic connection or some other ways of connecting, it affirms that physical life is linked to the spirit life. Some may understand this mental stage in a psychological or phenomenal manner, but largely our people think it has to do with spiritual connection with the past. Now the clash of world-views is very much a reality in our time. (Soa)

A Tongan participant had similar misgivings about the relationship between varying ways of diagnosing the core issues being manifested:

> It could also be seen that this person is not out of his mind, he is not hallucinating. He is dealing with the spirit, he is entering the spirit world, not necessarily Pulotu anymore, because that person may be very remote from

> 'aitu, but he is definitely dealing with the spirit world because his grandmother or mother or brother has come back to deal with him. (Mele)

The Conflict between Two Worlds

The early missionaries to Samoa and Tonga attempted to dislodge the spirit world from the minds of the natives. Outwardly, Samoans and Tongans adapted well to the new faith brought to them, but away from the missionaries' gaze, they kept in touch with the pre-Christian world of Pacific spirits. The area of physical and mental health is paradigmatic of the uneasy 'marriage' of western and indigenous points of view. Cluny Macpherson explains the struggle that developed when the missionaries' medicines failed to cure Samoans of the new diseases that were brought through contact with the West:

> The Samoans had in effect two options: to abandon the precontact medical paradigm, which by now was proving inadequate to explain the new diseases, or to extend it to provide explanations of the new range and types of illness. That they chose the latter course requires some explanation. First, the illnesses which their own paradigm had explained so well continued to afflict Samoans, and there was no reason to suppose that the *aitu* who had dominated their lives for so long had suddenly relinquished their power. Even the

> Samoans, who were converted to Christianity, did not, to the missionaries' despair, abandon their belief in the power of the *aitu*. The role of supernatural agents in sickness, then, was not denied. It is acknowledged today.[39]

Anthropologist Barbara Burns McGrath confirms that Tongans also had to address the same tensions:

> When things like good health, or *mana*, are as much under the influence of deceased relatives as the behavior of the individual, then a cure or salvation will be achieved only by considering the physical body, the soul, and the collective social and spiritual world. Thus, to some extent, Tongan spirits remain beyond the grasp of Christianity and outside of western biomedicine.[40]

It may even be that the continuing Samoan and Tongan socio-political discourses on spirit possession reveal a counter-colonial aspect, in addition to the simple jarring of conflicting claims about the origins of health and sickness. Certainly, this is Mageo's claim.[41] In this sense, the continuing attachment of Samoans and Tongans to their indigenous world of spirits functions today as a site of

39. Macpherson, 'Samoan Medicine', 3.
40. McGrath, 'View From the Other Side', 42–43.
41. Jeannette Marie Mageo, *Theorizing Self in Samoa: Emotions, Genders, and Sexualities* (Ann Arbor: University of Michigan Press, 1998).

resistance to the eradication of their traditional cultures and cosmologies.

One of the Samoan women participants expressed how, for her, there had been the gradual move toward holding together two contrasting perspectives:

> For me, even though I was born in Samoa, my upbringing was more a pālagi upbringing, especially growing up in the Seventh Day Adventist church. I might as well have been a pālagi through all my life, because this religion had its first arrival in Samoa. It almost taught that anything Samoan was evil . . . I grew up in that environment where any notion of the spirit world was very biblical for me, and even though I heard stories and sort of saw people who were supposedly possessed, I was still able to say to myself, oh yeah, that is just the evil spirit—until I was much older and started learning from my father. That's when I started to develop new respect for the spirit world, and it is respect that has grown in time, and I have even more so now than then. (Lavinia)

One of the Samoan male participants described this same conflict between two worlds through the paradigm of the struggle between genders:

> I believe that male domination was not part of the Samoan culture before the missionaries

and the Bible arrived. Though we have stories of mythological cruel male figures, the amazing story was that it was a female, Nafanua, who confronted the male cruelty to make a peace that united the whole country for the first time. She even unified the four main tribal titles of Samoa and conferred them to yet another woman, Salemasina, who became the first-ever political leader of the whole country. This same woman, Nafanua, prophesied the arrival of the white missionaries. The occasion was that one of the tribal chiefs, Malietoa Vainu'upo, went to Nafanua to ask for an *ao* (the right to govern) and a blessing, so that he could rule his district. Nafanua replied that she had no more ao left, but to go and await his ao, which would come from heaven. Nafanua prophesied that a time would come when all Samoan people would be under one governorship—the arrival of the missionaries (John Williams and the LMS missionaries arrived at Malietoa's village) and the sweeping conversion of all Samoans to the missionary God. But then it was perceived that because this was the new and supreme God, all things of the past would no longer be relevant. Largely unknown, the missionaries came with the scriptures and a culture that had a masculine-dominant view of life, and our people are still debating, even today, whether we should find meanings in our own stories, or should adopt

> this understanding of God that came with all the wrappings of western culture and perceived as part of God? (Soa)

Creative Tensions in Theology and the Church

How can we, as non-Pasifika Christians, understand the role of spirits in a Pasifika world which also claims to be heavily Christianised? Macpherson and Macpherson (1990) argue that from the beginning until today, the western Christian world-view has not displaced the traditional Samoan and Tongan involvement with spirits:

> Nor does the significance of the supernatural in Samoan life appear to have declined dramatically since contact. A new god was added to a set of pre-contact gods and assumed dominance over Samoan life but did not displace all pre-existing supernatural agencies . . . Even Christians accept the existence of *aitu*, which they liken to the demons which Christ cast out in Scripture to justify their belief.[42]

Thus, Samoan and Tongan Christians seem to move relatively easily between the two worlds of traditional culture (*fa'aSamoa, fakaTonga*) and the discourse of the Christian colonisers.

42. Macpherson and Macpherson, *Samoan Medical Belief*, 239.

A team of Pasifika and pālagi researchers, in an extensive, government-funded research project, reached the conclusion that even when Samoans and Tongans seek treatment from western mental health professionals, they still need the presence of both worlds in order for them to feel culturally met:

> Spirituality is raised throughout service provider, consumer, and family discussions in two ways. On the one hand it refers to traditional Pacific beliefs in ancient cosmology where the "spiritual" is manifested in beliefs in the ethereal connections between peoples, their ancestors, and the ancient Polynesian gods . . . On the other hand, spirituality also refers to more contemporary Pacific beliefs in Christianity. Interestingly, participants discussed spirituality using both conceptions without any sense of contradiction.[43]

This raises the question of how the word 'spirituality' is understood when used in a variety of venues, including mental health and Christian theology.

43. Francis Agnew and others, 'Pacific Models of Mental Health Service Delivery in New Zealand ("PMMHSD") Project', Clinical Research and Resource Centre, Waitemata District Health Board, Auckland, http://www.tepou.co.nz/file/PDF/publications/Pacific%20Models%20Report%20Final%20Sept%202004.pdf (accessed November 1, 2007).

Western Christians sometimes attempt to apply theologies of the Holy Spirit to Pasifika discourses about the presence and work of the supernatural. We believe this is an incorrect conflation of concepts, based solely on the coincidence of 'spirits' and 'Spirit'. As some writers have pointed out, the early missionaries took another approach, of labelling the indigenous spirits as 'evil' or as 'devils'.[44] But McGrath correctly points out that Pasifika spirits are not inherently evil; they are *tapu*.[45] To connect the world of Pasifika spirits with Christian understandings of evil is either a mistake on the part of the early missionaries, or a deliberate attempt to displace traditional cultural understandings with imported ones.

We believe that rather than connecting the Pasifika world of spirits with biblical concepts of evil and the demonic, it is more appropriate to connect the Pasifika spirits with the post-resurrection appearances of Jesus. Biblical scholar Deborah Thompson Price has analysed the post-resurrection appearances in Luke 24 in the light of the various post-mortem apparitions which are described in ancient Greco-Roman literature.[46] She concludes that this Lukan text intentionally explores a variety of possible understandings of how 'a spirit' (Jesus) could be felt as 'alive' among a group of people who remembered him so

44. Macpherson and Macpherson, *Samoan Medical Belief*, 67, 239; McGrath, 'View from the Other Side', 39, 42; Poltorak, 'Nemesis', 18–19; Wendt, *Mango's Kiss*, 50–51.
45. McGrath, 'View from the Other Side', 30–31.
46. Deborah Thompson Price, 'The 'Ghost' of Jesus: Luke 24 in Light of Ancient Narratives of Post-mortem Apparitions', in *Journal for the Study of the New Testament* 29, No 3 (2007).

clearly. Price explores four paradigms in particular: disembodied spirits (ghostly presences that can even eat and drink), revenants (re-animated corpses), heroes (the dead who are capable of physical contact with the living), and translated mortals (the 'disputed dead' who live in the afterlife as mortals). Price claims that in various ways, these paradigms more accurately explain the ways in which Jesus is presented in the Lukan post-resurrection appearances. Price's work could be useful in pointing toward a Christian theology which can understand and reach a peace with the the Samoan and Tongan sense of the spirit world, without having to reframe such events as expressions of pneumatology.

Certainly this resembles the manner in which one of the Samoan women participants recounted an experience of her beloved father making a spirited appearance in the midst of a significant family occasion:

> Remember how the two disciples had walked to Emmaus and they were going over the events of the day? I suppose they were reminiscing about Jesus going, poor Lord. It's almost like, very similar, to that time, because we were all sitting there wishing that our Dad could just be alive for one more time, just to see his little girl go to the beauty pageant. And then this blackbird flew straight into the sitting room, landed in front of the coffee table in front of us and we all turned around and said '*Oy, talofa li*', you know, cause we knew,

> we are thinking, look at him, he had to come. There was . . . maybe a bit of awe. (Lavinia)

Conclusion

In 2005, the World Council of Churches issued a policy document entitled 'Mental health as a key issue in the future of global health developments'. This report argued that mental health problems are particularly debilitating for 'the poor, homeless, unemployed, persons with low education, victims of violence, immigrants and refugees, indigenous populations, children and adolescents, abused women, and the neglected elderly'.[47] At the same time, the report recognised that many indigenous cultures honor the presence of 'spirits' in various forms, and that these are not always to be understood as forms of mental illness: 'culturally determined normal variations in thinking and behaving are not mental disorders.'[48] Whether mental illness or not, the church is never absolved from the responsibility to provide support and care to people who are in touch with the world of Pasifika spirits, in manners which do not pathologise or do violence to those experiencing contact with the 'invisibles', nor should we

47. Prathap Tharyan, Deepa Braganze, and Prasanna Jebarag, *Mental Health as a Key Issue in the Future of Global Health Developments,* World Council of Churches ecumenical consultation on 'The Global Health Situation and the Mission of the Church in the 21st Century', Breklum, Germany, September 2005, http://www.oikoumene.org/_(accessed February 2, 2007), 3.
48. Tharyan, Braganze, and Jebarag, *Mental Health as a Key Issue,* 2.

re-frame their world to fit our assumed sense of rationalism or European structures of theology.[49]

Bibliography

Agnew, Francis, Fuimaono Karl Pulotu-Endemann, Gail Robinson, Tamasailau Suaalii-Sauni, Helen Warren, Amanda Wheeler, Maliaga Erick, Tevita Hingano, and Helen Schmidt-Sopoaga. 'Pacific Models of Mental Health Service Delivery in New Zealand ("PMMHSD") Project'. Clinical Research and Resource Centre, Waitemata District Health Board, Auckland, 2004, http://www.tepou.co.nz/file/PDF/publications/Pacific%20Models%20Report%20Final%20Sept%202004.pdf (accessed November 1, 2007).

Anae, Melani. 'Draft of preliminary findings on the mental health of Pacific Islands people in New Zealand from a literature review undertaken by way of HRC seeding grant'. Auckland: Department of Anthropology, University of Auckland, 1999.

Azaunce, Miriam. 'Is It Schizophrenia or Spirit Possession?', in *Journal of Social Distress and the Homeless* 4/3 (1995): 255–263.

49. Special thanks are offered to our seven anonymous research participants, who entrusted us with their intimate spiritual experiences, and to the cultural consultant for this research, Ms Cabrini 'Ofa Makasiale. Gratitude is also expressed to the University of Auckland Human Subject Ethics Commmitte for granting permission to conduct this research, and to the Sainsbury Trust for funding it.

Bourguignon, Erika. *A World of Women: Anthropological Studies of Women in the Societies of the World* (New York: Praeger, 1980).

Bush, Allister, Sunny Collings, Kiwi Tamasese, and Charles Waldegrave. 'Samoan and Psychiatrists' Perspectives on the Self: Qualitative Comparison', in *Australian and New Zealand Journal of Psychiatry* 39 (2005): 621–626.

DeSouza, Ruth. 'Sailing in a New Direction: Multicultural Mental Health in New Zealand', in *Australian e-Journal for the Advancement of Mental Health* 5, No 2 (2006): 1–11.

Drozdow-St Christian, Douglass. *Elusive Fragments: Making Power, Propriety, and Health in Samoa* (Durham: Carolina Academic Press, 2002).

Freud, Sigmund. *Totem and Taboo: Resemblances between the Psychic Lives of Savages and Neurotics* (1913). In *The Standard Edition of the Complete Psychological Works of Sigmund Freud,* edited by James Strachey, 13:1–161 (New York: WW Norton, 1950).

Goodman, Felicitas. *Speaking in Tongues: A Cross-cultural Study of Glossolalia* (Chicago: University of Chicago Press, 1972).

Goodman, Richard A. 'Some Aitu Beliefs of Modern Samoans', in *Journal of the Polynesian Society* 80 (1971): 463–479.

Hau'ofa, Epeli. 'Our Sea of Islands', in *A New Oceania: Rediscovering our Sea of Islands,* edited by E Waddell, V Naidu, and E Hau'ofa, 2–16 (Suva: University of the South Pacific, 1993).

Hickling, Frederick, and Gerard Hutchinson. 'Post-colonialism and Mental Health: Understanding the Roast Breadfruit', in *Psychiatric Bulletin* 24 (2000): 94–95.

Keller, Mary. *The Hammer and the Flute: Women, Power, and Spirit Possession* (Baltimore: Johns Hopkins University, 2002).

Kenny, Michael. "Multiple Personality and Spirit Possession' , in *Psychiatry* 44 (1981): 337–358.

Lui, David. 'Spiritual Injury: A Samoan Perspective on Spirituality's Impact on Mental Health', in *Penina Uliuli: Contemporary Challenges in Mental Health for Pacific Peoples*, edited by Philip Culbertson, Margaret Nelson Agee, and Cabrini 'Ofa Makasiale, 66–76 (Honolulu: University of Hawai'i Press, 2007).

Macpherson, Cluny. 'Samoan Medicine', in *Healing Practices in the South Pacific*, edited by Claire Parsons, 1–15 (Honolulu: Institute for Polynesian Studies, Brigham Young University, 1985).

Macpherson, Cluny, and La'avasa Macpherson. *Samoan Medical Belief and Practice* (Auckland: Auckland University Press, 1990).

Mageo, Jeannette Marie. *Theorizing Self in Samoa: Emotions, Genders, and Sexualities* (Ann Arbor: University of Michigan Press, 1998).

McGrath, Barbara Burns. 'A View from the Other Side: The Place of Spirits in the Tongan Social Field', in *Culture, Medicine and Psychiatry* 27 (2003): 29–48.

Poltorak, Michael. 'Nemesis, Speaking, and *Tauhi Vaha'a*: Interdisciplinarity and the Truth of 'Mental Illness' in Vava'u, Tonga', in *The Contemporary Pacific* 19/1 (2007): 1–36.

Prince, Deborah Thompson. 'The Ghost of Jesus: Luke 24 in Light of Ancient Narratives of Post-mortem Apparitions', in *Journal for the Study of the New Testament* 29/3 (2007): 287–301.

Pulotu-Endemann, Fuimaono Karl. *Pacific Mental Health Services and the Workforce: Moving on the Blueprint* (Wellington: Ministry of Health, 2001).

Schopenhauer, Arthur. *Studies in Pessimism* (1851). In *The Yale Book of Quotations*, edited by FR Shapiro, 672. (New Haven: Yale University Press, 2006).

Tamasese, Kiwi, Carmel Peteru, Charles Waldegrave, and Allister Bush. '*Ole Taeao Afua*, The New Morning: A Qualitative Investigation into Samoan Perspectives on Mental Health and Culturally Appropriate Services', in *Australian and New Zealand Journal of Psychiatry* 39 (2005): 300–309.

Tamasese Efi, Tui Atua Tupua. 'In Search of Meaning, Nuance, and Metaphor in Social Policy.' Keynote address, The Social Policy Research and Evaluation Conference, Wellington, New Zealand: Ministry of Social Development, April 29-30, 2003, http://www.msd.govt.nz/documents/publications/msd/journal/issue20/20-pages49-63.pdf (accessed September 27, 2007).

Tavita, Terry. 'Samoa's Women with Spirit', in *Samoan Observer Online*, November 9, 2004, http://www.samoaobserver.ws/news/opinion/op1104/0911op001.htm (accessed December 26, 2006).

Teaiwa, Teresia. 'Militarism, Tourism, and the Native: Articulations in Oceania'. PhD dissertation, University of California, Santa Cruz, 2001.

Tharyan, Prathap, Deepa Braganze, and Prasanna Jebaraj. *Mental Health as a Key Issue in the Future of Global Health Developments.* World Council of Churches ecumenical consultation on 'The Global Health Situation and the Mission of the Church in the 21st Century', Breklum, Germany, September 2005, http://www.oikoumene.org/ (accessed February 2, 2007).

Walters, William. 'Community Psychiatry in Tutuila, American Samoa', in *American Journal of Psychiatry* 134/8 (1997): 917–919.

Wendt, Albert. 'Afterword: Tatauing the Post-colonial Body', in *Inside Out: Literature, Cultural Politics, and Identity in the New Pacific,* edited by Vilsoni Hereniko and Rob Wilson, 399–412. (Lanham: Rowman & Littlefield, 1999).

Wendt, Albert. *The Mango's Kiss* (Auckland: Vintage Books, 2003).

Wood, Houston. 'Three Competing Research Perspectives for Oceania', in *The Contemporary Pacific* 18/1 (2006), 33–55.

Spirit Possession and Mental Health in the New Zealand Context

Ann M Nolan

In the scientific and psychiatric literature, the notion of possession by spirits is most frequently and consistently interpreted or described as an archaic and non-scientific way of explaining mental illness. When individuals claiming to be possessed present to mental health facilities, mental health clinicians, or psychiatrists, the usual diagnosis is that the person has a delusional belief, which has no connection to the supernatural world. The belief is therefore able to be explained in psychodynamic, psychological, or psychiatric terms. Possession by demons or evil spirits is considered by the psychiatric community to be uncommon—indeed, rare. Globally speaking, then, current psychiatric, psychological, and medical models for treating delusional disorders subsume claims of spirit possession into a medical system of treatment using psychotropic medication, psychotherapy, and counselling.

The reason that psychiatry and psychological medicine must be concerned with claims of demon possession is that it is generally accepted that if people are to seek medical help at all, they will turn to these branches of medicine. This is so, practitioners claim, because the symptoms are often similar to those of particular types of mental illnesses. Some of the symptoms of mental illness, such as disturbed and bizarre behaviour, altered states of consciousness, and dissociative disorders, are very similar to those behaviours that appear in demon possession.

Philip Coons, Professor of Psychiatry at Indiana University School of Medicine, gives a clear and succinct description of the different types of psychopathological forms of disorder, including multiple personality disorder, trance possession disorder, delusions of possession, and demon possession. He focuses on the difference, for example, between ritual possession which is voluntary, and therefore does not require diagnosis and treatment, and involuntary possession. He acknowledges that while there has never been an official approved psychiatric diagnosis for what he describes as the possession syndrome, psychiatry grapples with questions of how to understand and treat the manifestations of this condition, moving towards the conclusion that it is vital for professionals to continue to seek answers to the question, 'who is qualified to discern possession, what professional works with what type of subject, what is an effective working relationship, and which techniques are truly effective'.[1]

1. Philip Coons, 'The Differential Diagnoses of Possession States', in *Dissociation* 1 (1993): 213–221.

During the historical period when rationalist philosophy and scientific inquiry began to demand evidence based on reasoned argument, western understanding moved away from viewing demon possession as a supernatural invasion of individuals to describing it as possession syndrome in psychiatry. Before giving a brief history of this development, it is important to define what is meant by 'unwanted spirit or demon possession' in order to show how this differentiation between what is possession and what is mental illness came about.

Definition of Spirit Possession

It is widely accepted by scholars who study spirit possession in different countries and cultures that the concept of possession by both good and evil spirits who are capable of taking control of human beings has existed universally from earliest antiquity across many different cultures.[2] Evil or demonic spirit possession, wherein a normal personality is displaced by a malevolent and harmful force, is referred to in several places in the Bible, as is the casting out of demons.

The chief characteristic of being possessed by a supernatural spirit is the invasion of an individual by a paranormal force which uses the body of the human victim as

2. See Coons, 'Differential States', 213–221; Miriam Azaunce, 'Is it Schizophrenia or Spirit Possession?', in *Journal of Social Distress and the Homeless* 4/3 (1995): 255–263; and SN Chiu, 'Historical, Religious, and Medical Perspectives of Possession Phenomenon', in *Hong Kong Journal of Psychiatry* 10/1 (2000): 14–18.

a vehicle for its own thoughts, words, and acts, causing the person physical, mental, and spiritual torment.[3] There is wide agreement amongst anthropologists and psychiatrists that these possessive states are not dissimilar to forms of trance, personality disorders, and dissociative disorders, because these too have the common manifestations of changes in behaviour, speech, mood, distorted body movements, and memory.

Certain types of mental illnesses which manifest as disordered personalities or strange behaviours, and symptoms such as those associated with epilepsy in earliest times, were poorly differentiated from behaviours found in persons believed to be possessed by demons or evil spirits, punished by the gods, or who had become mad under the spell of a witch doctor.[4]

History of Possession in Psychiatry

In Western Europe, up until the late Middle Ages, the psychiatric treatment of such 'disorders' was scarcely distinguishable from pre-scientific demonology wherein possession by evil spirits was an synonym for mental illness. Rather, the category that we now call mental illness was then seen as demonic possession. The treatment was

3. MF Unger, *Demons in the World Today* (Wheaton, IL: Tyndale House Publishers, 1971), 102–108.
4. AD Forrest, 'Concepts of Mental Illness: An Historical Introduction', in *Companion to Psychiatric Studies*, edited by AD Forrest, J Affleck, and A Zeall (Edinburgh: Churchill Livingstone, 1978), 1.

exorcism. Many mentally ill people were seen as witches and were persecuted.

As the Medieval period progressed into the Renaissance, the differentiation between mental illness and possession by spirits, even if the characteristics appeared to be the same or similar to the latter, was marked with the publication, in 1520, of the book *Diseases which lead to a Loss of Reason* by the physician Paracelsus (1491–1541). This significant book made it clear that mental disorders were not caused by spirits, but were natural illnesses and could be treated medically. Paracelsus' view provided a clear direction for the development of western psychiatry in the 1600s, whereby 'the range of disorders attributed to demonic possession' became 'gradually narrowed'.[5] The reason given for this narrowing was the rise of the philosophy of secular humanism, which was committed to the use of scientific methods of inquiry based on critical evaluation and reasoning when examining factual evidence. The employment of rational scientific methods excluded the supernatural.[6] Such logical and technical methods helped to inform and construct theoretical frameworks within which mental disorders could be explained.

5. Simon Kemp and Kevin Williams, 'Demonic Possession and Mental Disorder in Medieval and Early Modern Europe', in *Psychological Medicine* 17 (1987): 21–29. See also SN Chiu, 'Historical, Religious, and Medical Perspectives of Possession Phenomenon', in *Hong Kong Journal of Psychiatry* 10/1 (2000): 14–18.
6 Walter C Johnson, 'Demon Possession and Mental Illness', in *Journal of the American Scientific Affiliation* 34 (1982): 149.

> As Michael Stone points out, the sixteenth century was 'marked both by the culmination of the Inquisition and by the re-emergence of rational and humanistic thought—a movement spearheaded by philosophers' concerning mental life, opening up the way for 'a more reasoned, empirical, and compassionate treatment of the mentally ill'.[7]

In the seventeenth century, psychiatry continued to embrace rational empiricism, which sought to establish 'firm foundations and classification' based on demonstrable evidence. This evidence included such things as brain measurement—collecting physical anatomical samples for analysis and comparison. Findings could then be used to assist with diagnosis of mental problems.

By the Age of Enlightenment, the division between religion's being the 'healer' of demon possession, and secular medicine's having the responsibility to treat and restore mental illness to wellness, was complete. Psychiatry placed an ever greater reliance 'on direct observation and rational argument. Superstition and the dogmatism of the Church were on the wane, especially in those countries most influenced by the Reformation.'[8]

The strength and influence of the new sciences permeated not only medicine, but all other disciplines as well, especially those concerned with how both the universe

---

7. Michael H Stone, *Healing the Mind: A History of Psychiatry from Antiquity to the Present* (New York: WW Norton, 1997), 27.
8. Stone, *Healing*, 52.

and human society functioned. Church thinkers, too, were educated into considering the new scientific thought that penetrated philosophy and theology. Those who left Europe to go to the New World and beyond took these new ideas with them, including those that went to New Zealand in the 1800s. Both the pioneers and the missionaries that came to this land emerged out of the Enlightenment era, and were, by and large, just that: 'enlightened', accepting psychological or cognitive dysfunction or bizarre behaviours as resulting from mental illness, not from spirit possession. This is not to say that they did not believe in the possibility of spirit possession, but that the type of Christianity that the Anglican, Roman Catholic, and Presbyterian missionaries imparted was based on doctrine, the observation of religious principles and ethics in daily life, piety and devoutness in prayer, and religious observance of the sacraments. It is beyond the scope of this essay to provide a comprehensive history of the attitudes toward spirit possession held by the missionary evangelists and practising Christians in New Zealand, except to say that in mainstream New Zealand religion and psychiatry from that time forward, spirit possession has not featured as a prominent issue until Pentecostalism appeared, which is briefly addressed below.

By the nineteenth century, psychiatry had gained a firmer footing as a branch of medicine, demystifying the workings of the brain and its anatomical parts. As Stone points out, 'persecutions of witches became a rarity' and Sigmund Freud (1856–1939) became a household name.[9]

9. Stone, *Healing*, 68.

Freud strengthened the view of the classical psychoanalytic school that possession states conform to conditions of neurosis, thereby providing a psychoanalytic basis for understanding the supernatural world. Freud explained that that states of possession were no more than 'reprehensible wishes, derivatives of instinctual impulses that have been repudiated and repressed'.[10] The medical and psychological community was further influenced by Freud's anti-religious stance when he proposed, in his 1927 book *The Future of an Illusion*, that religion fostered neurotic influences lacking in logic and reason, and had an adverse effect on the human psyche, thereby strengthening the idea that religion and psychiatry are in conflict. The result, as I have pointed out earlier, has been that western psychiatry has continued to treat claims of possession as delusional, and to treat them pharmaceutically and therapeutically.

Nonetheless, the debate in the international literature, where contentious views about what belongs to psychiatry and what belongs to religion in matters of spiritual problems—including claims of demon possession—is ongoing. The claim made by both religious ministers and mental health practitioners, especially Christian psychologists and psychiatrists, that there is an increase in occultism in western culture has enlivened the debate about making a distinction between demon possession and the pathology of mental illness. For example, in a 1976 arti-

10. Sigmund Freud, 'A Seventeenth Century Demonological Neurosis', in *The Complete Psychological Works of Sigmund Freud*, edited by J Strachey (London: Hogarth Press, 1961), 19:67.

cle, Millard Sall, of the Anaheim Psychological Center in California, distinguished between demon possession and the pathology of mental illness in an attempt to sort out which was the appropriate pathway for restoring persons to wellness: psychotherapeutic or psychiatric treatment for those with identified mental health symptoms, or religious deliverance by ministers or faith healers in the cases of purported demon possession with symptoms which do not fit psychopathology.[11]

Sall's research sparked renewed interest concerning the debate on the place of psychotherapy as a part of the larger ministry of the church, especially in relation to spirit possession, as claimed by Paul Bach in his article on the relationship between demon possession and psychotherapy.[12] Since then, this theme has remained a recurrent debate in the literature on pastoral psychology, psychology and Christianity, and Christian psychiatry.

> In a recent article, Stafford Betty, professor of religious studies at California State University, Bakersfield, and specialist in the philosophy of religion and in spiritual and paranormal studies, claims there is growing evidence

11. Millard J Sall, 'Demon Possession or Psychopathology? A Clinical Differentiation', in *Journal of Psychology and Theology* 4/4 (1976): 286–290.
12. Paul J Bach, 'Demon Possession and Psychopathology: A Theological Relationship', in *Journal of Psychology and Theology* 7/1 (1979): 22–26, and Millard J Sall, 'A Response to "Demon Possession and Psychopathology: A Theological Relationship"', in *Journal of Psychology and Theology* 7/1 (1979): 27–30.

> for 'demonic possession', though considered by psychiatrists to be rare, and asking what psychiatry's response ought to be.[13]

Using case studies from China, India, and the United States, Stafford Betty examines the universality of spirit possession and its superhuman components, and evaluates the comparative success of deliverance and exorcism, as opposed to psychiatry, in order to suggest a psychiatric response to the this phenomenon. He does not base his definition of evil or demonic spirits on Christian theological descriptions, but universalises his classification to mean those spirits 'who are more or less intelligent beings, insensible to us, with a will of their own who seem to bother or oppress us, or in rare cases, possess our bodies outright, and with whom we can relate in a variety of ways'.[14] From his evaluation of case study evidence, he asks whether spirits are products of an aberrant brain, or whether they have an independent existence and, if so, how the person should be healed and who should do the healing. Betty argues that in the case of medicine, 'a correct diagnosis is essential to healing'.[15] Misdiagnosis leads not only to unsuccessful, but also to inapproriate treatment. If a psychiatrist tries to cure spirit possession with conventional medical treatment, he or she may not be

---

13. Stafford Betty, 'The Growing Evidence for "Demonic Possession": What Should Psychiatry's Response Be?', in *Journal of Religion and Health* 44/1 (2005): 13–30.
14. Betty, 'Growing Evidence', 14.
15. Betty, 'Growing Evidence', 20.

successful, because the person requires the healing rites conducted by exorcists or deliverance ministers. Betty is not able to provide adequate statistics showing the relative success or failure rates of such rites, but cautiously supports that the anecdotal evidence does point to more success than failure.[16]

A second theme that continues to be debated concerns diagnosis about what is delusional, the phenomenon and nature of dissociative disorders, and the use of the terms 'spirit' and 'demon possession'. Ivey Gavin, for example, claims that, in the mainly secular psychiatric literature, the terms 'evil' and 'demonic possession' are useful metaphors for 'understanding destructive elements of human psychological functioning, and that, despite their historical location in supernatural discourses, they are comprehensible in secular psychological terms because psychoanalysis uses rational terms to understand the claimed supernatural origins of this phenomenon'.[17]

Spirit possession in the New Zealand medical literature is quite different. The emphasis is on the acknowledgement that the different cultures that make up the New Zealand population, not only Māori, but also people from the Pacific and Asia in particular, have their own beliefs about the spirit world and how that world impacts on the lives of people. These beliefs shape the way they respond to mental illness.

16. Betty, 'Growing Evidence', 22.
17. Ivey Gavin, 'Diabolical Discourses: Demonic Possession and Evil in Modern Psychopathology', in *South African Journal of Psychology* 32/4 (2002): 54–59.

The trend in the New Zealand literature is to seek better ways of understanding the belief systems of these many cultures, in order to build a culturally appropriate mental health system which can meet the needs of everyone. This approach is clear in the main medical journals, namely the *New Zealand Medical Journal* and the *Australian and New Zealand Journal of Psychiatry*. The interface between psychiatry and religion does not come up for debate in this mainstream literature.

In one of the rare exceptions to this state of affairs, psychiatrist Laurie Gluckman has summarised Samoans' views on mental illness, since this is the largest Pacific Island group in New Zealand and the one most published about. He points out that Samoans have unique culture-bound syndromes because they suffer illnesses as a result of the violation of Samoan customs or of offending an ancestral spirit.[18]

A good example of what Gluckman and others have described is the 1979 case of a Samoan boy possessed by a spirit. This case report examined the instance of a boy who was found not to have a mental illness, but to be possessed by a spirit, as identified by a Samoan health worker. This highlighted how differently Samoan people see the cause of possession—as coming from links with ancestors—and how their traditional approach to healing is quite different to that of medical clinicians in mental health. A Samoan traditional healer was brought in to

18. Laurie K. Gluckman, 'Clinical Experience with Samoans in Auckland', in *Australian and New Zealand Journal of Psychiatry* 11 (1997): 101–107.

assist with restoring the boy to wellness, which he did successfully. What this case illustrated was how the belief system of the Samoan persons involved was respected. Furthermore, it demonstrated that the willingness on the part of the mental health clinicians to accept the explanation that the cause of the problem was supernatural helped to facilitate the appropriate method of healing in a culturally suitable and effective way.[19]

While there is less written about Tongan mental health, Dr Leopino Foliaki reported that the term *angaangaua*, meaning 'two characters', refers to people who appear to have two personalities. Just as Samoans believe that they can be invaded by a dead person's spirit, the illness *te'ai* is very similar for Tongan people. Tongans, Foliaki said, believe that migraines and severe depression are caused by ancestral spirits.[20] The use of traditional healers is important to this community, as described by Toafa, Moata'ane and Guthrie, providing good insight into what needs to be integrated into the mainstream mental health system for Tongans.[21]

> The substantive work on demon possession in New Zealand, written in 1985 by Simon

19. PJ Kinloch and M Short, 'Samoan Spirit Possession: Case Report', *New Zealand Medical Journal* 90 (1979): 498–499.
20. Ministry of Health, 1993 Unpublished minutes of a fono on Pacific Islands mental health, Wellington. www.moh.govt.nz/moh.nsf/Files/chap4/$file/chap4.pdf (accessed December 16, 2007).
21. Viliami Toafa, Losa Moata'ane, and Barbara Guthrie, 'Tongan Medicine and the Role of Traditional Tongan Healers in New Zealand', in *Pacific Health Dialog* 8 (2001): 78–82.

Kemp of the Department of Psychology, University of Canterbury, Christchurch, argues that historically-speaking, demon possession was only applied to a narrow range of disorders, and that most people believed in physical causes of mental disorders.[22] Then in 1987, with Kevin Williams, also from the Department of Psychology, Kemp described how the western European belief in demon possession as a cause of mental illness changed through the medieval and early modern periods, showing why this phenomenon is now considered by psychiatrists and psychologists to be very uncommon.[23] Kemp and Williams do, however, make two important points relevant to this essay. First, they say that in 'in present-day western countries, two types of possession are reasonably common in Christian Pentecostal sects'.[24] They identify the first of these as marked by 'speaking in tongues', attributed to the Holy Spirit, and the other as 'believed to be of diabolical origin and regarded with horror.'[25] Second, they note that 'whatever the reason, the possession syndrome appears more commonly in the Pentecostal Christian

22. Simon Kemp, 'Modern Myth and Medieval Madness: Views of Mental Illness in the European Middle Ages and Renaissance', in *New Zealand Journal of Psychology* 14/1 (1985): 1–8.
23. Kemp and Williams, 'Demonic Possession', 21–29.
24. Kemp and Williams, 'Demonic Possession', 22.
25. Kemp and Williams, 'Demonic Possession', 22.

> subculture than in the western community at large, and most such cases appear to escape clinical attention.'[26]

Approaches to Mental Health Issues in New Zealand

Before addressing possession syndrome in the Pentecostal Christian subculture and relating it to the New Zealand context, it is important to examine how the New Zealand public health system has responded to the challenge to provide an effective mental health service to the culturally-diverse population, for it is in the public policy literature that spirit or demon possession is discussed most often. I will mention the most significant documents published after the establishment of Regional Health Authorities in 1993, because these authorities were set up to purchase health services. To do so, these authorities engaged many working parties and commissioned much research on how to improve the health system. The *Blueprint for Mental Health Services: How Things Need To Be*, published by the Mental Health Commission in 1998, is particularly noteworthy because it is considered to have broken new ground in recognising the needs of Māori and Pacific people. Its strong emphasis on eradicating discrimination against people with mental illness, and the need to create an environment which included such sufferers, underpinned the *Blueprint* initiatives. A whole section on the needs of Māori was included. For example,

26. Kemp and Williams, 'Demonic Possession', 22.

the *Blueprint* called not only for improved quality and access to mainstream services for Māori, but also for the inclusion and encouragement of Māori elders to work alongside both Māori and non-Māori clinicians in order to provide a fuller, more comprehensive, and culturally-sensitive treatment for people. The *Blueprint* set the standards for the ongoing task of building a mental system that is responsive to all cultures.

As well as the needs of Māori, the needs of Pacific people came under scrutiny. The Ministry of Health, in response to the growth in the proportion of Pacific people from 0.1% in 1945 to 4.9% in 1991, published a significant report concerning its understanding of and responsibility to care for the mental health of Pacific people in this country.[27] The report gives very clear descriptions of how different Pacific cultures view mental well-being as 'not separate from, but considered to be part of, the overall well-being of the body, soul and spirit'.[28] In general, the report supports the observations of Gluckman and Foliaki, that Pacific people consider that a decline in mental well-being or mental illness is brought about by an external spiritual force in the form of 'ancestral spirits who have taken possession of the person because the person or the person's family have broken a certain custom or offended the spirits in some way'.[29] The belief is common across

27. Peter M Ellis and Sunny CD Collings, *Mental Health in New Zealand from a Public Health Perspective* (Wellington: Public Health Group, Ministry of Health, 1997).
28. Ellis and Collings, 'Mental Health', 106.
29. Ellis and Collings, 'Mental Health', 106.

the different Pacific cultures that there is an ongoing spiritual and physical communication between ancestors and living people. The report described how traditional healers are the ones sought out to treat sufferers, giving an example of the Samoan approach. Certain spirits are associated with different *matai* (chiefs) or families, so those possessed by those spirits 'seek out the appropriate matai to conduct the exorcism'.[30] Inspired by the intention of the *Blueprint*, the document called for fuller participation by Pacific people in mainstream mental health services, including the involvement of traditional healers.

The report, *Coordinated Care for Māori: Issues for Development*, also published in 1998, was commissioned by the Māori Policy Unit of the Ministry of Health. The unit recognised that Māori were not enjoying the same levels of health as the rest of the population, not only because of the relatively poor socio-economic status of some Māori,[31] but also because the holistic view of health adopted by Māori was not being properly catered for. This view encompasses the *Whare Tapa Whā* model, which identified the four dimensions of health as outlined in the *Blueprint*: *taha wairua* (spirituality), which includes belief in the relationship between the spirit world and living people; *taha hinengaro* (thoughts and feelings); *taha tinana* (physical well-being); and *taha whānau* (family). Traditional remedies such as *mirimiri* (massage) and *rongoā* (herbal treatments), combined with the use of traditional healers

30. Ellis and Collings, 'Mental Health', 127.
31. Ministry of Health, *Coordinated Care for Māori: Issues for Development* (Wellington: Te Kete Hauora, Ministry of Health, 1998), 5.

who incorporate *karakia* (prayer) in order to include the spiritual dimension as part of the healing, are accepted as culturally proper.[32]

Coordinated Care for Māori advocated for the mainstream medical model to be extended to include a range of traditional healing approaches at a time when Regional Health Authorities were constrained in their capability to spend their resources on 'non-health' services. The report recommended that the development of a more integrated and coordinated care system for Māori could go a long way to meet Māori aspirations and improve Māori health. This meant including 'non-health' services that are integral to Māori identity. As Mason Durie pointed out, a secure Māori identity 'depends on access to the cultural, social and economic resources of *te ao Māori* (the Māori world), especially Māori language, family networks and customary land'.[33] This necessarily includes traditional Māori medicine and healing in the appropriate setting.

The New Zealand Public Health and Disability Act 2000 (Part 3) states that district health boards are to 'reduce health disparities by improving health outcomes for Māori and other population groups'. The New Zealand Health Strategy 2000 and the New Zealand Disability Strategy 2001 address this issue. These strategies contain the government's health priorities, considered to be of utmost importance for the good health and well-being of all

32. Mason Durie, *Whaiora: Māori Health Development* (Auckland: Oxford University Press, 1998.
33. Mason Durie, 'Mental Health and Maori Development', in *Australian and New Zealand Journal of Psychiatry* 33/1 (1999): 5–12.

New Zealanders. Included is the commitment to ensure accessible and appropriate services for Māori, which includes support for Māori holistic models of health and wellness such as those laid down in the articles of the *Blueprint*.

In the same year, the Ministry of Health published two important documents on Māori health, which included Māori mental health: *He Korowai Oranga: Māori Health Strategy* and *Whakatātaka: Maori Health Action Plan 2002-2005*.[34] Each of these builds on and extends the insights of the 1998 document on coordinated care for Māori. A particularly significant focus of both the strategy and the action plan is that they value and recognise the veracity of Māori models of health and traditional healing. The Ministry of Health then will support, in both planning and funding, the delivery of health services which include the support of mainstream and traditional healing practices that promote the spiritual, mental, and physical wellness of Māori whānau. District health boards in New Zealand have Māori advisors for culturally-sensitive protocols for Māori, including traditional healers as well as clinicians, used both in assessment and treatment in order to maintain a holistic approach, including the spiritual dimension important to Māori. This is also true for the different Pacific groups, particularly Samoans and Tongans. As in the

34. *He Korowai Oranga* literally means 'the cloak of wellness'; *He Korowai Oranga: Māori Health Strategy* (Wellington: Ministry of Health, 2002), ii; *Whakatātaka* is the weaving of strands, creating a pattern step by step; *Whakatātaka: Māori Health Action Plan 2002–2005* (Wellington: Ministry of Health, 2002), ii.

case for Māori, district health boards have developed and maintained a positive recruitment of different health professionals from the different ethnic groups, who in turn maintain links with traditional healers and advisors, both within and outside the health system.

Te Orau Ora: Pacific Mental Health Profile, published in 2005 by the Ministry of Health, was commissioned to provide up-to-date information on the mental health status of Pacific peoples in order to provide relevant information to district health board funders and planners, so that the needs of this population might be more appropriately met.

Te Orau Ora drew attention to the marked difference between the way western medicine and Pacific people view mental health. In particular, it stressed that for Pacific people, 'holistic' meant that 'the spiritual, physical, emotional, and family—need to be in harmony', and that western terms such as 'chemical imbalance' or 'biological cause' are not concepts 'that Pacific peoples easily identify with'.[35] In a discussion in response to the 'spiritual dimension', the report pointed out that, while the Ministry of Health does have a commitment to incorporating traditional healing processes with western models, in 'modern western psychiatric practices, discussion, and literature, there is a tendency to either pathologise or ignore spiritual experiences'.[36] Consequently, the report found evidence that Pacific people are more likely to go to general practi-

35. Ministry of Health, *Te Orau Ora: Pacific Mental Health Profile* (Wellington: Ministry of Health, 2005), 17.
36. Ministry of Health, *Te Orau Ora*, 17.

tioners, and less likely to interact with mental health services, showing that there is a need to 'build and maintain links between non-mental health services and general Pacific health services, and the mental health sector'.[37] What the report has highlighted is that, despite positive steps to integrate Pacific peoples into the full range of the western health system, there is still work to be done.

A noteworthy article published in 2005 outlined means of assisting Pacific peoples to develop a pathway towards being fully integrated into the mental health system in a culturally-appropriate way. This was described as a new research method for Samoan people called *Fa'afaletui,* which was thought also to be of use to other Pacific cultures which have a strong sense of collective identity.[38] The Fa'afaletui concept is a method 'which facilitates the gathering and validation of important knowledge within the culture', wherein gender-separated groups met to share knowledge, and to discuss issues of cultural protocol and *tapu* which could not be discussed openly in mixed-gender groups. Representatives of each group then met to thread and rethread the information among the relational houses 'until all were agreed that the specific knowledge pieces were valid and authentically reflected the collective experience of the participants'.[39] 'Relational houses'

37. Ministry of Health, *Te Orau Ora*, 37.
38. Kiwi Tamasese, Carmel Peteru, Charles Waldegrave, and Allister Bush, '*Ole Taeao Afua*, The New Morning: A Qualitative Investigation into Samoan Perspectives on Mental Health and Culturally Appropriate Services', in *Australian and New Zealand Journal of Psychiatry* 39 (2005): 300.
39 Tamasese and others, '*Ole Taeao Afua*', 302.

in this context refers to the separate gender-based elder groups composed of health professionals and representatives from the Samoan community deemed appropriate to participate. When this method was applied to the issue of culturally-appropriate Samoan mental health services, through the process of Fa'afaletui, the study concluded that the Samoan sense of self as a relational self was 'crucial to an understanding of what constitutes mental well-being for Samoan people', and that spirituality must be addressed in the mental health care of Samoan people.[40] In a manner similar to that by which Kaupapa Māori mental health services have established collective whānau-centred practices to address all the needs, including the spiritual needs, of Māori as crucial to securing Māori identity and mental well-being, the report concluded that understanding Pacific identity in the mental health context is the positive way forward.

During the 1980s, and up until 1990, most of the research into the mental health of Asian people focused on refugees and trauma. Between 1991 and 2001, Asian people were forming the fastest-growing ethnic population in New Zealand, making up 6.4 percent of the population.[41] Consequently, in 2002, the Mental Health Commission charged the Department of Geography at the University of Waikato to produce a report which identified mental health problems in Asian communities, and which was

40. Tamasese and others, *'Ole Taeao Afua'*, 307.
41. Elsie Ho, Sybil Au, Charlotte Bedford, and Jenine Cooper, *Mental Health Issues for Asians in New Zealand* (Wellington: Mental Health Commission, 2003).

published the following year. The report highlighted two important points.

The first point was that mental illness 'is highly stigmatising in many Asian cultures who consider that illnesses like schizophrenia are conceived of as supernatural punishments for wrong-doings, and as such entail intense shame and stigma'.[42] The second point was that because Asian people use traditional health practices often in tandem with western medicine, and do not necessarily inform western mental health professionals, mental illness amongst Asians was seen as 'a critical research issue', because 'growing population diversity raises concerns for increased sensitivity to and respect for differences in beliefs and cultural practices'.[43] The report's recommendations reinforced the necessity of providing information and support systems constructed to encourage increased participation in New Zealand society and the New Zealand health system, and ongoing research into how to address Asian mental health problems more effectively.

Because there are still gaps to be filled, the *Te Rau Hinengaro: The New Zealand Mental Health Survey*, published in 2006, has reaffirmed the need to continue to support Māori and Pacific health initiatives and providers. The work of breaking down barriers to health service use and mental health service delivery needs to continue. New primary mental health initiatives aimed at Māori need ongoing support, as does primary health care for Pacific peoples, because there are still gaps to be filled.

42. Ho and others, *Mental Health*, xiii.
43. Ho and others, *Mental Health*, xiv.

Treatment options, the report said, need to take into account more fully the range of beliefs about the causes of mental unwellness.

What this survey of the responses of government and mental health professionals in the New Zealand context shows is that the 'commitment to understand' includes enshrining in public policy the different ways that this country's diverse cultures comprehend the spirit world and spirit possession as related to their mental well-being. Professional psychiatry, which is guided by public policy, is open to trying to provide appropriate treatment to members of those cultures which hold that ancestral spirits are able to have adverse effects on the physical, psychological, and spiritual well-being of people. Mental health practitioners, whose expertise is the psychosocial and emotional assessment of individuals, are thus supported strongly by policy and practice to include the spiritual dimension of a person's life in assessment and treatment. Even though there is still work to be done to strengthen this holistic approach to the many cultures in New Zealand, the task of ensuring culturally-sensitive responses is a goal shared by government and clinicians alike.

Conclusion

I wish to return to the point made by Kemp and Williams, that demon possession is most likely to occur in Pentecostal sects and most likely to escape clinical attention. This raises some quite serious questions. There has been a significant increase in Pentecostal communities and churches in New Zealand. The attraction of Pentecostalism is the 'receiving and retaining of the Holy Spirit' to meet human needs, with an emphasis on healing and being delivered from evil.[44] If persons are told they are possessed, or believe they are possessed by a demon or evil spirit, then a deliverance or exorcism is performed. The rationale for this practice is based on the belief that the tradition of doing so is 'regarded as a continuation of the New Testament tradition and was a feature of the ministry of healing evangelists', with their gift of deliverance ministry.[45] If there is an increasing Pentecostal population in New Zealand, and if we assume there is an increase in exorcism/deliverance of demons, there could well be unidentified cases of mental illness. What enables pastors and ministers to diagnose what is demon possession, versus what are symptoms of an identifiable, treatable mental illness? What about people from Māori, Pacific, or Asian cultures who also belong to Pentecostal churches? How is Christian demonic possession distinguished from the beliefs that different ethnic groups have about spirit possession and that spring from their own cultural understandings about the spirit world and spirit possession? To what extent do pastors and ministers have power to call people 'possessed' who are not insane by any other standards?

44. John Wilson and Harvey K Clow, 'Themes of Power and Control in a Pentecostal Assembly', in *Journal for the Scientific Study of Religion* 20/3 (1981): 244.
45. Allan Anderson, *An Introduction to Pentecostalism* (Cambridge: Cambridge University Press, 2004), 223.

> The concern for psychiatry and mental health clinicians, then, is not that people are being possessed by demons, but rather that if their faith community believes they are, and exorcism is not working, they will neither seek, nor are likely to be encouraged to seek, assistance from mental health services. If people are being deprived of a full diagnosis which might show that they have a treatable mental illness, then self-harm, stigmatisation, or isolation from the wider community might result, with tragic effects.

Bibliography

Anderson, Allan. *An Introduction to Pentecostalism* (Cambridge: Cambridge University Press, 2004).

Azaunce, Miriam. 'Is it Schizophrenia or Spirit Possession?', in *Journal of Social Distress and the Homeless* 4/3 (1995): 255–263.

Bach, Paul, J. 'Demon Possession and Psychopathology: A Theological Relationship', in *Journal of Psychology and Theology* 7/1 (1979): 22–26.

Betty, Stafford. 'The Growing Evidence for Demonic Possession: What Should Psychiatry's Response Be?', in *Journal of Religion and Health* 44/1 (2005): 13–30.

Chui, SN. 'Historical, Religious, and Medical Perspectives of Possession Phenomenon', in *Hong Kong Journal of Psychiatry* 10/1 (2000): 14–18.

Coons, Philip. 'The Differential Diagnoses of Possession States', in *Dissociation* 1 (1993): 213–221.

Durie, Mason. 'Mental Health and Māori Development', in *Australian and New Zealand Journal of Psychiatry* 33/1 (1999): 5–12.

--------. *Whaiora: Maori Health Development* (Auckland: Oxford University Press, 1998).

Ellis, Peter M, and Sunny CD Collings. *Mental Health in New Zealand from a Public Health Perspective* (Wellington: Public Health Group, Ministry of Health, 1997).

Forrest, AD. 'Concepts of Mental Illness: An Historical Introduction', in *Companion to Psychiatric Studies*, edited by AD Forrest, J Affleck and A Zeally (Edinburgh: Churchill Livingstone, 1978), 1–7.

Freud, Sigmund. 'Seventeenth Century Demonological Neurosis', in *The Complete Psychological Works of Sigmund Freud*, edited by James Strachey (London: Hogarth Press, 1961), 19:67–105.

Gavin, Ivey. 'Diabolical Discourses: Demonic Possession and Evil in Modern Psychopathology', in *South African Journal of Psychology* 32/4 (2002): 54–59.

Gluckman, Laurie K. 'Clinical Experience with Samoans in Auckland', in *Australian and New Zealand Journal of Psychiatry* 11 (1977): 101–107.

Ho, Elsie, Sybil Au, Charlotte Bedford, and Jenine Cooper. *Mental Health Issues for Asians in New Zealand* (Wellington: Mental Health Commission, 2003).

Johnson, Walter C. 'Demon Possession and Mental Illness', in *Journal of the American Scientific Affiliation* 34 (1982): 149–154.

Kemp, Simon. 'Modern Myth and Medieval Madness: Views of Mental Illness in the European Middle Ages and Renaissance', in *New Zealand Journal of Psychology* 14/1 (1985): 1–8.

Kemp, Simon, and Kevin Williams. 'Demonic Possession and Mental Disorder in Medieval and Early Modern Europe', in *Psychological Medicine* 17 (1987): 21–29.

Kinloch, PJ, and M Short. 'Samoan Spirit Possession: Case Report', in *New Zealand Medical Journal* 90 (1979): 498–499.

Ministry of Health. Unpublished minutes of a fono on Pacific Islands mental health. Wellington: Ministry of Health, 1993. www.moh.govt.nz/moh.nsf/Files/chap4/$file/chap4.pdf (accessed December 18, 2007).

Ministry of Health. *Coordinated Care for Māori: Issues for Development* (Wellington: Te Kete Hauora, Ministry of Health, 1998).

Ministry of Health. *Te Orau Ora: Pacific Mental Health Profile* (Wellington: Ministry of Health, 2005).

Ministry of Health. *Whakatātaka: Māori Health Action Plan 2002–2005* (Wellington: Ministry of Health, 2002).

Ministry of Health. *Oranga: Maori Health Strategy* (Wellington: Ministry of Health, 2002).

Prins, H. 'Besieged by Devils—Thoughts on Possession and Possession States', in *Medical Science and the Law* 32 (1992): 237–246.

Sall, Millard J. 'A Response to 'Demon Possession and Psychopathology: A Theological Relationship', in *Journal of Psychology and Theology* 7/1 (1979): 27–30.

--------. 'Demon Possession or Psychopathology? A Clinical Differentiation', in *Journal of Psychology and Theology* 4/4 (1976): 286–290.

Stone, Michael H. *Healing the Mind: A History of Psychiatry from Antiquity to the Present* (New York: WW Norton, 1997).

Tamasese, Kiwi, Carmel Peteru, Charles Waldegrave, and Allister Bush. '*Ole Taeao Afua,* The New Morning: A Qualitative Investigation into Samoan Perspectives on Mental Health and Culturally Appropriate Services', in *Australian and New Zealand Journal of Psychiatry* 39 (2005): 300–309.

Toafa, Viliami, Losa Moata'ane, and Barbara Guthrie. 'Tongan Medicine and the Role of Traditional Tongan Healers in New Zealand', in *Pacific Health Dialog* 8 (2001): 78–82.

Unger, MF. *Demons in the World Today* (Wheaton, IL: Tyndale House Publishers, 1971).

Wilson, John, and Harvey K Clow. 'Themes of Power and Control in a Pentecostal Assembly', in *Journal for the Scientific Study of Religion* 20/3 (1981): 241–250.

A *Moana* Rhythm of Well-Being

Winston Halapua

This essay is essentially about the concept of well-being, within which spirit possession is located and analysed theologically. As the notion of well-being is explored in relation to spirit possession, so some actions are suggested. This contribution provides an Oceanic perspective on spirit possession, and needs to be seen in relation to other contributions in this volume.

I have structured my exploration in six parts: (a) A Tongan understanding of spirit possession; (b) Jesus casting out demons; (c) the Tongan concept of *'avea* (spirit possession); (d) a *moana* (Oceanic) methodology for reflecting on the concept of well-being; (e) the natural rhythm of well-being; and (f) a Christ-centred challenge of who the spirit-possessed are.

There are marked differences in the way Tongans and most other people in Oceania understand spirit possession, from the way in which it is understood in other parts of the world. The focus of this essay is an exploration of the deep theological understanding of spirit possession in an Oceanic context and its relationship to the issues of mental disorder and to the wider community.

In this chapter, I write of spirit possession in the context of Tonga. The Tongans are Polynesians. As a kingdom and independent nation, Tonga is one of the Pacific nation states. The author speaks from a Polynesian perspective, but at the same time acknowledges that within Oceania there will be many common experiences relating to spirit possession.

A Tongan Understanding of Spirit Possession

One of my first memories of my childhood in Tonga is of an incident which happened when I was about six years old. It remains a vivid, indelible memory. My parents were going low-water fishing to gather shellfish and seaweed. The location was about five miles from our home. To carry the catch, a horse would be needed. As a small boy, I rode on the back of the horse which my father led, my mother walking alongside. Near our isolated destination was the grave of a young man who had been a very promising youth, but who had died in a tragic accident. Suddenly, as we neared the grave, the horse became agitated and reared. Its head moved from side to side. Its nostrils flared and steamed. The terrified horse attempted to turn and run before my father grabbed the bridle. I was thrown in the air and had a bad fall onto the dirt track. My mother screamed.

It seemed that the previously docile horse really refused to pass the grave. Its behaviour was unexpected and inexplicable except in terms of the location. I survived the frightening incident and the fall. It was only my father's strong presence, and my trust in him and my mother, that enabled me to go back to the horse and continue the journey. But as years passed I came across similar stories associated with that particular place.

My father became a priest, and later a bishop. I remember that he was often called to minister to parishioners, extended family, and others, whose minds and behaviour were disturbed and who were regarded as spirit-possessed. This spirit possession in Tonga was and is not regarded as uncommon in the community. My father was a man of prayer and was regarded as having great *mana* (charisma). People acknowledged that the victim of spirit possession would calm even before my father reached the home of the one affected. On reaching the home, my father would call the whole family together and he would lay hands on the possessed person and pray. If he felt it necessary, he would refer the person to a doctor to receive additional help. Healing was in the context of a family—often, extended family—and in the context of other help and expertise within the community.

My early experience reminds me that forms of what we may call spirit possession are common in Tonga. 'Spirit possession' in Tonga may be linked with the atmosphere of a location, with tragedy, and with disturbance. Animals, like the horse of my childhood, may exhibit a sense of foreboding that there is spiritual disturbance. Spirit possession in Tonga, and in many Pacific Island communities, may be linked to particular locations. It is always seen in the context of a community and that community's interrelationships.

In Tonga, people with strange behaviour and emotional disturbance may be regarded as spirit-possessed. Such behaviours and disturbances may be clearly connected to some tragic events, or may be inexplicable. An important dimension of the healing of those regarded as spirit-possessed is the presence of someone who is trusted, people with whom they feel safe, and someone perceived to have a strong spirituality, or *mana.* This is illustrated above by my father's strong presence in the incident with the horse. I trusted my father and that trust prevailed. It illustrates my father's gifts of prayerful, strong, and wise presence when called upon to exercise ministry.

Jesus Casting out Demons (Mark 5:1–20): A Tongan Perspective

The story of the healing of Gerasene Demoniac is an extremely dramatic story in Mark's gospel. Jesus crossed the lake in a boat and, after the stilling of the storm, he and his disciples reached the country of the Gerasenes. Jesus is in a location which is Gentile, and therefore regarded as a place which is essentially unhealthy. On stepping out of the boat, Jesus is immediately confronted with a man who lived among the tombs and whose behaviour was so disturbed that shackles and chains could not hold him. The man confronts Jesus, acknowledging the strength of Jesus' presence: 'What have you to do with me, Jesus, Son of the most High God? I adjure you by God, do not torment me.' For Jesus had said to him, 'Come out of the man, you unclean spirit.'

Tongans would identify with this story and appreciate the different features which they could relate to from their own village experiences. Tongans would see that the unhealthy environment (Gentiles and tombs), the episode of the reacting animals (pigs), the torment of the man, and his isolation from the community were all interrelated. What is happening on the land, what is happening among the animals, what is happening among people are all connected and have bearings on the health and behaviour of individuals. In the story, the man who is possessed recognises the strong presence of God in the person of Jesus. Here, in Jesus, there is a power that is greater than his torment. Tongans understand that sense of awe and presence, and the healing which will arise from an encounter with a person of great *mana*.

Names are important in Tonga. They tell of identity and relationship. Names sometimes speak of events in history—which may be of happiness or trauma. When Jesus asks the name of the tormented man, he replies, 'My name is Legion, for we are many.' If the English word 'Legion' is used, it is not difficult, given the significance of names, for Tongans to interpret that the man is referring to the many dimensions of trauma arising from Roman occupation. In the Tongan language, the man is called 'Kongakau'—a strict translation is 'A part of many parts'. What a Tongan listening to the story hears is that unwellness is part of a more complex situation. Who I am is the result of what has happened to me, who I am is stemming from my isolation in the tombs, my behaviour is an expression of being pushed out of the village. Who I am is because I have no longer a place in community. The possessed man acknowledges there is no place for him, and therein lies his agony and his despair. He sees no way out of his isolation.[1]

The story goes on: 'He begged him earnestly not to send them out of the country.' Now on the hillside, a great herd of swine was feeding and the unclean spirits begged him (Jesus), 'Send us into the swine let us enter them.' So he gave them permission. 'And the unclean spirits came out and entered the swine, and the herd, numbering about two thousand, rushed down the steep bank into the sea and were drowned.' Animals in Tonga, as we have seen, sometimes are acknowledged as giving expression to disturbance. The herd of pigs in this context carries the expression of the trauma. The unclean spirits, which are the result of the complex trauma of a man who has no place in the community, are cast out. The spirits of 'un-belonging', of 'no place', are given a place in the pigs as they rush to the sea. The void in the man's life is swallowed up in the chaos of the sea.

The story of the Gerasene Demoniac in Mark's gospel, read through Tongan eyes, would illustrate the importance of the community in healing. The man is restored to a place of belonging in the friendship of Jesus. The man wants to stay with Jesus, but Jesus says to him, 'Go home to your friends, and tell them how much the Lord has

1. See the essay later in this volume, by Elaine Wainwright, on this same passage from Mark.

done for you, and what mercy he has shown you'(Mark 5:19).

The impact of Jesus' healing activities on those who are spirit-possessed reveals the dawn of the new age in the reign of God. Healing of the spirit-possessed is healing that has a spiritual dimension, and is about the restoration of a person's ability to relate to God and to others within the community.

An Oceanic understanding of spirit possession foregrounds and affirms the relationship between those deemed possessed and the wider environment and their communities, as the stories above illustrate. There is, in Oceania, a respect for the place of location, the network of relationships, and the ancestors. In the Oceanic worldview before the impact of the missionaries, the honouring of gods and spirits was closely linked to the earth and the sea, the flora and the fauna, all of which were integral to the people's lives. Spirit possession in an Oceanic paradigm is seen in the context of a whole range of relationships. It is a holistic tragedy, not an individual one.

'Avea in Tongan Tradition

I am a lay person in the area of psychiatry and the medical world. However, I have come to believe that there is a broad overlapping relationship between what the Bible terms as spirit possession, and mental disorders. Mental disorders include schizophrenia, depression, and other psychiatric conditions.

Mapa Ha'ano Puloka, the first Tongan psychiatrist, has written extensively on the topic of mental disorders within a Tongan context. His Tongan word for mental disorder, including spirit possession, is *'avanga.* In his article on concepts of mental illness, he writes: 'Avanga is a Tongan concept which is couched in culture-specific idioms. It has mystical phenomena with pathological manifestation that is characterised by disassociation. In its popular Tongan conceptualisation it means an acute, short duration sickness caused (or believed to be caused) by a spook.'[2]

The ancient Tongan word for spirit possession is 'avea. 'Avanga and 'avea have the same roots in Tongan. 'Avea was the word first written down by the Christian missionaries who initially translated the Bible into Tongan, thereby introducing the culture of the written word into our context. By their use of ancient Tongan words to express biblical realities and profound human experiences, the missionaries have preserved words which are deep and rich, some of which have now faded from common use.

The word 'avea is now not in common use, due to the fact that popular English words for mental disorders have been Tonganised.[3] English words for mental disorders have been given a Tongan ring, but these words do not stem from within the culture. Profound human experiences, then, are described with alien words, though attempts have been made at translation.

The depth of meaning in the word 'avea is closer to expressing the understanding of spirit possession in the

2. Mapa Ha'ano Puloka, "*Avanga*: Tongan Concepts of Mental Illness', in *Pacific Health Dialog* 6/2 (1999): 268.
3. See Michael Poltorak, 'Nemesis, Speaking, and *Tauhi Vaha'a*', in *The Contemporary Pacific* 19/1 (2007): 1–36.

Bible. According to the Hebrew understanding, the spirit and the body are interwoven and not separated. 'Avea is more than spirit possession; it is about networks of relationship. Tongans are born into an extended family, and it is common for people to trace their ancestry. When a Tongan person is considered 'avea, the response of other Tongans is to view the person within the web of relationships: their place in the family, where the family come from, and what the responsibilities of that person are within a larger range of activities. Tongans see the person considered 'avea as a person with a name and with an understanding of how that name has been handed down through generations. Tongans who belong to the whole extended family see the person with 'avea as belonging to them, and so treat that person with compassion. If there is stigmatisation, or the person is made fun of, then the indication is that the mockers are outside the wider relationships of the extended family.

As in many other Oceanic island communities, 'avea, for Tongans, is deeper than a psychiatric problem, disease, or possession. Individual Tongans are seen in their totality: the names they bear, the rights, privileges, and responsibilities which go with those names, the family tree, the composition of the extended families to which they belong, the power of an ancestral line, and the place of each person in the community. In addition, a person is a unique individual with particular achievements, failures, or choices. The person with 'avea remains, in essence, with his or her relationships intact, but the sickness has hijacked the person's life, taking away the ability to fulfil a role completely within the community. When individuals are deprived of fulfilling their potential due to 'avea, the extended family steps in to assume the sick person's normal responsibilities. The person with 'avea does not leave a gap in the family; the person remains an important part of the whole family and is held by the whole family, as life goes on.

'Avea indicates deprivation from living as a full person because of a sickness beyond one's control. Interestingly then, in the Tongan use of 'avea, there is a suggestion not so much of possession, but of dispossession. A person with 'avea is seen clearly as a significant member of the family and is held within that family, but the person is dispossessed of a unique and productive life, and of fulfilling responsibility, due to a sickness which is mostly not of the person's own making.

Moana Methodology and the Theological Hermeneutic of Moana Well-being

Moana methodology is a hermeneutic by which 'spirit possession' can be explored theologically from an Oceanic perspective. It is a way of attempting to engage spirit possession through the eyes of well-being.

Moana is one of the ancient Polynesian words for the ocean. Moana is also a generic word for the ocean. The ocean accounts for nearly three-quarters of the surface area on this planet Earth. Today, our immense moana is grouped into five regions—the Pacific Ocean, the Atlantic Ocean, the Indian Ocean, the Arctic Ocean and the Antarctic Ocean. The reclaiming of the moana as a fundamental world-view, as opposed to large land masses, is a conscious move to articulate the integrity and uniqueness of an Oceanic identity. Moana methodology proposes that an Oceanic world-view has a significant and distinct con-

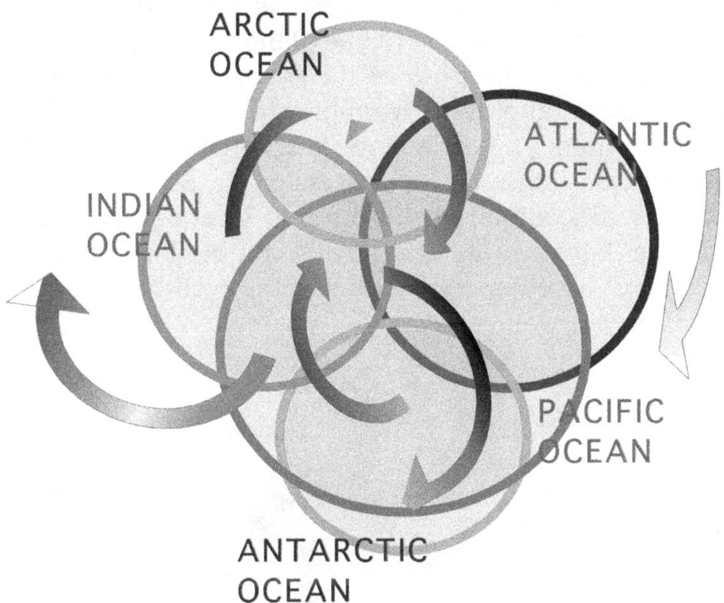

tribution to offer to issues of well-being and spirit possession.

The foundational position of moana methodology attempts to honour the integrity of an Oceanic world-view which asserts the interconnectedness of all creation. The moana is acknowledged, in essence, as a gift of the Creator. The interconnectedness of the moana (now known as the five oceans) to the sun, moon, stars, the wind, the atmosphere, continental shelves, the deep, the land, all species including humanity, is celebrated. The flowing and the interwovenness of the five oceans are integral to the whole rhythm of the moana. The cross-flowing rhythm and interaction of the oceans, and the vast differences of each region, gift life to the whole planet Earth in so many ways. The interacting life of the oceans affects climate, oxygen, space, and home for most species on Earth. Moana methodology offers an interconnected world-view to an understanding of spirit possession. In this paradigm, moana is conceptualised by the holistic interconnection of all life. Each set of values finds completion in all the others, and together contributes to the well-being of the community.

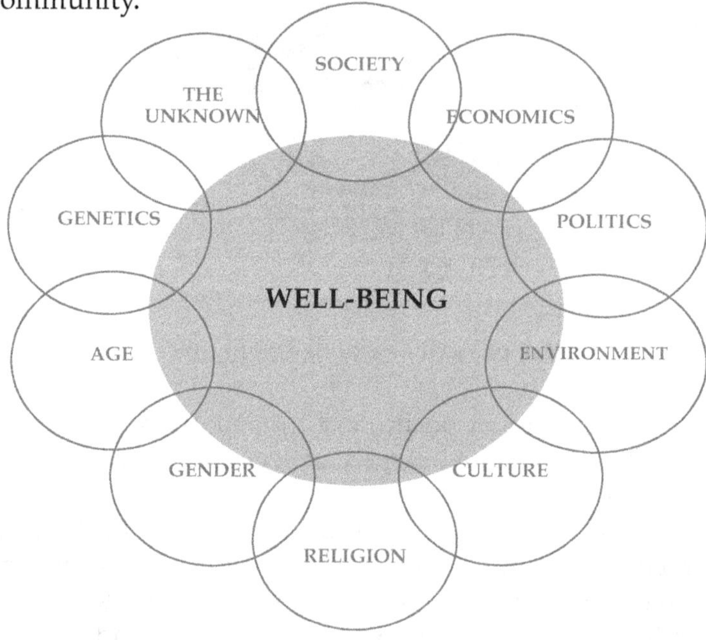

The five oceans have particular resources and aspects, but at the same time each finds completion in the others, and together all contribute to the well-being of life on planet Earth—the essence of global wholeness. As the oceans are different yet interacting, so this essay proposes that there is no single way of approaching, investigating, and contributing to the issues of spirit possession. Moana methodology would underline that, while there are many ways of investigating and analysing, a theological contribution is one approach with a unique gift. The uniqueness of the methodology, this writer asserts, is the emphasis that in Christ we encounter the fullness of God's love and the source of our interconnectedness, informing us in our engagement with all others, including those perceived as spirit-possessed.

The Rhythm of Well-being

A moana perspective, from the outset, is about working together and receiving one another's contributions as gifts with their own integrity. From a moana perspective, spirit possession is not the totality of a person. A person's whole life is not coloured by it. The illness is a part of a far bigger picture. To give an example, a person who is perceived as spirit-possessed already has an ancestral or family name. She or he, single or married, has a family tree and a rich history. The context of the person in relation to the community and the land is recognised. A person has individual dreams and aspirations. A person in Oceania is born into a community of belonging, and for the most part, the community holds that person with her or his illnesses and inner disturbance, even though the person may find difficulty in relating in the usual way.

In the healing stories of Jesus presented by the gospels in relation to spirit possession, a whole new avenue of understanding well-being is exposed. Jesus unveils the rottenness of oppressive and unjust structures which dispossess the powerless. He engages with victims who are suffering huge trauma, and in doing so, exposes the root and violent causes of people's acute suffering. Jesus is not condemning the victims; he is releasing them to fullness of life so that they might return to community. He is asserting well-being and is challenging whatever mitigates against that.

In Jesus, we have one whose love embraces all, including those perceived as spirit-possessed. Jesus addresses not just the suffering of individuals, but also that which is dislocated in society. In this way, Jesus is deeply contextual. He sees people in their total environment. His love provides the rhythm of well-being which embraces the totality of a person, and then embraces them in their relationship with God and in community.

Who are the Spirit-Possessed?

Jesus' embrace of the spirit-possessed has prompted this writer to pose the question: 'Who *are* the possessed?'

Spirit possession in the gospels is associated with those who have been isolated by the community on one level. They are regarded as possessed by demons. But Jesus addressed the question of well-being far more broadly. He spoke into a web of violent and exploitative relationships that isolated and abused powerless people and labelled them as 'spirit-possessed'. The challenging question remains: 'What is health or well-being?' Jesus does not allow a narrow view of health. He is about promoting the health of the whole community. I would argue that today, those who engage in perpetuating any unjust system should be challenged, just as were the religious and political leaders of Jesus' day.

To what extent is spirit possession acknowledged in the psychiatric world of mental disorders? How can spirit possession be located, analysed, and treated within a holistic understanding of well-being? The World Health Organisation has a broad understanding of health. It is more than just absence of physical illness: health comprises a 'state of complete physical, mental, and social being'.[4] Beaglehole and Bonita argue that 'The foundations of health are common to all and include basic requirements such as adequate food, safe water, shelter, safety, and hope. In addition, information, education, and a sense of community are essential if people are to develop their potential'.[5]

The contribution of spiritual well-being is not emphasised in the WHO definition, or in Beaglehole and Bonita.

---

4. National Health Committee, *The Social, Cultural and Economic Determinants of Health in New Zealand: Action to Improve Health.* A report from the National Advisory Committee on Health and Disability (Wellington: Ministry of Health, June, 1998), 20, http://www.nhc.health.govt.nz/moh.nsf/0/BC21C8CFF2D8D5DFCC2572AC0016BBC7 (acccessed June 19, 2007).
5. R. Beaglehole and R. Bonita, *Public Health at the Crossroads: Achievements and Prospects*, second edition (Cambridge: Cambridge University Press, 2004), 4.

Spirituality tends to be assumed, or put as an appendix, in the published strategies of the Ministry of Health (2001),[6] the Ministry of Health for Disability Issues (2001),[7] and the Auckland District Health Board (2002).[8] Prominent place is given in these documents to the socio-economic, political, and academic dimensions of health. Many other needs of those with mental disorders are also included: for example, a safe environment, housing, food, and education. Spirituality seems to be only an afterthought. Yet, living in acknowledgement of the ancestors, and in relationship with the environment and to the community, are sacred dimensions of Oceanic people, a crucial part of their whole view of what constitutes well-being. To deny this most basic part of the makeup of Oceanic peoples is to totally dislocate them as human beings, and to deny their rights. To separate an Oceanic person from the value of living in interconnectedness with her or his God, the environment, and fellow human beings is like expecting an island to exist without an ocean.

---

6. Ministry of Health, *Primary Health Care Strategy* (Wellington: Ministry of Health, 2001), http://www.moh.govt.nz/moh.nsf/pagesmh/756 (accessed August 13, 2007).
7. Minister for Disability Issues, *The New Zealand Disability Strategy* (Wellington: Ministry of Health, 2001), http://www.nzds.govt.nz (accessed August 10, 2007).
8. Auckland District Health Board, 'Hei Oranga Tika Mo Te Iti Me Te Rahi: Healthy Communities, Quality Healthcare. Proposed Strategic Plan for the Auckland District Health Board 2002–2007' (Auckland: Auckland District Health Board, 2002), http://www.adhb.govt.nz/downloads/publications/reports/2002/short-summary-version.pdf (accessed July 20, 2007).

David Lui's chapter entitled 'Spiritual Injury; A Samoan Perspective on Spirituality's Impact on Mental Health' points out how rarely spirit possession, as defined above, is given a place within modern health systems.[9] Western paradigms and scientifically-driven health systems which reject spirit possession directly undermine the ancient worldviews of the Oceanic people.

Spirit possession may be understood in various ways: mental disorder, psychiatric illness, abnormality, dysfunction, or being possessed by external forces or demons. I would argue, from a theological perspective, that spirit possession is related to the God who embraces all life with God's love, including those perceived as being spirit-possessed. A Christian contribution to an understanding and compassionate embrace of the marginalised and powerless within our communities, including the spirit-possessed, is imperative. People, like the five oceans (Diagram 1), live and share life with each other (Diagram 2). In order to be whole, people need each other. Each section of the community exists for others and through others. For Christians, relationships which link them to others, and their interconnectedness to each other, are modelled in Christ.

9. David Lui, 'Spiritual Injury: A Samoan Perspective on Spirituality's Impact on Mental Health', in *Penina Uliuli: Contemporary Challenges in Mental Health for Pacific Peoples*, edited by Philip Culbertson and Margaret Nelson Agee, with Cabrini 'Ofa Makasiale (Honolulu, University of Hawai'i Press, 2007), 72.

> Christ, as the revelation of God's love in the power of the Spirit of God, provides a deeper understanding of well-being than do many of the definitions supplied by the western world-views. I would argue that Oceanic perspectives more fairly represent the wider understandings of health, in that they include relationships to the extended family, the environment, and God.[10] The health of human beings in Jesus' healing stories moves beyond physical and mental well-being. Jesus' compassionate care and healing offer spiritual well-being to complete the package, by including full restoration of a person to self, the household, the community, and God.

Conclusion

The ancient word 'avea, as the fullest Tongan expression for spirit possession, conveys that there are people who are dispossessed and deprived of the totality of their humanity, which stems from their place in community and their relationship with God. 'Avea, in a nut shell, is about people deprived not through their doing, but by forces beyond their control. 'Avea can be located and analysed from the perspective of socio-economics,[11]

10. Sitaleki A Finau, 'Cultural Democracy', *Maori and Pacific Island Health* 33/5 (2006): 313–318.
11. James Rarick, 'Abstracts from the Pacific Global Health Conference', in *Pacific Health Dialog* 13/2 (2006): 163–196.

gender,[12] culture,[13] political policies,[14] and many other factors. 'Avea signals that the undermining of the place of God, from an Oceanic perspective, is a fundamental issue of justice. Those with 'avea as human beings are to be restored with compassion to their place in the community, and this means addressing all that dislocates people in society. The illness of the whole community is the pressing issue.

> The writer would only feel able to speak from an understanding of health which acknowledges the context and the web of relationships in which a suffering individual is located. A moana well-being approach is a relational and holistic paradigm in regard to spirit possession. Such an approach is concerned with what makes for the wholeness of people. It

12. Vivian Lin, Helen L'Orange, and Kate Silburn, 'Using Gender-sensitive Health Indicators to Help Achieve Equity and Equality in Mainstream Policy Development and Programme Delivery', in *Development Bulletin* 71 (2006): 49–54.
13. Madhukar Pande, Sitaleki Finau, and Graham Roberts, 'Retaining Pacific Cultural Values in Modern Health Systems', in *Pacific Health Dialog* 11/1 (2004): 107–113.
14. Debbie Peterson, *I Haven't Told Them, They Haven't Asked: The Employment Experiences of People with Experience of Mental Illness* (Auckland: Mental Health Foundation of New Zealand, 2007), 55–57, http://www.mentalhealth.org.nz/resources/I-havent-told-experiences.pdf (accessed November 16, 2007); Roland Schultz, 'Community Mental Health', in *Pacificentric Health Research Methods: Anthology Series No 1* (Suva, Fiji: Pacific Health Research Council, 2003), 189–196.

recognises the interconnectedness of social, mental, physical, economic, political, environmental, religious, gender, and spiritual factors to the field of health. An Oceanic understanding of interconnectedness gives energy to this approach. The writer would argue that this approach resonates with the approach of Jesus to people who are marginalised, including people with spirit possession. Jesus' understanding of and love for an individual in her or his totality is evident throughout his whole ministry.

Bibliography

Auckland District Health Board, 'Hei Oranga Tika Mo Te Iti Me Te Rahi: Healthy Communities, Quality Healthcare. Proposed Strategic Plan for the Auckland District Health Board 2002-2007' (Auckland: Auckland District Health Board, 2002), http://www.adhb.govt.nz/downloads/publications/reports/2002/short-summary-version.pdf (accessed July 20, 2007).

Beaglehole, R, and R Bonita. *Public Health at the Crossroads: Achievements and Prospects*, second edition (Cambridge: Cambridge University Press, 2004).

Bromley, Geoffrey W. *Theological Dictionary of the New Testament* (Grand Rapids: William B. Eerdmans, 1985).

Carter, Warren. *Matthew and the Margins: A Socio-Political and Religious Reading* (Maryknoll: Orbis Books, 2005).

Finau, Sitaleki A. 'Cultural Democracy', in *Maori and Pacific Island Health* 33/5 (2006): 313–318.

Lin, Vivian, Helen L'Orange, and Kate Silburn. 'Using Gender-sensitive Health Indicators to Help Achieve Equity and Equality in Mainstream Policy Development and Programme Delivery', in *Development Bulletin* 71 (2006): 49–54.

Lui, David. 'Spiritual Injury: A Samoan Perspective on Spirituality's Impact on Mental Health', in *Penina Uliuli: Contemporary Challenges in Mental Health*, edited by Philip Culbertson and Margaret Nelson Agee, with Cabrini 'Ofa Makasiale (Honolulu: University of Hawai'i Press, 2007), 66–76.

Minister for Disability Issues. *The New Zealand Disability Strategy* (Wellington: Ministry of Health, 2001), http://www.nzds.govt.nz (accessed August 10, 2007).

Ministry of Health. *Primary Health Care Strategy* (Wellington: Ministry of Health, 2001), http://www.moh.govt.nz/moh.nsf/pagesmh/756 (accessed August 13, 2007).

National Health Committee. *The Social, Cultural and Economic Determinants of Health in New Zealand: Action to Improve Health.* A report from the National Advisory Committee on Health and Disability (Wellington: Ministry of Health, June, 1998), http://www.nhc.health.govt.nz/moh.nsf/0/BC21C8CFF2D8D5DFC-C2572AC0016BBC7 (acccessed June 19, 2007).

Pande, Madhukar, Sitaleki A. Finau, and Graham Roberts. 'Retaining Pacific Cultural Values in Modern Health Systems', in *Pacific Health Dialog* 11/1 (March 2004): 107–113.

Peterson, Debbie. *I Haven't Told Them, They Haven't Asked: The Employment Experiences of People with Experience of*

Mental Illness (Auckland: Mental Health Foundation of New Zealand, 2007) http://www.mentalhealth.org.nz/resources/I-havent-told-experiences.pdf (accessed November 16, 2007).

Poltorak, Michael. 'Nemesis, Speaking, and *Tauhi Vaha'a'*. in *The Contemporary Pacific* 19/1 (2007): 1–36.

Puloka, Mapa Ha'ano. ''*Avanga*: Tongan Concepts of Mental Illness', in *Pacific Health Dialog* 6/2 (1999): 268–275.

Rarick, James. 'Abstracts from the Pacific Global Health Conference', in *Pacific Health Dialog* 13/2 (September, 2006): 163–196.

Schultz, Roland F. 'Community Mental Health', in *Pacificentric Health Research Methods: Anthology Series No 1* (Suva, Fiji: Pacific Health Research Council, 2003), 189–196.

Stanton, Graham. *A Gospel for a New People* (Edinburgh: T&T Clark, 1992).

Demons in Early Judaism: Demonic Influence and Political Oppression

Keith Stuart

As a teenager in the 1970s, I joined a predominantly Catholic charismatic youth group in Auckland. The prayer meetings swelled with teenagers, and were exciting and, at times, scary. The group regularly had 'deliverances' of teens supposedly possessed by evil spirits. I remember that at one meeting I raised my hands in prayer, as was the custom for the group, and an older member whispered in my ear, 'Not now, it's probably an evil spirit trying to influence you'. I felt frightened for weeks afterwards, frightened that I was at risk of being taken over by a spiritual being over whom I had no control. I felt powerless, like Sarah in the book of Tobit. Sarah's husbands were killed by an evil demon on their marriage night. She was powerless to stop it. That memory stayed with me for over thirty years. It was only after studying biblical literature and working as a counsellor that I understood what was happening in that situation and what relationship the practice of 'deliverance' had to the biblical record. In this essay, I will explore the Jewish background to demonic possession, using a framework taken from the discipline of sociology, a framework I have found useful in interpreting my own experience.

The Book of Tobit

While most Christians are familiar with the exorcising of demons in the Second Testament, the practice has its roots in the First Testament and intertestamental literature. One such Jewish story is recounted in the Book of Tobit, written approximately two hundred years before the earliest text in the Second Testament. The Book of Tobit is found in the Apocrypha.[1] The book tells the story of two related healings—of Tobit who was blind, and of Sarah. In the story, Sarah, a young woman, was troubled by the demon Asmodeus. Seven times in a row, this demon had killed Sarah's new husband on their marriage night. Sarah prayed to God to die rather than to continue to live with

1. Tobit is found in Catholic and Orthodox Bibles but not in Protestant Bibles. For the purpose of this paper I will use the English text from *The Holy Bible: New Revised Standard Version* (Nashville: Thomas Nelson Publishers, 1989). The Book of Tobit exists in both long and short versions in the Greek. The discovery of fragments of the book written in Hebrew and Aramaic amongst the Dead Scrolls has led to the longer version being seen as the earlier text. Benedikt Otzen, *Tobit and Judith*, edited by Michael Knibb, Guides to Apocrypha and Pseudepigrapha (London: Sheffield Academic Press, 2002), 63. The *NRSV* follows the longer version of the text.

the affliction caused by the demon (Tob 3:10–15). The rest of the story is summarised in Tob 3:16–17:

> At that very moment, the prayers of both of them were heard in the glorious presence of God. So Raphael was sent to heal both of them: Tobit, by removing the white films from his eyes, so that he might see God's light with his eyes; and Sarah, daughter of Raguel, by giving her in marriage to Tobias son of Tobit, and by setting her free from the wicked demon Asmodeus. For Tobias was entitled to have her before all others who had desired to marry her.

Skilful narration keeps the reader engaged for the remaining eleven chapters as the author reveals how the healing is accomplished.

The story has been described as a 'Jewish novel'. Although a novel is not usually used to fill in the details of history, we can gain insight into the lives of real people by asking appropriate questions, such as: Who was the story written for? How do the intended audience and the work itself compare to similar stories in the period and world in which the novel was written?

The period and world in which the book was written are not the same as the setting of the book. The story is set outside the Jewish homeland in the time of Assyrian rule (eighth to seventh centuries BCE). Internal evidence from the book indicates that it was written much later, namely, in the second century BCE. Hence, the rulers at the time of writing were the Greeks.[2]

The description, in the book, of life in exile under foreign rule is grim. The Jews face a constant threat of murder, bodies are left unburied in the streets, and some exiles are giving up the practice of their religion and assimilating into the foreign culture. This setting provides the purpose of the book. It was written to teach the Jews how to live under Hellenistic domination in both Palestine and the Diaspora. The key to living in this situation was to 'remain faithful to the Lord and the Law'.[3]

---

2. The writer shows knowledge of events that occurred after the period in which the book is set, and uses phrases that are dated later than the setting, for example, the fall of Nineveh to the Babylonians and the rebuilding of the temple under the Persians (Tob 14:4–5). These events may indicate that the book was written sometime after the end of Assyrian Rule, 333 BCE. Lester L. Grabbe, '"The Exile" under the Theodolite: Historiography as Triangulation', in *Leading Captivity Captive: "The Exile" as History and Ideology*, edited by Lester L Grabbe (Sheffield: Sheffield Academic, 1998), 91. The author uses the phrases 'the law of Moses' (Tob 1:8; 7:13) and 'the Book of Moses' (Tob 6:13; 7:11,12). These phrases occur in the Book of Chronicles and in books written after Chronicles, but not in earlier books. I Chronicles has been dated around 400 BCE Robert North, 'The Chronicler: 1-2 Chronicles, Ezra, Nehemiah', in *The New Jerome Biblical Commentary*, edited Raymond E Brown, Joseph A Fitzmyer, and Roland E Murphy (London: Geoffrey Chapman, 1990), 363. This places the time of writing of the Book of Tobit after 400 BCE.
3. Carey A Moore, *Tobit—A New Translation with Introduction and Commentary*, edited by William Foxwell Albright and David Noel Freedman, The Anchor Bible (New York: Doubleday, 1996), 24; also, Joseph A Fitzmyer, *Tobit*, edited by Loren T Stuckenbruck,

A Framework for Interpreting the Story

The story includes the burning of fish organs as part of Sarah's healing process. This is not, to my knowledge, a healing activity used in modern medical practice. While the story may have nothing to add to our understanding of empirical medicine,[4] from an alternative viewpoint it could provide insights into the practice of healing at the time it was written. The framework I will use to identify these insights is from the discipline of sociology.[5]

Sociology observes that healing processes take place in systems. A system of healthcare can be described as a set of interacting resources and strategies that are intended to prevent or cure illness in a particular community.[6] Pilch,

---

Commentaries on Early Jewish Literature (Berlin, New York: Walter de Gruyter, 2003), 31.

4. In his commentary on Tobit, Fitzmyer appears to take the viewpoint of modern empirical medicine. He notes that the book has primitive conceptions and beliefs about angels subduing demons and supplying remedies for bodily afflictions. 'They all make a good folktale, but hardly convince one of their historical substance.' Fitzmyer, *Tobit*, 33.
5. Sociology is defined as the systematic investigation of human societies. To simplify this task, sociology breaks down human societies into three categories: infrastructure (the material and economic factors), structure (includes politics, family patterns and power relationships), and superstructure (mental and symbolic aspects). The application of this method to ancient human societies relies on the availability of evidence. This evidence includes texts, records, remains, and artefacts that the society produced. See Jon L Berquist, *Judaism in Persia's Shadow* (Minneapolis: Fortress Press, 1995), 242.
6. Hector Avalos, *Illness and Healthcare in the Ancient Near East*, edited

who used a sociology framework when exploring healing in the Second Testament, identified a number of functions performed by a healthcare system.[7] These included providing a set of cultural values and beliefs around health; telling those who belong to the culture how to experience illness; giving order to illness by labelling, classifying, and explaining it; and providing healing activities that are in line with the previous three functions.

Cross-cultural and historic studies on spirit possession have also identified social functions that are similar to those of a health care system. The social functions identified include the support of the power and belief structures of a group, and providing a means of proselytising new believers while strengthening the faith of existing believers.[8]

Social functions are supported by roles in a society. There are the roles of the 'sick' and the 'healer'. In the case of possession, the roles are the 'possessed' and the 'exorcist'. I intend to identify these functions of healing within the Book of Tobit, as well as applying observations

by Peter Machinist, Harvard Semitic Museum Monographs, vol 54 (Atlanta: Scholars Press, 1995), 23.

7. John J Pilch, *Healing in the New Testament* (Minneapolis: Fortress Press, 2000), 27ff.

8. Nicholas P Spanos, *Multiple Identities and False Memories: A Sociocognitive Perspective* (Washington, DC: American Psychological Association, 1996), 145–82. Spanos wrote from the perspective of psychology. From 1975 to 1994, he was Director of the Laboratory for Experimental Hypnosis at Carleton University, Ottawa, Ontario, Canada, where he was a Professor of Psychology.

from historical studies in spirit possession to further the understanding and interpretation of the story of Sarah.

Beliefs Associated with Illness

The central belief concerning healing in the Book of Tobit is that God is the one healer (Tob 3:16). As the one healer, God is presented in the book as the source of the knowledge of healing activities. God reveals the activities through a messenger, the angel Raphael (Tob 6:4-9), who is contrasted with the evil demon 'Asmodeus' (Tob 3:8; 5:4–12:20). The presence of these characters indicates a belief in angels and demons.[9]

Demons are found in the First Testament, although there is not a single term which can be consistently and unquestionably translated as *daimonion* in the LXX (the Greek translation of the Hebrew Testament), and subsequently, 'demon' in the English translation.[10] The frag-

9. *The Anchor Bible Dictionary* presents a number of theories about the development of demons in Jewish literature. The starting point for this development was a general belief in demons as independent evil spirits, which was always a part of Israel's theology (particularly on the popular level). This belief simply was expanded in later periods. These expansions included separation into 'good' spirits (angels) and 'evil' spirits (demons), and the development of independent evil figures as it became theologically unacceptable to present evil events and elements as aspects of God. Joanne K. Kuemmerlin-McLean, 'Demons: Old Testament', in *The Anchor Bible Dictionary*, edited by David Noel Freedman (New York: Doubleday, 1996), 2:139.
10. Kuemmerlin-McLean, 'Demons: Old Testament', 2:138.

ments of the Book of Tobit found at Qumran can be used to identify the Hebrew term that the Greek texts of the book translate as *daimonion*.[11] The Aramaic fragments of the book use the Semitic word *šd*.[12] References to this word in the First Testament (*'dym*) appear in the context of the worship of demons equated with new or false gods, for example:

> They sacrificed to demons, not God, to deities they had never known, to new ones recently arrived, whom your ancestors had not feared. (Deut 32:17)

> They sacrificed their sons and their daughters to the demons; they poured out innocent blood, the blood of their sons and daughters, whom they sacrificed to the idols of Canaan; and the land was polluted with blood. (Ps 106:37)

In these and other references to angels and demons in the First Testament, there is usually no mention of personal names. In contrast, the author of the story of Tobit provides the angel and the demon with names and roles, in order to allow them to interact with the other characters

11. The critical edition of the Greek texts of Tobit are edited by Robert Hanhart, *Tobit, Septuaginta, Vetus Testamentum Graecum* (Gottingen: Vandenhoeck & Ruprecht, 1983).
12. 4QTob 196–197 (Aramaic): 196; 6:15, 6:18, 197; 6:8, 6:15, 6:16. Martínez Florentino García and Eibert JC Tigchelaar, *The Dead Sea Scrolls Study Edition*, 2 vols, vol 1 (Leiden: Brill, 1997).

in the story. The angel Raphael had the role of testing (Tob 12:14) and healing (Tob 3:16). The demon Asmodeus had power to afflict humans (Tob 3:6). The names add to the story by revealing more about the characters. The name of the angel, Raphael (*rp'l*), is a Hebrew word-play meaning 'God heals'. The derivation of the name Asmodeus is uncertain. It is often taken to come from *Aeshma Daeva*, 'the wrath demon', of the Zoroastrian Avesta. Alternatively, according to popular Jewish etymology, the name comes from *Ashmedai* (which is translated as Asmodeus in the Greek), which was derived from *'md*, 'destroy, exterminate'.[13]

Demons with personal names and roles are included in other literature from the period in which the Book of Tobit was written. Two examples are The First Book of Enoch (1 Enoch) and the Book of Jubilees. 1 Enoch interprets the events of Genesis chapters 6 to 9 (Noah and the flood) as a prototype of judgment and restoration, in which evil that originated in demonic rebellion would find its cure in divine intervention.[14] The demons of this rebellion and angels involved in the divine intervention are named in 1 Enoch 8:3 – 9:3.

> Shemihazah taught incantations and how to cut roots; Hermoni taught how to undo sorcery, magic, and skills; Baraq'el taught

13. Moore, *Tobit*, 147.
14. George WE Nickelsburg, 'Enoch, First Book', in *The Anchor Bible Dictionary*, edited by David Noel Freedman (New York: Doubleday, 1996), 2:509.

> the signs of the shafts; Kokab'el taught the signs of the stars; Zeq'el taught the signs of the lightning; 'Ar'teqof taught the signs of the earth; Shamshi'el taught the signs of the sun; Sahari'el taught the signs of the moon. And all began to reveal secrets to their wives, and because of this doing men expired from the earth, and the outcry went right up to the heaven. Then Michael, Sariel, Raphael, Gabriel gazed from the sanctuaries of the heavens to the earth and saw much blood poured upon the earth, and all the earth was filled with wickedness and violence perpetrated upon it. Hearing this, the four of them went and said to themselves that the outcry and the wail for the destruction of the sons of the earth went right up to the gates of heaven.[15]

Like 1 Enoch, the Book of Jubilees rewrote and reinterpreted the events of Genesis.[16] In chapter 10 of the Jubilees, illness is explained by evil spirits who hurt people.

> All of the evil ones, who were cruel, we bound in the place of judgement, but a tenth of them we let remain so that they might be subject

15. García and Tigchelaar, *The Dead Sea Scrolls Study Edition*, 1: 403.
16. Larry P Hogan, *Healing in the Second Temple Period* (Gottingen: Vandenhoeck & Ruprecht, 1992), 78.

> to Satan on earth. And the healing of their illnesses together with their seductions we told Noah (Jub 10:11).[17]

Not only does the book of 1 Enoch reinterpret the events of Genesis; it also reinterprets Hellenistic mythology. In Greek mythology, the offspring of intercourse between the gods and humans are heroes, for example, Hercules.[18] In 1 Enoch, heavenly beings have sex with humans and produce giants who set about destroying the world. The books also appear to reinterpret the Greek Prometheus story. While Prometheus revealed fire to humans, the demons reveal and teach evil.

These two works provide evidence that belief in individuated demons was part of the mythology of Jews at the time of writing of the Book of Tobit, a mythology developed to counteract that of the Hellenistic rulers. The author of Tobit draws on this mythology for the book.

The Experience and Explanation of Illness

Belief in demons is used to explain Sarah's illness. Sarah's family provides the social framework in which she experiences her illness. Each member of the family has a role. The inability to fulfil these roles is an indicator of illness in the book. Sarah cannot fulfil her role as wife and provider

17. RH Charles, *Apocrypha and Pseudepigrapha of the Old Testament*, edited by RH Charles (Oxford: Clarendon Press, 1915), 76.
18. Rainer Albertz, *A History of Israelite Religion in the Old Testament*, 2 vols, vol 2 (London: SCM Press, 1994), 578.

of an heir (Tob 3:15). Throughout history, demonic possession was used as one explanation for certain behaviours that were socially disruptive, or considered abnormal.[19] Sarah's lack of a husband and children is considered abnormal, and she is labeled as 'afflicted by a demon'.[20]

The lack of a husband leaves Sarah powerless in her community. She is also powerless as an exile living under Hellenistic domination. She is labelled and given the role of 'possessed'.[21] This is in keeping with observations made from subsequent historical manifestations of demonic possession in Christian Europe: 'Those who became demoniacs were usually individuals with little social power or status who were hemmed in by numerous social restrictions and had few sanctioned avenues for protesting their dissatisfactions or improving their lot.'[22] In patriarchal cultures, adult demoniacs were more frequently women than men.[23] Historical studies also show that people are often trained into the roles of 'the possessed' and the 'exorcist'.[24] The training of Sarah is not apparent, although one could surmise that after seven attempted marriages, she had some practice. The training

19. Spanos, *Multiple Identities*, 160.
20. Sarah's maids accuse her of killing her husbands (Tob 3:8), although this explanation is not developed in the book. Murder is certainly a socially disruptive behaviour. The explanation the author used is that a demon killed them.
21. It is noted that the term 'possession' is a Second Testament expression and is not found in the book of Tobit.
22. Spanos, *Multiple Identities*, 163.
23. Spanos, *Multiple Identities*, 163.
24. Spanos, *Multiple Identities*, 149.

of Tobias in the role of 'exorcist' is, however, obvious. Raphael teaches him on his journey:

> The two continued on their way together until they were near Media. Then the young man questioned the angel and said to him, 'Brother Azariah, what medicinal value is there in the fish's heart and liver, and in the gall?' He replied, 'As for the fish's heart and liver, you must burn them to make a smoke in the presence of a man or woman afflicted by a demon or evil spirit, and every affliction will flee away and never remain with that person any longer.' (Tob 6:7–9).

The Healing Activity

The healing of Sarah is in three parts. She is married to Tobias (Tob 7:12–13), then freed from the demon (Tob 8:1–8). To complete the process, the couple prays together. In the marriage ceremony, the father gives the bride to her prospective husband, and this is followed by an oral statement of the marriage, 'Take her to be your wife'. This statement includes the affirmation that it is in accordance with the decree of the Law of Moses. The decree referred to is probably Deuteronomy 25.

> When brothers reside together, and one of them dies and has no son, the wife of the deceased shall not be married outside the family to a stranger. Her husband's brother shall go

> in to her, taking her in marriage, and performing the duty of a husband's brother to her. (Deut 25:5)

The author of the book of Tobit reinterprets this passage, applying it to Sarah's status as an only child (Tob 3:15), rather than to descendants of the first husband. Following the affirmation of the Law, the father blesses the couple and the ceremony ends with a meal. The marriage clearly fits in with the author's purpose of remaining faithful to the law.

After the wedding, Tobias and Sarah are led to the bedroom to consummate their marriage. It is in this situation that the evil demon has in the past killed Sarah's husbands (Tob 3:8). Tobias remembers the instructions given to him by Raphael, and uses the fish organs to make a foul smell (Tob 8:2). The notion that foul smells would drive away demons was common in the ancient world. Josephus reports that an exorcist named Eleazar, who drove out demons, used a ring embedded with an aromatic herb:

> And he left behind him the manner of using exorcisms, by which they drive away demons, so that they never return; and this method of cure is of great force unto this day; for I have seen a certain man of my own country, whose name was Eleazar, releasing people that were demoniacal in the presence of Vespasian, and his sons, and his captains, and the whole multitude of his soldiers. The manner of the cure was this: He put a ring that had a root of one

> of those sorts mentioned by Solomon to the nostrils of the demoniac, after which he drew out the demon through his nostrils; and when the man fell down immediately, he abjured him to return into him no more, making still mention of Solomon, and reciting the incantations which he composed. [25]

Literature of the period not only supports the use of smells to exorcise demons,[26] but also seems to sanction the role of 'exorcist' as played by Tobias. The Prayer of Nabonidus, from the Qumran documents (4Q242), gives witness to the role of 'exorcist' in Jewish tradition in the late second/early first century BCE:

> . . . I was afflicted with an evil ulcer for seven years . . . and an exorcist pardoned my sins. He was a Jew from among the children of the exile of Judah, and he said, 'Recount this in writing to glorify and exalt the name of the Most High God.'[27]

25. Flavius Josephus, *The Antiquities of the Jews*, trans. William Whiston (London: Ward & Lock, 1987), 214.
26. Further evidence for the practice is documented by Bernd Kollman, 'Göttliche Offenbarung Magisch-Parmakologischer Heilkunst Im Buch Tobit', in *Zeitschrift für die Alttestamenttliche Wissenschaft* 106 (1994): 289–299.
27. Geza Vermes, *The Complete Dead Sea Scrolls in English* (London: Allen Lane, The Penguin Press, 1997), 573.

This and other findings at Qumran indicate that there was a highly developed practice of exorcism within the Qumran community, and therefore suggest that exorcism was one of the healing practices of early Judaism.

Once the demon is repelled, in Tob 8:3, Raphael binds the demon hand and foot. The phrase, 'bind hand and foot', may be a technical term during the period for incapacitating demons, as 1 Enoch 10:4 also uses the phrase: 'Again the Lord said to Raphael, "Bind Azazyel hand and foot".' The involvement of Raphael ensures that the belief in God as the one healer is preserved. Tobias cannot free Sarah from the demon by the use of remedies alone. God, through Raphael, completes the cure.

The prayer of Tobias and Sarah is the final action the healing of Sarah. The prayer includes an allusion to the Genesis creation story (Gen 2:18ff.) that defines the role of women as that of helper. This can be interpreted as an affirmation of the healing of Sarah, and her restoration to her place in society as wife, provider of an heir for the family, and helper. The prayer concludes with a statement of what Sarah and Tobit expect for their future: a long life together.

> You made Adam, and for him you made his wife Eve as a helper and support. From the two of them the human race has sprung. You said, 'It is not good that the man should be alone; let us make a helper for him like himself. I now am taking this kinswoman of mine, not because of lust, but with sincerity. Grant that she and I may find mercy and that we

> may grow old together.' And they both said, 'Amen, Amen.' Then they went to sleep for the night. (Tob 8:6–9)

The story of the freeing of Sarah takes the reader into the bedchamber on her wedding night. While the 'exorcism' appears to be very private, it is made public by narrating the event. In Europe from the fifteenth to the eighteenth centuries, exorcisms were often public events. 'Every exorcism represented a dramatic moral confrontation between the power of God and that of the Devil. Consequently, successful exorcisms illustrated the power of the Church, affirmed its beliefs and values, and helped maintain its authority . . . Thus a successful exorcism was a powerful tool for converting unbelievers as well as redoubling the faith of believers'.[28] The same function of exorcism can be seen in operation in the book of Tobit. Sarah's successful freeing from the demon Asmodeus, made public in the reading of the story, is used to redouble the faith of the Jews in exile. The event furthers the purpose of the book: 'remain faithful to the Lord and the Law'.

Asmodeus as a Metaphor for Greek Domination

The author parallels illness with the exile of the Northern Kingdom. Illness becomes a metaphor for the exile.[29] The

28. Spanos, *Multiple Identities*, 172.
29. Rainer Albertz, *Israel in Exile: The History and Literature of the Sixth Century BCE*, edited by Dennis T Olsen and Sharon H Ringe (Atlanta: Society of Biblical Literature, 2003), 33.

expulsion of Asmodeus can be seen as symbolic of the expulsion of the occupying forces and the culture responsible for the exile. The story presents a positive outcome for Sarah. However, the book does not present a positive outcome for the children of Israel. Ultimately, healing will come to the previous inhabitants of the Northern Kingdom, when God brings them back to the land of Israel:

> But God will again have mercy on them, and God will bring them back into the land of Israel; and they will rebuild the temple of God, but not like the first one until the period when the times of fulfilment shall come. After this they all will return from their exile and will rebuild Jerusalem in splendour; and in it the temple of God will be rebuilt, just as the prophets of Israel have said concerning it. (Tob 14:5)

It is interesting to observe that the rates of demonic possession have varied at different times in Christian history. For example, once Christianity became the state religion in the fourth century CE, the frequency of stories of exorcisms decreased. During the Reformation and Counter-Reformation, the frequency of stories appears to have increased. These changes in the frequency of stories of demonic possession can be linked to the competition for converts.[30] Perhaps the same could be said of early Judaism. The author of Tobit indicates that Jews were assimi-

30. Spanos, *Multiple Identities*, 172.

lating into the dominant Hellenistic culture, for example, Tob 1:10 (cf Tob 3:3; 4:4). This story of demonic possession is used to discourage conversion to Hellenistic religion, increase the faith of the Jewish exiles, and gain converts. While the book focuses on the Jews in exile, the possibility of converts is reflected in Tob 14:6–7:

> Then the nations in the whole world will all be converted and worship God in truth. They will all abandon their idols, which deceitfully have led them into their error; and in righteousness they will praise the eternal God.

The Story Revisited

Earlier in the chapter, I gave a synopsis of the story. Following this investigation I would like to present an alternative synopsis to the story of Sarah: Sarah is a powerless woman. She is powerless as a Hebrew living in exile under Greek domination. She is even powerless in her own community, as she is not married and cannot produce an heir for the family. Using the mythology of the time, she is labelled as 'afflicted with a demon'. The author uses the public act of freeing her from the demon to provide hope to other Hebrew exiles—hope that, just as Sarah was freed from the demon and was able to resume her place in her community, the exiles will be freed from the domination of the Greeks.

Epilogue

Let me return the charismatic youth group I mentioned at the beginning. When I reflect on those events now, instead of fear, I feel anger at being used. Rather than interpreting the experience as being at the mercy of an evil spirit, I see myself being at the mercy of a group process. The practice of deliverance was used as a tool for proselytising and strengthening the faith of those in the group, just as the healing of Sarah from the evil demon Asmodeus was used to strengthen the faith of the Jews in exile. The whisper in my ear was a way of training me in the role of 'the possessed', so that those in the role of 'exorcist' could perform their function, showing the strength of God.

Bibliography

Albertz, Rainer. *A History of Israelite Religion in the Old Testament*, 2 vols (London: SCM Press, 1994).

———. *Israel in Exile: The History and Literature of the Sixth Century BCE,* edited by Dennis T Olsen and Sharon H Ringe (Atlanta: Society of Biblical Literature, 2003).

Avalos, Hector. *Illness and Healthcare in the Ancient Near East*, edited by Peter Machinist, Harvard Semitic Museum Monographs, vol 54 (Atlanta: Scholars Press, 1995).

Berquist, Jon L. *Judaism in Persia's Shadow* (Minneapolis: Fortress Press, 1995).

Charles, RH. *Apocrypha and Pseudepigrapha of the Old Testament*, edited by RH Charles. (Oxford: Clarendon Press, 1915).

Fitzmyer, Joseph A. *Tobit*, edited by Loren T Stuckenbruck (Berlin: Walter de Gruyter, 2003).

García, Martínez Florentino and Eibert JC Tigchelaar. *The Dead Sea Scrolls, Study Edition*, 2 vols (Leiden: Brill, 1997).

Grabbe, Lester L. '"The Exile" under the Theodolite: Historiography as Triangulation', in *Leading Captivity Captive: 'The Exile' as History and Ideology*, edited by Lester L Grabbe (Sheffield: Sheffield Academic, 1998), 80–100.

Greenspoon, Leonard J. 'Between Alexandria and Antioch: Jews and Judaism in the Hellenistic Period', in *The Oxford History of the Biblical World*, edited by Michael D Coogan (New York: Oxford University Press, 1998), 317–351.

Hanhart, Robert. *Tobit*, Septuaginta, Vetus Testamentum Graecum (Gottingen: Vandenhoeck & Ruprecht, 1983).

Hogan, Larry P. *Healing in the Second Temple Period* (Gottingen: Vandenhoeck & Ruprecht, 1992).

Josephus, Flavius. *The Antiquities of the Jews*, translated by William Whiston (London: Ward and Lock, 1987).

Kollman, Bernd. 'Göttliche Offenbarung Magisch-Parmakologischer Heilkunst Im Buch Tobit', in *Zeitschrift für die Alttestamenttliche Wissenschaft* 106 (1994): 289–299.

Kuemmerlin-McLean, Joanne K. 'Demons: Old Testament', in *The Anchor Bible Dictionary*, edited by David Noel Freedman (New York: Doubleday, 1996), 2:138–140.

Moore, Carey A. *Tobit—A New Translation with Introduction and Commentary*, edited by William Foxwell Albright and David Noel Freedman. The Anchor Bible (New York: Doubleday, 1996).

Nickelsburg, George WE. "Enoch, First Book, In *The Anchor Bible Dictionary,* edited by David Noel Freedman (New York: Doubleday, 1996) 2:508-516.

North, Robert. 'The Chronicler: 1-2 Chronicles, Ezra, Nehemiah', in *The New Jerome Biblical Commentary,* edited by Raymond E Brown, Joseph A Fitzmyer, and Roland E Murphy (London: Geoffrey Chapman, 1990), 362–398.

Otzen, Benedikt. *Tobit and Judith,* edited by Michael Knibb. Guides to Apocrypha and Pseudepigrapha (London: Sheffield Academic Press, 2002).

Pilch, John J. *Healing in the New Testament* (Minneapolis: Fortress Press, 2000).

Spanos, Nicholas P. *Multiple Identities and False Memories: A Sociocognitive Perspective* (Washington, DC: American Psychological Association, 1996).

Vermes, Geza. *The Complete Dead Sea Scrolls in English* (London: Allen Lane, The Penguin Press, 1997).

Heavenly Visitors: God's Messengers

Alice M Sinnott

Accounts of spirit possession share several common characteristics. In each of them, we meet assumptions about a Deity and a spirit world intimately involved with the human community, and active in the lives of human beings. These assumptions generally underpin accounts of spirit possession, and are expressed in a variety of interpretations of a fundamental notion that God and human beings, collectively and individually, are inextricably interconnected. Views of the world based on a notion that God and a world of spirits are intimately engaged in the lives of human beings offer, for some, a way of explaining and interpreting calamities and human suffering. Within such belief systems, all or some of their communities may diagnose as spirit possession the unique suffering of individuals burdened with mental illness. Such diagnoses pose serious questions about how and why such a diagnosis is made, and what, if any, treatment should be made available. Sometimes, communities subscribing to the notion that some forms of mental illness are, in fact, expressions of spirit possession invoke biblical texts to legitimate treatments and therapies provided for individuals.

In this essay, I shall attempt to examine a perception of spirit possession that is contrary to the above understanding of spirit possession. This is the belief in some cultures that heavenly visitors or creative spirits inspire people such as gifted storytellers, thinkers, writers, artists, and musicians, and includes acceptance of those who are sometimes called free spirits—people who think and act differently from what the majority of the population considers the norm. I shall focus my discussion of the above notion of spirit possession in the biblical Book of Tobit,[1] and in the parallel novel *Miss Garnet's Angel,* by Salley Vickers.[2] Discussions about spirit possession today usually de-accentuate or ignore this understanding of spirit possession. My intention is to challenge the conventional wisdom, which suggests that notions of spirit possession always centre on questions of illness ascribed to demonic or spiritual powers, and represent spiritual possession

1. For the Book of Tobit, see New Revised Standard Version of the Bible with the Apocrypha. Bible references in this paper are taken from this version. The Book of Tobit is part of the Catholic and Orthodox biblical canon, but is placed among the Apocrypha in the Protestant canons. It is not included within the Tanakh (Hebrew Bible), but is found in the Greek Old Testament (the Septuagint), and Aramaic and Hebrew fragments of the book were discovered in Cave IV at Qumran in 1952.
2. Salley Vickers, *Miss Garnet's Angel* (London: Fourth Estate, 2000).

as an explicitly negative experience. I shall consider the routes taken by the spirit-possessed and spirit-accompanied characters in the two narratives to transcend the sufferings, conditions, and dilemmas they encounter. In the novel *Miss Garnet's Angel,* Salley Vickers presents examples of positive cases of spirit possession by using thematic parallels and intersections to combine the biblical Book of Tobit—a book that has much to say about good and bad spirits—with a contemporary narrative about Miss Julia Garnet, a retired history teacher who has been practicing 'economies of the spirit' throughout her life. Julia's journey of self-discovery leads her to embrace the spirit of creativity and discovery that eventually guides her to redemption from loneliness and loss, and to the consolation of human relationships and spiritual riches.

Walking with Heavenly Messengers

Miss Garnet's Angel provides a subtle depiction of how a woman whose life had been circumscribed and dictated by economies of the spirit first tentatively catches the light, and gradually embraces all that the creative spirits and heavenly guides offer her. Sally Vickers' novel charts the late coming-of-age of Julia Garnet, a retired English schoolteacher, who spends six months in Venice after her lifelong companion, Harriet, dies. Vickers mentioned in an interview that her choice of Venice as the setting for her novel was apposite, as it is a meeting of land and sea, East and West, material and spiritual wealth. Venice evokes a sense of the close connection between good and ill, light and dark, love and death—the themes of *Miss Garnet's*

Angel that are also central to the story of Tobit. Venice, the place where Julia comes face-to-face with beckoning angels and heavenly spirits, has a transforming effect on Julia, a committed Communist. Inexplicably, she begins to let go of her antipathy toward religion when she encounters the story of Tobit rendered in art in the Church of the Angelo Raffaele, which has sculptures of Tobias and the Angel Raphael above the portal at the entrance, and an organ loft decorated with seven paintings by Giantonio Guardi, based on the Book of Tobit, a story that makes ample use of spirit characters.[3] Guardi's paintings enthral Julia. Consequently she sets about acquiring a copy of the book so she can read the entire narrative. Her reading of the story leads her to embark fully on her own journey of discovery and she begins befriending the previously unknown Raphael.

---

3. In Chiesa dell' Angelo Raffaele, a doorway sculpture by Sebastiano da Lugana, depicts Tobias with his dog and the angel Raphael. Tobias is holding the hand of the Angel Raphael and has a fish in his other hand. In the organ loft and above the altar, a series of paintings illustrate the Book of Tobit: *The Departure of Tobias; The Angel Appears to Tobias; The Healing of Tobias's Father; The Marriage of Tobias,* all by Giantonio Guardi, c1750. The paintings show vibrant, flickering figures bathed in shimmering light against backgrounds suggested by a few indefinite forms. The artist used a style of coloured handwriting, often calligraphic, and sometimes cloudy. Surfaces are full of light, vitality, and texture. The paintings have a luminous atmosphere in which figures appear only as far as light defines them in the compositions that are framed by trees, set within decorative fronds and branches. The church of the Carmini, near Chiesa dell' Angelo Raffaele, also has representations of the Tobias story.

Vickers interweaves Julia's journey with the journey taken by the biblical Tobias in response to a request by his elderly, blind father Tobit to go to Media to recover a family debt and allow him to die in peace. Both stories establish dual meanings for blindness: as a physical condition on one hand, and as a more abstract reference to the capacity for empathy, love, self-awareness, and community on the other. On his journey, Tobias is accompanied by a hired merchant guide, Azarias, who is the Angel Raphael disguised in human form.[4] Julia, now possessed by the story of Tobit and enamoured of the angel Raphael, embarks on a personal and spiritual journey which parallels that of Tobias.

A virgin in her sixties, Julia is still haunted by the spectre of her tyrannical, abusive father. It was her belief that there are two kinds of people in the world: those willing to tangle with their fate, who endeavour to shape the course of their lives, and those who bear their circumstances with little or no struggle. Cut adrift by the sudden death of Harriet Josephs—for more than thirty years Julia's companion in a small West London flat—Miss Garnet decides to spend six months in Venice—a decision that ignites her spirit of adventure. As Julia explores Venice and simultaneously identifies with Tobias's journey, she herself embarks upon a life-altering journey of the spirit, as everywhere she goes in Venice the all-prevalent spirit of the Angel Raphael possesses her. Julia falls in love, for the first time in her life, with the art dealer, Carlo, but eventu-

4. The name Raphael, meaning 'the healing of God', appears only in the Book of Tobit.

ally realizes she is as blind as Tobit in her understanding of his affection. She meets Toby and Sarah, self-described twins, who are working to restore the fourteenth century Chapel-of-the-Plague in Venice, a church of miracles of healing attributed to the Angel Raphael. In this relationship, Julia plays the role of the angel, protecting and guiding two people who are young enough to be her children as they struggle with demons from their shared past.

Tobias's journey, in company with Raphael/Azarias, brings him some strange encounters, such as when a large fish jumps at him from the River Tigris, and Azarias instructs him to capture it. Later, he tells Tobias to use the liver, gall, and heart of the fish to cast out demons from Sarah, so that Tobias can safely marry her, thus avoiding being strangled on his wedding night by the demon Asmodeus, as her previous seven husbands had been. On returning home, Tobias uses the fish liver, gall, and heart to cure his father's blindness. Raphael then announces, 'When you and Sarah prayed, it was I who brought and read the record of your prayer before the glory of the Lord, and likewise whenever you would bury the dead . . . God sent me to heal you and Sarah your daughter-in-law. I am the angel Raphael, one of the seven angels who stand ready, and enter before the glory of the Lord' (Tob 12:12–15, cf Rev 8:2).[5]

5. Mention is made of the devil in many passages of the Bible, but no full account of his character is given in any one place.

Tobit's Spirit of Alienation

At the beginning of the story, Tobit introduces himself as one who 'walked in the ways of truth and righteousness all the days of my life. I performed many acts of charity for my kindred and my people who had gone with me into exile' (Tob 1:3–19). We realise that we are to hear a tale of loss and restoration, persecution and redress. The introductory chapter highlights themes of isolation, suffering, and death that run throughout the narrative, and allows the reader to glimpse the happy conclusion that eventually lies in store. Tobit's works of justice and compassion bring him no happiness (2:50), and his neighbours regard his works of mercy as worthless. When he returns home one day after burying an Israelite, he falls asleep outside the wall of the courtyard and bird droppings fall into his eyes, eventually causing him to go blind. As Tobit can no longer be the breadwinner, Anna, his wife, takes on work outside the home, a situation that he finds very humiliating. He responds to Anna's success by doubting her honesty.

A spirit of alienation possesses Tobit and renders him incapable of perceiving and appreciating his connections with his wife, his son, and his community. Such physical and mental blindness is not responsive to human healing. His experience of alienation and loneliness is echoed by Julia when she observes, 'We cannot commission desire', referring to herself and Carlo. However, Julia's disappointment over Carlo, and her subsequent break down, enlarge her vision and give her the ability to see the Archangel Raphael when others cannot. When Tobit embraces the living human community that surrounds him, the film that obscures his vision will vanish. Meantime, a spirit of sadness and alienation circumscribes Tobit's very existence; he groans, weeps, and prays at the height of his misery as a spirit of despair threatens to overwhelm him (3:1). In this moment of imminent spiritual danger, he turns to God, as the author of just works and discerning activity (3:2). This God is both righter of wrongs and perceiver of reality. Where Tobit has failed to see clearly, God will surely discern the truth. Ironically, the audience knows that healing will come with Tobias and the accompanying angel.

Tobit does not recognise his own inner blindness, nor does he acknowledge the failure of his judgement. Although he invokes God's merciful compassion, he can see only one solution to his grief: a quick and painless death. He asks that God remember him and not punish him (3:3), yet the punishment he seeks to avert is not death, but a life of continued suffering. In his death wish, he seeks release from alienation and suffering: 'Command my spirit to be taken up from me so that I may be released from the face of the earth and become dust' (3:6). Tobit's words, 'it is better for me to die than live' (Tob 3:6), echo those of Jonah (4:3, 8), who also sought death because he refused to accept God's decision to save the people of Nineveh. This refusal rested upon Jonah's notion of election that did not include gentiles. Like Tobit, he isolated himself by his inability to think in terms of the inclusion of all humanity. God responded to Jonah's complaint by emphasising that God's mercy includes gentiles and Jews (Jonah 4:11).

Sarah's Spirit of Alienation

A spirit of alienation also possesses Sarah, who has tried seven times to marry, and seven times has failed because the demon Asmodeus controls her, and has killed, in succession, each of the bridegrooms who entered her chamber (Tob 3:8).[6] Though Asmodeus does not physically harm Sarah, he kills anyone who desires to approach her (6:15), so his activities prevent her from becoming a wife and mother in the community that she so much desires. She has witnessed the strangling in her room of seven potential husbands. To compound her misery, she suffers mockery from her maids, who accuse her of murdering the seven men. They taunt her, 'Why do you whip us, because your husbands are dead? Go with them!' (3:8). Such accusations shed light on Sarah's spirit of alienation and her harshness towards those who serve her (3:9).

A spirit of sadness, bitterness, and alienation possesses Sarah, like Tobit. She, too, gives way to grief, and longs for death, but cannot justify taking her own life, as that would bring disgrace upon her family and lead her father in sorrow to the grave (3:10). She elects to place her life in God's hands and begs for mercy, which she equates with

---

6. M Hutter, 'Asmodeus', in *Dictionary of Deities and Demons of the Bible*, edited K van der Toorn and others (Leiden: Brill, 1995), 106–8. The name of the demon mentioned in the Book of Tobit (3: 8) is probably derived from the Hebrew root meaning, 'to destroy', so he is probably connected with the demon called Abaddon the Destroyer in Rev 9:11. In Aramaic, a demon also signifies one who destroys. The name most likely derives from a compound meaning 'demon of wrath'.

sight or the ability to see clearly, 'I have given my eyes to you, my eyes have regained sight' (3:11–12). Interestingly, while Tobit asked God to look upon him (3:3), he himself could not turn his face to God or to the people around him, as his eyes remained clouded by suffering. Sarah, on the other hand, has begun to view herself in relation to others (3:10). However, she does not yet see any reason to continue living because she knows of no human being with whom she can unite in life. She has neither sister nor brother; neither does her father have any close relative or intimate friend whom she might marry. While she has no apparent hope of establishing a family or community, she begs God to free her from her plight (3:15).

Healing Spirits

Prayers uttered by Sarah and Tobit reach God as one prayer (3:16), and the narrative shifts dramatically as God enters the story and commissions Raphael to heal them both. Interestingly, Raphael imparts the means for healing to Tobias, who becomes the healer for Sarah and Tobit. The plan for healing includes sending away the cataracts from Tobit's eyes so he will 'see the light of God with his eyes' (Tob 3:17). Raphael himself binds the demon Asmodeus, thus setting Sarah free from the demon's power, and protecting Tobias from death as he marries Sarah. This marriage will not only initiate a new family, but will also link Sarah, Tobit, and their families. The celebration of their marriage initiates a celebration of life, an affirmation of joy in the face of suffering in the midst of Raguel and Sarah's community, who will bear their burdens with them. In order to accomplish this double healing, the angel Raphael assumes human form and takes on the name Azariah, 'YHWH helps', a name that communicates God's active role in creation. Through this angelic intermediary, God is present as both healer and helper. Indeed, when Raphael finally reveals his identity, he says, 'it is good to unveil the works of God' (12:11), and describes his role in bringing their prayers before God (12:14). At his urging, they praise 'these marvellous deeds God had done when the angel of God appeared to them' (12:22).

Raphael is not God, yet Raphael's deeds are God's deeds—he re-presents God, acting on behalf of the Deity, and symbolising God's presence among God's people and in creation. If the angel may serve as God's agent for healing and helping, so too can human beings, as we will see in the remainder of this story. By observing God at work through the angelic intermediary, the human actors discover how they might communicate and receive God's gifts of healing through one another. Raphael does not perform the planned acts of healing himself, but imparts the means of healing to others. He instructs Tobias about how to prepare the medicines that will both drive away the demon Asmodeus, and remove Tobit's blindness (6:5, 8–9). It is Tobias who burns the fish liver and heart upon the embers, banishing Asmodeus forever (8:2), and Tobias uses the fish gall to cure his father's blindness (11:11–13). Raphael plants the seeds of love for Sarah in Tobias's heart (6:11–18), but Raguel, Sarah's father, unites them in marriage (7:11–13).

Community Links Lives

God commissions Raphael, a good spirit, to initiate a process of healing 'so that Tobit might again see God's light with his eyes' (3:17).[7] Tobit's spirit of isolation does not allow him to perceive the light that shines for him through his son, his wife, family, and friends. Tobit's deliverance from the spirit of despair is inextricably bound up with his recognition of the community that surrounds him. It is through human connections and entering into life-giving relationships that the greater illnesses of isolation as experienced by Tobit and Sarah, and Julia and the twins, find healing. When they suffered alone, they were tempted to choose death over life. Those burdened by grief, isolation, or alienation need caring and nurturing communities to grieve with them, care for them, help carry their burdens, and free them to choose life and rejoice in its blessings. On his arrival in Nineveh, Raphael, the healing angel, greets Tobit, 'Joyous greetings to you!' and Tobit retorts, 'What joy is left for me anymore? I am a man without eyesight; I cannot see the light of heaven, but I lie in darkness like the dead who no longer see the light. Although still alive, I am among the dead. I hear people, but I cannot see them' (5:10). Tobit mistakenly identifies his blindness as the cause of his perceived isolation from others.

Raphael, however, offers encouragement to Tobit by assuring him that God has healing in store for him. Tobit seems to brighten, and begins to call Raphael brother and asks to what tribe and family Raphael belongs. Ra-

7. Anna calls Tobias 'the light of my eyes' (10:5) as does Tobit (11:14).

phael, in turn, responds with an ironic question: 'Are you seeking a tribe and family?' 'Why? Do you need a tribe?' (5:12). Tobit does need to acknowledge his tribe and a family in order to be freed from his spirit of isolation and alienation. When Raphael instructs Tobias about healing Tobit's blindness, he says, 'Your father will regain his sight and see the light' (11:8), and on regaining his sight, Tobit exclaims, 'I now see my son Tobias!' (11:15).

Family language pervades the conversation of Tobias and Raphael as they journey towards Ecbatana, accompanied by Tobias's dog (Tob 5:6).[8] The audience also embarks on a parallel journey through the narrative, which drives out isolation and alienation, and overcomes danger to arrive at an experience of joy and freedom. In a way, the comedy of Tobit does not merely engage its readers; its creative spirit offers corporeal ways of sustaining hope in the face of disaster. When Tobias first speaks to Raphael, he calls him 'brother' (6:7). Raphael responds in kind, saying, 'Tonight we must stay with Raguel, who is a relative of yours', adding, 'you are Sarah's closest relative' (6:11–13), and proposes that Tobias marry Sarah. In 6:11–13, we find eleven explicit references to blood relationships (brother, father, daughter, relative), and seven to marriage and engagement. Family and kinship relationships are uppermost throughout the narrative.

A bond of kinship ignites Tobias's love for Sarah: 'When Tobias heard the words of Raphael and learned that she

8. Tobias's dog may suggest some Zoroastrian influence. Zoroastrians regarded dogs as those who lead souls across the threshold of life and death. See Vickers, *Miss Garnet's Angel*, 309–10 & 340.

was his kinswoman, related through his father's lineage, he loved her very much, and his heart was drawn to her' (6:18). This joining of Tobias and Sarah will provide the focus around which their families and tribe will build a new community. Their marriage occasions a marvellous wedding feast, fourteen days of uninterrupted celebration that transform their lament into feasting, reversing the earlier catastrophes. Raguel's instruction to Tobias, 'you shall bring joy to my daughter's sorrowing spirit' (8:20), again highlights the awareness of the spirit of sorrow. Embracing Tobias, Tobit says, 'Be of good cheer, my son! I am your father, Edna is your mother, and we belong to you and to your beloved now and forever. So be happy, son!' (8:21). Thus Raguel affirms and welcomes the spirit of unity and happiness, as does Edna later when she says, 'From now on, I am your mother' (10:13).

Sarah, too, finds a welcoming spirit when her father instructs her to honour her new mother and father: 'from now on they are as much your parents as the ones who brought you into the world' (10:12). The cause for celebration and joy proves to be not merely the joining of two individuals, but the union of two families and, through this union, the growth of community. Even Tobit's kinsman, Gabael, hastens to join the celebration, thanking God that he can be reunited with his beloved kin: 'Blessed be God, because I have seen the very image of my cousin Tobit!' (9:6). The wedding celebration continues even beyond the fourteenth day, when Tobias and Sarah leave Ecbatana full of happiness and joy (10:14), and once more Tobias's dog follows them (Tob 11:4).

On arriving in Nineveh, Tobias bids his father to take courage and, holding him, removes the cataracts from his eyes (11:11–13). Seized by a spirit of joy, Tobit weeps and exclaims, 'I can see you, son, and the light of my eyes!' (11:14). With the recovery of his sight, Tobit rejoices in his family and community, now aware of his blessings of belonging. He moves forward to welcome Sarah, his new daughter-n-law, thanks God for leading her to his family, and invites her to enter his house. 'So on that day there was rejoicing among all the Jews who were in Nineveh' (11:19).

Happy Conclusions

A spirit of gladness pervades the concluding section of Tobit, with Tobias and Sarah enjoying life together and, in time, a happy death (14:12–14). Transformation of sorrow into joy in this story does not negate the reality of suffering or the experiences of failure and frustration by the characters, but it does refuse to accept ultimate defeat. Happy conclusions provide a spirit of consolation for those who suffer or are alienated, for though the story is fantastic, it is nonetheless 'true'. The author of Tobit created a world in which the readers can empathise with Tobit, Sarah, and their kin, and experience their eventual liberation and freedom from suffering and alienation. The Book of Tobit and *Miss Garnet's Angel*, like all good stories possessed by heavenly spirits, create secondary worlds into which their audiences enter. Within these worlds, what the writer relates is true. Audiences believe, as long as they remain within the story. With Tobit, Sarah, Julia, and the many other characters, readers recover, or claim for the first time, sight, love, beauty, faith, and art—the ability to see what is familiar with new eyes. Stories make possible such discoveries by exorcising angry, fearful, sad, and alienated spirits, and awakening the imaginations and hearts of their readers to choose joy in the face of pain, and human community over isolation and alienation. As Julia observes, 'history does not repeat itself; but perhaps when a thing was true it went on returning in different likenesses, borrowing from what went before, finding new ways to declare itself'.[9]

Humour Heals

Tobit provides much cause for laughter, particularly in the author's use of irony, as so ably discussed by George Nickelsburg. Irony pervades the miserable but righteous Tobit's assurances to Tobias that good works will earn him a good reward from God. Likewise, there is irony in Tobit's assertion, on first meeting Azariah, that a good angel will go with Tobias (5:21), given that Tobit does not yet know Azariah's identity as the angel Raphael. Readers' knowledge of this allows them to laugh along with the author. Nickelsburg likewise notes a series of comic double-entendres, and the ironic pleasure which readers experience through knowledge that the characters do not yet possess (5:1–21).[10] Irene Nowell, exploring the function

9. Vickers, *Miss Garnet's Angel*, 330.
10. GWE Nickelsburg, *Jewish Literature between the Bible and the Mishnah: A Historical and Literary Introduction* (Philadelphia: Fortress, 1981),

of such irony and humour in Tobit, comments that 'irony provides a window through which discerning readers can see their own lives'.[11] Irony serves not merely to entertain readers, but also enables them to place themselves within the story, so that they can reassess and discover truths about their own lives in Tobit and in *Miss Garnet's Angel*. As Julia says 'When I came to Venice I'd never really seen beauty before . . . I'd never really let it inside me . . .'[12] Miss Garnet is awakened to the world around her and, for the first time in her long life, she forms meaningful relationships.

Fantasy and humour of many kinds pervade both the Tobit story and *Miss Garnet's Angel*. Bizarre happenings include unexpected encounters with twin birds whose droppings leave Tobit blind for four years; a terrifying fish that leaps out from the water at Tobias and attempts to swallow him whole (6:2); and the faithful dog that runs to keep up with Tobias and Raphael adds the delight of the unexpected (6:2; 11:4). Entertaining imagery, speech, and situations do not demean the very real pain of the characters, but highlight the paradoxes that face the characters, as well as the readers. The laughter generated by such writing opens a way to freedom from constraints and rules, and celebrates life as it is, drawing us to discover unforeseeable connections and a common existence where imaginary and real life come together. Laughter

---

31.

11. Irene Nowell, 'Irony in the Book of Tobit', *The Bible Today* 33 (1995): 83.
12. Vickers, *Miss Garnet's Angel*, 228.

can also enable an irreversible reformation of a person's worldview. Readers can empathise with the blindness, despair and alienation experienced by the characters in both stories. Tobit, Sarah, and Julia also reflect the comic elements of everyday life that offer readers a way to transformation in the face of suffering by reminding them that humour and laughter are legitimate responses to catastrophes. Laughter, accompanied by a spirit of joy and courage, sustains those who bring healing to Tobit, Sarah, and Julia, and enables them to prevail over calamity and to transform sorrow into joy. Fantastic angels and demons, whimsical fish and sparrows, Julia and her angel take us on captivating journeys and reveal characters who abandon their customary prudent behaviours, their familiar categories, and challenge beliefs that have been integral to their lives by opting for spiritual and emotional transformations. *Miss Garnet's Angel* and the Book of Tobit portray characters who welcome into their lives heavenly spirits of joy, courage, healing, and redemption from numb solitude, suffering, blindness, and loneliness, to find concrete ways of lightening their own and others' afflictions with the unique consolations of personal relationships, spiritual nourishment, laughter, and celebration.

Bibliography

Hutter, M. 'Asmodeus', in *Dictionary of Deities and Demons of the Bible*, edited by K van der Toorn, Bob Becking, and Pieter W Van der Horst (Leiden: Brill, 1995), 106–108.

Nickelsburg, GWE. *Jewish Literature between the Bible and the Mishnah: A Historical and Literary Introduction* (Philadelphia: Fortress Press, 1981).

Nowell, Irene. 'Irony in the Book of Tobit', *The Bible Today* 33 (1995): 79–83.

Vickers, Salley. *Miss Garnet's Angel* (London: Fourth Estate, 2000).

'Clothed and In his Right Mind': An Exploration of Spirit Possession in Early Christianity

Elaine M Wainwright

On 7 April, 2006, a New Zealand Court of Appeal judgment was handed down in the case of *R v Lee* in which Mr Lee appealed his 2001 conviction of the manslaughter of Joanna Lee who 'died while an exorcism was being performed on her by Mr Lee'.[1] The proceedings speak of it being 'the role of two of the members of Mr Lee's Church . . . to point out the demons in Joanna's body and where they were located'.[2] Another witness testified that 'the exorcism at the house finished with a cry from Joanna to expel the last of the demons. Just before the exorcism ended, there were still about two demons left in Joanna's body but they had gone when Mr Lee had finished the

1. *R v Lee*, New Zealand Court of Appeal, CA437/04 (unreported decision). April 7, 2006: 1.
2. *R v Lee*: 15.

deliverance'.[3] Around this same time, Anthony Molloy, QC, approached the School of Theology to undertake research on behalf of the Sainsbury Trust, whose terms of reference were 'spirit possession in Aotearoa New Zealand and . . . well-being'.

In the rational and scientific era that characterised the twentieth century and has seeped over into the early twenty-first century, one wonders where this language of demons being expelled from a human body, or spirit/s possessing a person, might come from and what it might mean, especially if such belief and the actions associated with it can lead to the death of a young woman. In the context of his claim that we 'discern the weakness of a social system' when we 'discover what it excludes from conversation', Walter Wink suggests that '[a]ngels, spirits, principalities, powers, gods, satan—these, along with all other spiritual realities, are the unmentionables of our culture'.[4] Indeed, in the late eighties and early nineties of the last century, Wink's analysis may have been correct, but there has been a significant change, in that now one finds his 'unmentionables' characterising streams of popular culture. *Ghost Whisperer* and *Medium* show weekly on New Zealand television, and a New Zealand film-maker, Glenn Standrig, has recently written and directed the documentary film, *The Truth about Demons*.[5]

3. *R v Lee*: 30.
4. Walter Wink, *Unmasking the Powers: The Invisible Forces that Determine Human Existence,* vol 2 of *The Powers* (Philadelphia: Fortress, 1986), 1.
5. *Truth about Demons,* written and directed by Glenn Standring, produced by Dave Gibson (Sydney: Siren Visual Entertainment/21st

Other contributors to this volume have explored the language and claims of spirit and demon possession, and phenomena associated with it, from a variety of perspectives: linguistic, cultural, sociological, anthropological, historical, and theological. In this article, I will turn attention to the Second Testament as a significant source of belief in and language of spirit possession. Using a variety of approaches characteristic of contemporary Second Testament scholarship, I will examine the story of the healing of the Gerasene Demoniac (Mark 5:1-20) in the context of the Graeco-Roman world and first century Christianity, in order to provide a backdrop to later development of belief in, and practices relating to, demon or spirit possession.

From One to Many—of Names and of Spirits/Demons

Using Mark 5:1–20 as a lens on the gospels, particularly the Synoptics where the language of demons, evil and unclean spirits, the devil, and Satan seems to cluster, one finds a particular choice of language in this text. The author of the Gospel of Mark speaks of a man (*anthrōpos*) with an unclean spirit (*en pneumati akathartō*) (Mark 5:2). In v 8, Jesus commands the unclean spirit to come out of the man, the singular form of the noun and adjective still being used. On inquiring of the name of this spirit, however, Jesus discovers that the spirit is 'Legion', and hence, in v 13, the narrator refers to 'them', in the plural form, as unclean spirits who come out of the man and

Century Pictures, 2000).

enter the two thousand swine. The/se spirit/s are beings separate from the human community, but inhabiting the same world. They are given language that is shared with the human community in this and other gospel narratives (Matt 12:43–44; Mark 1:23–24, 3:11; Luke 4:33–34, 8:29-30, 11:24). The naming of this spirit as *akarthartos*, or unclean, conforms to the Jewish mapping of people and places according to purity laws.[6] It was named as a source of disorder in the community's symbolic universe.[7] Interestingly, however, there is no reference to a spirit that is clean or pure in the Second Testament, but rather only a spirit that is *hagios* or holy,[8] one associated with what is of God, the

---

6. Jerome H Neyrey, 'The Symbolic Universe of Luke-Acts: "They Turn the World Upside Down"', in *The Social World of Luke-Acts: Models for Interpretation*, edited by Jerome H Neyrey (Peabody: Hendrickson, 1991), 271–304, uses the perspectives of cultural anthropology to explore the ways in which the first century Jewish community mapped its world so as to maintain an ordered universe. The categories of clean and unclean were foundational to the ordered symbolic universe that was thereby being constructed. The unclean was what was out of place, dis-ordered, or contravening the right order of things in this constructed universe. For this perspective on the Markan Gospel, see David Rhoads, *Reading Mark, Engaging the Gospel* (Minneapolis: Fortress, 2004), 140–175.
7. The phrase 'unclean spirit' occurs nineteen times in the gospels (two in Matthew; eleven in Mark; six in Luke, and none in John). It is clearly a preferred Markan term, with only five other occurrences in the Second Testament. It appears only once in the LXX, at Zech 13:2. Mark does not use the phrase 'evil spirit'/*pneuma ponēron,* which occurs in only nine verses of the Second Testament, four of which are in Luke and four in Acts, with only one occurence in Matthew.
8. The article by Helen Bergin in this volume discusses this notion of

Holy One, and given to Jesus and the Jesus community.[9]

The man of Mark 5:1–20 with the unclean spirit is not named personally, but only in relation to his situation: he is an *anthropos*/human with an unclean spirit. After Jesus drives out the unclean spirits, however, the man is referred to as *ho daimonizomenos*, or the one being demon-ised, being under the power of a *daimonion*/*diamōn*/ demon, the participle being in the present passive tense (5:15, 16).[10] The man is named according to the condition that he had at the beginning of the story, with the passive tense directing attention to the *daimonion*. Even

---

a h/Holy spirit.

9. References to a holy spirit or the holy spirit in the Second Testament are too numerous to list here. The phrase occurs in ninety-four verses: five in Matthew, four in Mark, thirteen in Luke, and seven in John. The greatest concentration is in Acts, where it is found in forty verses, and is then scattered across the remainder of the texts. For the parallel phrase *en pneumati tō hagiō* or equivalent, see Matt 3:11; Mark 1:8, 12:36; Luke 3:16, 4:1, 10:21; John 1:33; Acts 1:5, 11:16, 20:28 and *passim*.
10. It should be noted that the word 'possession' or 'possessed' is not inherent in this verb. Rather, the verb carries the connotations of the earlier description of the man in Mark 5:2 as being *en pneumati akathartō*, or imbued with a spirit. It is not difficult to see, however, how the notion of possession developed. Second Testament authors speak readily of being in God (*en tō Theō*—1 John 3:24; 4:13, 15; cf John 10:38; 14:10) or in Christ (John 14:20; 15:4) to convey the sense of submitting oneself to the power and influence of God or Christ. Similarly, therefore, being in/*en* an unclean spirit can likewise mean the submitting of the person to the power and influence of that spirit, hence being possessed by that spirit. Contemporary interpreters therefore read this verb as meaning possessed by a demon.

though the unclean spirits have been driven out by Jesus, the narrator, who is giving expression to the perspective of those who come out from the city and the countryside (5:14), uses the descriptive participle, indicating that the man has been named according to his previous condition. In 5:18, the aorist passive participle is used, carrying with it the recognition that the man's condition of being taken over by a demon/s is now in the past.

This Markan story seems to move between the language of 'unclean spirit' and 'demon', and hence gives greater access to the world that this language is creating in the first century of the Common Era. The word *daimonion*/demon is used in fifty-three verses across the gospels (eleven in Matthew; thirteen in Mark; twenty-three in Luke; and six in John), and in ten other verses in the remainder of the Second Testament. The verb *daimonizomai* is used thirteen times, twelve of which are in the participial form describing, as in Mark 5:15, 16, and 18, the one having, or being in the possession of, a demon. All of these occur in the gospels. Given this world which the gospels are constructing of demons or spirits which are unclean or unholy, it comes as a surprise to discover that the presence of demons in the world construction of the LXX is extremely limited, the noun *daimonion* appearing only seventeen times, seven of which are in Tobit, and others of which are scattered across just five other books, most of which are of late origin.[11] The verb *daimonizomai*

11. Two essays in this volume give attention to the book of Tobit and its concentration of demon language, namely, those of Keith Stuart and Alice Sinnott.

does not occur at all. There has been, therefore, a significant development of a language world of demonology in the Hellenistic and early Roman period, leading into the first century of the Common Era.

Contemporary awareness of intertextuality enables us to recognise that the Markan, synoptic, and Second Testament language world is constructed interactively with that of the MT, LXX, Jewish Apocryphal and Pseudepigraphical writings, and other texts too numerous to give account of in this article. I have already noted how few times *daimonion* occurs in the LXX, where it creates meaning within the predominantly monotheistic worldview of the Jewish people. It generally refers to other-worldly beings who are not divine, but who are mistakenly perceived to be so by those who stray from Israel's God. They do not, therefore, threaten the sovereignty of the God to whom both good and evil can be attributed.[12] Under the influence of Persia and the East during and after the Babylonian captivity, and with the rise of an apocalyptic worldview, demons become more manifest in the reli-

12. For a much more extensive analysis of this word set from the classical Greek world through the influence of the East into Hellenism and Rabbinic Judaism, see Heinrich Schlier, *'daimōn'*, in *The Theological Dictionary of the New Testament*, edited by Gerhard Kittel, translated by Geoffrey W Bromiley (Grand Rapids: Eerdmans, 1964), 2:1–21, and Ken Frieden, 'The Language of Demonic Possession: A Key-word Analysis', in *The Daemonic Imagination: Biblical Text and Secular Story*, edited by Robert Detweiler and William G Doty (Atlanta: Scholars Press, 1990), 41–52. Apart from the demon encountered in the book of Tobit, see Deut 32:17; Pss 91:6, 96:5, 106:37; Is 13:21, 34:14, 65:3; and Bar. 4:7, 35.

gious language of Israel. They now seem to function independently of God as evil spirits that inhabit the world between divinity and humanity.[13] They seduce or tempt members of the human community to evil rather than fidelity to God (Jub 10:1; 48:9; 1 En 19:1). A worldview was emerging in which these spirits, both good and evil who inhabit the in-between space, are at odds. Schlier summarises it thus: 'in the doctrine of ill-disposed angels and demons who seek to do harm to life and limb, it became obvious that the present world order, with all its suffering, want, and mortality is in conflict with the will of God'.[14]

What I have not addressed in this linguistic study is a related language field, namely that of *diabolos* and *satanas* which emerge from the LXX as almost interchangeable terms for an explicit embodiment of the force/s or power/s of evil. *Diabolos* is used in the LXX to translate the Hebrew *ha-satan* of Job (thirteen times in ten verses). There are only nine other uses of the term *diabolos* in the entire LXX. Mark does not use the term *diabolos* at all, but does use *satanas* in five verses (Mark 1:13; 3:23, 26; 4:15; 8:33). Both Matthew and Luke use *diabolos* four times in their temptation narratives (Matt 4:1–11; Luke 4:1–13), and then only twice and once respectively beyond those narratives. Significantly across the gospels, *diabolos* is always used with the definite article when referring to the personified evil one. This would warrant a different study to the one being undertaken here, and hence, I will limit

13. The prince of evil spirits is named Maestema in Jub. 10:8; 48:2, 9; 49:2, and Beliar in T. 12 Ptr.—Simeon 5:3; Naphtali 3:1; Joseph 20:3.
14. Schlier, *'daimōn'*, 16.

my exploration to the language world encountered in Mark 5:1–20, namely that of demons and unclean spirits.

The language of the Second Testament, and especially the synoptic gospels, gives expression to a world view or a cosmology that developed during the prior three centuries, in which angels/good spirits and demons/unclean or evil spirits play a crucial role, 'midway between gods and men',[15] according to Plutarch.[16] It is *a* cosmology, and one that differed from cosmologies evident in the First Testament and classical Greek texts. It functioned interactively with health care systems; with political, socio-economic and cultural factors; and with apocalyptic and other worldviews and perspectives within the varied contexts of the first century from which the gospels arose. It is appropriate, therefore, that the next lens I turn on the text of Mark 5:1–20 will be the socio-cultural, exploring the encoding of aspects of political, social, and cultural worlds in that text.

Before turning to that exploration, however, it is well to consider questions that might arise from this study of a Second Testament text that one can address to contemporary uses of the language of spirit or demon possession, such as that in the Lee appeal case cited at the beginning of this article. These questions would include:

15. Plutarch, *De Defectu Oraculorum* 415A.

16. For a collection of texts that give access to the development of this world view, see Wendy Cotter, *Miracles in Greco-Roman Antiquity: A Sourcebook for the Study of New Testament Miracle Stories* (London: Routledge, 1999), 75–119.

> *What is the language world constructed by those who speak today about demons and demon or spirit possession?*
>
> *What is the cosmology which they construct and which shapes and is shaped by their worldview?*
>
> *What are the intertexts which inform this construction?*

No One Had the Strength to Subdue Him: of Power and Possession

Reading on in Mark 5:1–20, beyond v 2 in which we encounter the man with an unclean spirit as noted in the previous section, readers are given a very vivid description of this man:

> . . . [he] lived among the tombs; and no one could bind him any more, even with a chain; for he had often been bound with fetters and chains, but the chains he wrenched apart, and the fetters he broke in pieces; and no one had the strength to subdue him. Night and day among the tombs and on the mountains he was always crying out, and bruising himself with stones. (Mark 5:3–5)

The narrator seems to pile up social descriptors characteristic of possession by an evil or unclean spirit. He was divided within himself, as the move between the singular and plural referents for the spirit indicates, and as we saw above (5:2, 6, 7 and 9, 10, 12, 13). His behaviour is excessively 'strange and bizarre', to use Hollenbach's terminology, as he lives among the tombs and on the mountains, unable to be bound.[17] The reader is not told if the bonds are to protect the man from himself, or to protect others from him. Strangely, however, the narrator informs the reader that the people from the city and the country are afraid when they see the man 'clothed and in his right mind'. If they had expelled the man from their midst, carrying in his body the force and power of what was unclean or demonic, would his return in his right mind have left a vacuum for the community? On whom would the demonic now rest; who would be the community's scapegoat? The description of the man's behaviour begins to raise such questions of the social encoding in this text.

Social scientific approaches to biblical interpretation, as well as postcolonial theories, have provided insights into the dynamics of spirit possession that we encounter in this text of Mark 5:1–20. First-century Palestine was a colonised nation, but resistance to such colonisation was mounting during the early decades of the latter half of that century, only to be crushed in the early 70s as the Roman army marched down from the north into Jerusalem, destroying its temple and scattering its citizens.[18] Frantz

17. I am in dialogue here with the article of Paul W Hollenbach, 'Jesus, Demoniacs and Public Authorities: A Socio-historical Study', in *Journal of the American Academy of Religion* 99/4 (1981): 570–572, in which he sets forth the ways in which a society identifies its 'demoniacs'.

18. Hollenbach, 'Jesus, Demoniacs and Public Authorities', suggests

Fanon's study, *The Wretched of the Earth*, informed by his experience in colonial Algeria during its war for independence, provides insights into the psycho-social dynamics of colonisation such as it may well have been experienced in the Syro-Palestinian and Decapolis regions of the Roman Empire in the first century. Fanon points to the way in which the experience of oppression is subsumed into and then obscured by language of spirits or demons and the divine, a process which characterised the periods of both Hellenistic and early Roman oppression of the East, including Palestine and its Jewish population.[19]

In such a context, the colonised can become divided within themselves, as is the man with the unclean spirit, with this division manifesting in strange and bizarre behaviour, as noted above. Such behaviour would be, therefore, the outcome of the social conflict experienced by the person. On the other hand, individuals may take into, or manifest in their bodies, the divisive, strange, and bizarre experiences that characterise their colonisation. The possession may, therefore, be the result of colonisation or a protest against it, but either way, it needs to be controlled within the community of the oppressed, for fear that the

---

that 'it was probably the very appearance of the cultural disruptions of the Hellenistic period that brought the demon symbolism into common parlance, beginning with the third century BCE. These included political and economic domination and exploitation and, particularly, the threatened erosion of long held traditional customs and beliefs' (580).

19. Frantz Fanon, *The Wretched of the Earth*, translated by Constance Farrington (New York: Grove Press, 1963), 54–58. He uses the term 'mystification' to describe this process.

colonisers might destroy the entire community as a result of this behaviour.[20] Possession by an individual cannot be separated, therefore, from the social and communal, as is manifest in Mark 5:1–20. The man is put outside the community. He is bound with chains so that he cannot be a source of retaliation by the occupying forces.

Another feature of the social world of the first century, encoded in the text of Mark 5:1–20, is its health care system. Jesus is met by a man with an unclean spirit as he gets out of a boat on the eastern shore of the Lake of Galilee. This would evoke for readers the prior characterisation of Jesus in the Markan narrative in relation to the spirit world. John the Baptist associates Jesus with the *pneuma hagios* (the spirit of holiness or holy spirit—1:8), and he promises that Jesus will baptise with or in this holy spirit. Presumably, then, it is this same spirit which comes down on Jesus from the heavens following his being baptised with water by John (1:10) and which drives Jesus out into the wilderness (1:12), where he is put to the test by Satan (1:13). From the beginning of the Markan story of Jesus, he is intimately connected with the world of the spirits, both holy and adversarial. The first action narrated of Jesus, following the declaration of his preaching the *basileia* of God in 1:14–15, and his initial move to establish a new fictive kinship group to undertake this task with him, is

20. Both Hollenbach, 'Jesus, Demoniacs and Public Authorities', 573–575, and Michael Willett Newheart, *'My Name is Legion': The Story and Soul of the Gerasene Demoniac* (Collegeville: Liturgical Press, 2004), 79–85, discuss the significance of Frantz Fanon's theory for the interpretation of the text of Mark 5:1–20.

his encounter with an unclean spirit in the synagogue at Capernaum (1:21–28). He confronts the unclean spirit and commands it to leave the man, and the crowds recognise his authority. In the subsequent summary passage (Mark 1:32–34 and 39), Jesus is characterised as a folk healer who heals the sick and who casts out demons, the two actions being closely related and within the ambit of the proclamation of God's *basileia*.[21] Jesus' *exousia* (1:28), his authority or power, linked, it would seem, to his charismatic association with the spirit of holiness, is what is recognised as enabling him to engage with and gain power over a spirit named as unclean in order to free the man possessed.[22] The health care system, therefore, includes illnesses in which spirits were involved or whose emic description is explicitly that of spirits and demons.[23]

21. For a brief discussion of health care as a system and its division into professional, the non-professional or folk, which can be secular and magico-religious, and the popular, which was generally associated with the home, see Arthur Kleniman, *Patients and Healers in the Context of Culture: An Exploration of the Borderland between Anthropology, Medicine, and Psychiatry* (Berkeley: University of California Press, 1980), 50–53. In a later summary passage, Mark 3:11–12, the unclean spirits recognise Jesus, and he confronts and orders them, again exercising his *exousia*, or power.

22. Graham H Twelftree, *Jesus the Exorcist: A Contribution to the Study of the Historical Jesus* (Peabody: Hendrickson, 1993), 46, following a study of exorcisms and exorcists in first century Palestine, concludes that certain exorcists such as Apollonius of Tyana, Rabbi Simeon, and Hanina ben Dosa performed successful exorcisms because of who they were. Note that in 3:15, the Markan Jesus authorises the twelve appointed ones to cast out demons with power, or *exousia*, and hence to share in his healing activity.

23 John J Pilch, *Healing in the New Testament: Insights from Medical and*

Midway en route to the story of Jesus' encounter with the Gerasene demoniac, Jesus himself, the folk healer who casts out demons by the power of the spirit of holiness that came on him in his baptism, and with which he is said to baptise, is accused of being demon-possessed himself. The first accusation comes from *hoi par' autou*, or those around him, who seem to be concerned that his healing activity among the crowds is such that he does not even have time to eat. The scribes who come down from Jerusalem are more explicit in their accusation: he is possessed by Beelzebul and, by the prince of demons, he casts out the demons (3:22). Within the Jewish health care system, there is contention over authority to heal, a contention which may well be around *exousia*, or authority, among healers, but which also may have social overtones, which we will see as we engage with the text of Mark 5:1–20 through these socio-cultural lenses.

At the end of the previous section I raised questions to address to contemporary uses of the *language* of spirit or demon possession today in the Lee appeal CA437/04, in the Sainsbury Trust brief, and in other contexts in which such language is current. So, too, at the end of this second section, I wish to raise questions of *power*, of *control*, and of *health care systems* as these emerge in relation to contem-

Mediterranean Anthropology (Minneapolis: Fortress, 2000), 104–106, includes illnesses associated with demons or spirits in his exploration of gospel taxonomies. The *emic* perspective is that of the cultural participants in the health care system—the way they tell their stories of illness and healing toward well-being.

porary claims of spirit possession and well-being beyond such possession.

> *What are the power dynamics within the community using language or claiming experience of spirit/demon possession?*
>
> *Does this group experience itself as oppressed, without power or influence, even endangered by a superior power—politically, socially, economically, or religiously?*
>
> *How does this relate to its claims of spirit possession of individuals or groups within its midst?*
>
> *What are the emic claims in relation to the person/s designated as spirit-possessed, and who in the community is voicing these claims?*

Demoniac/Clothed and in His Right Mind - Of Readings and Meanings

The opening verse of the story takes the reader into a context with mythological as well as socio-political overtones. The 'other side of the sea' is an unknown place in which Jesus' preaching and enacting of the *basileia* of God has not yet been encountered, in contrast to the known space of the Galilee. Reference to the country of the Gerasenes evokes Gerasa or Gadara, one of which is approximately fifty kilometers south-east of the Sea of Galilee, and the other, eight. Both of these locations appear problematic as contexts for the story because of their distance from the edge of the sea, but both represent the Roman Empire as major cities of the Decapolis. Jesus enters, for the first time, the 'other side of the sea' and the Decapolis, and he does so as a charismatic folk healer in conflict with the first century world of demons and unclean spirits. He is also preaching good news of a *basileia* that is not Rome.

The Markan account of the man on the other side of the sea in the country of the Decapolis is the most vivid description of the effects of an unclean spirit found in the Second Testament. The man is described as being alone, outside of the familial and communal structures that were characteristic of a dyadic first century society.[24] So drastic is the man's situation of living among the tombs and on the mountains, breaking free of any attempts to bind him, crying out when no one is there to hear, and harming himself, that it would seem that this is more than a colonised Gerasene enacting his opposition to Rome. Rather, it could be argued that colonisation has driven him mad, with the symptoms being described in first century language of possession by an unclean spirit.[25] As one reads on in the story, however, the Gerasene's resistance to the Empire is manifest in his naming the unclean spirit/s as

24. For a brief description of the dyadic characteristic of first century Mediterranean society, see John J Pilch and Bruce J Malina, editors, *Biblical Social Values and Their Meaning: A Handbook* (Peabody: Hendrickson, 1993), 49–52.

25. Hollenbach, 'Jesus, Demoniacs, and Public Authorities', 581, suggests that '[i]t is likely that the tension between his hatred for his oppressors and the necessity to repress this hatred in order to avoid dire recrimination drove him mad.'

Legion, and his skilful negotiating with Jesus that the spirits should enter the great herd of swine. This would seem to suggest he has made a choice for this liminal state of what was named as demon possession in order to oppose symbolically the oppression of Rome. It is significant that neither the man from whom the unclean spirit has gone out, nor Jesus, seem to be named as responsible for the destruction of the Legion with the drowning of the pigs, and yet both stand symbolically opposed to Rome, which the Legion represents.

Symbolic or actual resistance to oppression by an individual is not without its import for the person's community, especially, as noted above, in a dyadic society in which the individual is always defined by social and communal interconnections such as ties to family and kinship, city or region, and at times, nation. When read through the lens of both Fanon and Girard's theory of scapegoating, the violence expressed in and through the body of the man with the unclean spirit can be seen as an enactment of the violent resistance which the man's kin feel toward Rome but are too afraid to express. Their violence and fear is transposed onto the body of the individual. Walter Wink says in this regard that:

> the townspeople need him to act out their own violence. He bears their collective madness personally freeing them from its symptoms . . . Yet he secretly lives out the freedom to be violent that they crave: he is the most liberated among them, shattering chains, parading naked, free from taxes and tribute and

> the military service due Rome. Yet he is the more miserable for it, and they insure that he remains so.[26]

The initial focus of this story has been on the man who is named as being demon-possessed. It is only in v 6 that the narrator shifts attention to Jesus. The man does not flee from Jesus as one would expect, given the description of the social outcast with its politico-cultural overtones. Rather, he runs to him and kneels before him, engaging with him. The story is told in a way which conveys the ambivalence around the naming of a person as spirit-possessed. It is unclear whether it is the man or the unclean spirit authoring these actions which are characteristic of supplicants approaching a healer.[27] If the action of kneeling before Jesus is that of the man, then he could be seen as approaching Jesus as one in whom he recognises the power to heal, to free him of this possessing spirit.[28]

The shout that goes out from the man in v 7 takes the reader into the language world and cosmology of the gospel—the one with the unclean spirit is drawn into encounter with the one with the holy spirit, and the struggle which characterises that spirit world is played out in the narrative. Jesus, the healer, has commanded the unclean

---

26. Wink, *Unmasking the Powers*, 46.
27. Mark uses the verb *proskeuneō* (to kneel), which only occurs in this verse and at 5:19 in the Markan Gospel, but which characterises the supplicant in Matthew 8:2, 9:18, and 15:25.
28. This is one of the options proposed by Bruce J Malina and Richard L Rohrbaugh, *Social-Science Commentary on the Synoptic Gospels* (Minneapolis: Fortress, 1992), 208.

spirit to come out (v 8), and that spirit then challenges Jesus by recognising and naming him as belonging to God, being named as son of God, belonging to the realm in which the spirits belong, between the heights of God and the human community's earth. The struggle between the two powers is conveyed in the use of the name. The spirit names Jesus and Jesus then demands the name of the spirit, only to find that they are 'Legion'. Here the world construction in which naming gives power[29] and the politico-cultural features of occupation come together, as the name the spirit claims is that of the occupying Roman Army and their legions.

The ambivalent language of this section of the narrative, indicating the multi-layered texture of the text and the world it has created, continues in vv. 10–12. 'He' begs Jesus not to send 'them' out of the country (v 10), and then the 'unclean spirits' of v 12 continue the dialogue. The experience of occupation and a cosmology of warring spirit factions seem to be reflected in the very shifting aspects of the man and the spirit/s portrayed in this section of the text. What is more difficult to interpret is the seemingly strange language and imagery of v 13: the rush of the unclean spirits into the herd of pigs, and their careening down the steep bank into the sea. Fanon's theory of the 'mystification' of oppression referred to earlier is distinctly at work—the oppressor is destroyed symbolically.

The process of mystification can be seen in the identification of the unclean spirit as 'Legion', or 'many', and their desire not to be sent out of the country. The power

29. Malina and Rohrbaugh, *Social-Science Commentary*, 208.

of Rome is evoked very explicitly in the naming of 'Legion', as is its encroaching on the region in the desire of the unclean spirit not to be sent out of the country. The language of v 13b continues this process. The verb translated as 'rush', *hormaō*, is intransitive in this sentence, but in the transitive, it can mean to stir up, to incite, to urge on, and so carries traces of inciting or urging a Roman Legion to battle or to destruction, the very thing feared by the inhabitants of the Decapolis, as well as of Galilee. The sea, too, in the symbolic world of the Markan narrative, evokes not only the Lake of Galilee,[30] a small inland body of water, but also the Mediterranean, ringed as it was by lands under the power of Rome.[31] Richard Horsley suggests that this language of mystification extends even further, to the final phrase of v 13, 'they were drowned in the sea', recalling the Song of the Sea which Moses sang to celebrate Israel's triumph over the oppression of Pharaoh and the Egyptians.[32] What the people of the occupied

30. Twice, the Markan narrative explicitly names *thalassa* (sea) with the qualifier 'Galilee' (Mark 1:16; 7:31), the first being its initial use, and the second to distinguish it from the Mediterranean when narrating Jesus' return from the Mediterranean region of Tyre and Sidon to the Lake.
31. Luke, on the other hand, never uses *thalassa* for the Lake.
32. The phrase *eis . . . thalassan* or *en . . . thalassē* (in or into the sea), which occurs twice in Mark 5:13, appears four times in the Song of the Sea (Ex 15:1–18: vv 1, 4 [twice], 8, and cf v 10). I have taken this insight from my own notes on the paper of Richard A Horsley, 'My Name is "Legion": Demon-Possession and Exorcism as Responses to Roman Domination', (paper presented at the annual meeting of the Society of Biblical Literature, San Diego, CA, November 17, 2007).

Decapolis, including the man with the unclean spirit, secretly desired was the expulsion of Rome, but in their oppression, they could only dream of it. Their fear of Roman power, and their desire to control any possible retaliation against even their dreams, is laid upon the man whom Jesus encounters among the tombs, howling and bruising himself with stones. Jesus, who is associated with another power, that of the Most High God (v 6), confronts the power of Legion, utterly defeating it.

This reversal is manifest not only in the destruction of the unclean spirits, but also in the description of the man healed. The people from both the city and the country see the demoniac 'sitting there, clothed and in his right mind' (v 15). This description could be said to belong to the final stage of a healing narrative, as modeled by Arthur Kleinman, namely, the sanctioning of a new label that is generally a reversal of the 'culturally legitimated name' given to the illness.[33] This healing, or this casting out of an unclean spirit, like other such actions in a society characterised by a dyadic approach to personality, does not result in transformation or change only for the person, but also for the society. And it is the invitation to change that confronts the people when they see the transformation in the man. They are 'afraid', and they 'beg Jesus to leave their neighbourhood' (vv 15, 17). They have lost their scapegoat, the one who carried all their ambivalence and their guilt, their wanting Rome destroyed as were the pigs, but their not-wanting to draw down upon themselves their own destruction that their acting against

33. See Arthur Kleinman, *Patients and Healers*, 243.

their oppressors would cause. The man who is clothed and in his right mind has negotiated such a change, such a transformation, through his encounter with Jesus. For the others, however, this remains too risky. Jesus departs, as they wish, but he commissions the man who has been possessed but is now freed to tell what God, the one who is greater than any intermediary powers or spirits and greater than Rome, has done.

The story closes with v 20 narrating how the man proclaimed in the Decapolis, not what God had done, but rather, what Jesus had done for him. The narrative itself places Jesus not on the side of Beelzebul, the prince of demons, but on the side of God in the first century battle between the intermediary powers (see Mark 3:20–27). The story also closes as it opened, 'on the other side'. The region of the Decapolis, which previously had not encountered Jesus' preaching of a *basileia* alternate to Rome, has now not only encountered the power that accompanied Jesus' proclamation, but also hears the message of healing and transformation that Jesus wrought, not only in the man, but also in the region.

The questions that arise from this interpretive task are:

> *Who does a community demonise or cast out?*
>
> *What does this person symbolise for the community, or what burden of the community is the person made to carry?*

> *How does the community deal with the restoration of this person to the community, 'healed and in right mind'?*

Conclusion

The language of spirit possession is powerful. It is not only about power but it also functions powerfully. It emerged more prominently within the biblical tradition at a time when Israel/Palestine was oppressed, first by Greece and then by Rome. Contemporary social scientific theories such as those of Fanon and Girard have provided us with tools for analysing, in new ways, gospel stories of demon possession which arose out of such a context. These tools, in turn, are essential for understanding the social and cultural features and manifestations of power and oppression which may be operative when contemporary communities and individuals within strongly integrated social groups use the language and stories of demon possession and the casting out of demons. They give rise to some of the questions that I have suggested could be addressed to contemporary experiences named as spirit possession and to processes used to bring the person/s involved to wholeness or well-being. Perhaps it is to such as these that the dramatic and powerful story of Jesus' healing and restoration of the Gerasene demoniac directs us, so that to cases such as that of *R v Lee*, we can say—never again!

Bibliography

Cotter, Wendy. *Miracles in Greco-Roman Antiquity: A Sourcebook for the Study of New Testament Miracle Stories* (London: Routledge, 1999).

Fanon, Frantz. *The Wretched of the Earth*, translated by Constance Farrington (New York: Grove Press, 1963).

Frieden, Ken. 'The Language of Demonic Possession: A Key-Word Analysis', in *The Daemonic Imagination: Biblical Text and Secular Story*, edited by Robert Detweiler and William G Doty, *AAR Studies in Religion 60* (Atlanta: Scholars Press, 1990), 41–52.

Girard, René. *The Scapegoat*, translated by Yvonne Freccero (Baltimore: The Johns Hopkins University Press, 1986).

Hollenbach, Paul. 'Jesus, Demoniacs and Public Authorities: A Socio-Historical Study', in *Journal of the American Academy of Religion* 99/4 (1981): 567–88.

Horsley, Richard A. 'My Name is "Legion": Demon-Possession and Exorcism as Responses to Roman Domination'. Paper presented at the annual meeting of the Society of Biblical Literature, San Diego, CA, November 17, 2007.

Kleinman, Arthur. *Patients and Healers in the Context of Culture: An Exploration of the Borderland between Anthropology, Medicine, and Psychiatry* (Berkeley: University of California Press, 1980).

Malina, Bruce J, and Richard L Rohrbaugh. *Social-Science Commentary on the Synoptic Gospels* (Minneapolis: Fortress, 1992).

Neyrey, Jerome H. 'The Symbolic Universe of Luke-Acts: "They Turn the World Upside Down"', in *The Social*

World of Luke-Acts: Models for Interpretation, edited by Jerome H Neyrey (Peabody: Hendrickson, 1991), 271–304.

Newheart, Michael Willett. *'My Name Is Legion': The Story and Soul of the Gerasene Demoniac Interfaces* (Collegeville: Liturgical Press, 2004).

Pilch, John J. *Healing in the New Testament: Insights from Medical and Mediterranean Anthropology* (Minneapolis: Fortress, 2000).

Pilch, John J, and Bruce J Malina, editors. *Biblical Social Values and Their Meaning: A Handbook* (Peabody: Hendrickson, 1993).

Plutarch. *Moralia; De Defectu Oraculorum*, translated by FC Babbitt, WC Helmbold, and PH De Lacy. 15 vols, vol 5 (London: Heinemann, 1927–1969).

R v Lee, New Zealand Court of Appeal, CA437/04 (unreported decision), April 7, 2006.

Rhoads, David. *Reading Mark, Engaging the Gospel* (Minneapolis: Fortress, 2004).

Schlier, Heinrich. '*daimōn*', in *The Theological Dictionary of the New Testament*, edited by Gerhard Kittel, translated by Geoffrey W Bromiley, vol 2 (Grand Rapids: Eerdmans, 1964), 1–21.

Standrig, Glenn. *The Truth about Demons*. Produced by Dave Gibson. Sydney: Siren Visual Entertainment/21st Century Pictures, 2000.

Twelftree, Graham H. *Jesus the Exorcist: A Contribution to the Study of the Historical Jesus* (Peabody: Hendrickson, 1993).

Wink, Walter. *Unmasking the Powers: The Invisible Forces That Determine Human Existence*. Volume 2 of *The Powers* (Philadelphia: Fortress, 1986).

Naming the Spirit of God 'Holy'

Helen Bergin

Millions of believers, from many religious traditions, acclaim as 'holy' the God in whom they believe. I wish to address, from a Christian perspective, the topic of God's 'holiness' in relation to God's Spirit, or, as it is often called, God's 'Holy Spirit'. The word 'holy' often means 'separated from' or 'not ordinary',[1] with the quality of 'holiness' belonging, in an ultimate sense, to God. Biblical scholar Andy Johnson grounds divine holiness in Jesus of Nazareth, who embodied God's offer of reconciliation, compassion, and joy.[2] Theologian Nicola Slee speaks

1. See for example, WRF Browning's definition of holiness: 'what is separated from ordinary or profane use is "holy".' Browning then adds, 'Hence, above all, God is holy (Isa 6:3).' See 'Holiness', in *A Dictionary of the Bible* (Oxford: Oxford University Press, 1997), 174.
2. Andy Johnson, 'Holiness', in *The New Interpreter's Dictionary of the Bible: D-H* (Nashville: Abingdon Press, 2007), 2:846–847.

of God's Spirit as encouraging 'holism, integration and inclusivity'.[3] In this chapter, I will explore aspects of the Spirit's holiness with the above descriptions in mind. By focusing on God's 'holy' Spirit, I hope to provide a counterpoint to some chapters in this collection which, by contrast, refer to spirits which do not make holy.

Initially, I will examine the spirit world prior to, and into which, Jesus preached the reign of God. I will then reflect briefly on God as Spirit in the Hebrew Scriptures. Both aspects will provide a background for Second Testament descriptions of God's Spirit as 'holy'. In the major section of the essay, drawing from the above and with the assistance of Christian tradition, I will offer three ways of understanding God's Spirit as 'holy'. I will describe God's Spirit as enabling *freedom*, exhibiting *power*, and encouraging *wholeness*. It is my hope that these three descriptions will point to God's Spirit as 'holy'. In addition, such descriptions might offer an alternative vision to that in which lesser spirits can cause a reduction of liberty, a distortion of power, and a lack of wholeness in both individuals and communities.

Spirit World and God's Spirit in Scriptures

Prior to the time of Jesus Christ, the Israelite community understood spiritual transcendent beings (whether good or evil) as under Yahweh's control. Such beings were sub-

3. Nicola Slee, 'The Holy Spirit and Spirituality', in *The Cambridge Companion to Feminist Theology*, edited by Susan Frank Parsons (Cambridge: Cambridge University Press, 2002), 182.

ject to God's purposes. 'Angels' were God's trustworthy messengers, and 'spirits' generally were supernatural beings attempting to pervert divine purposes. With the advent of Jesus, spirits (that is, evil spirits) encountered someone who obstructed their power. At the same time, Jesus' defeat of evil spirits made clear that in his person and message of Good News, a new age was dawning in history.[4] In Jesus' day, the spirit world was most familiar.

The Israelites, likewise, were familiar with the Spirit of God. Often, 'God' and 'the Spirit of God' were acknowledged as alternative ways of speaking of Yahweh. God's Spirit was linked with creative power, both at the dawn of creation (Gen 1:2) and when communities needed renewing (Ezek 37:1–14). The Spirit was linked with the gathering of communities, as witnessed through charismatic leaders such as Moses and Joshua (Josh 1:16–18). God's Spirit was connected with prophetic individuals who challenged community attitudes and behaviour, as seen in Jeremiah (Jer 19:1–14) and Amos (Amos 5:1–24). God was experienced as actively committed to the people through the agency of God's Spirit.

In the First Testament, however, it was rare for God's Spirit to be named 'holy'. Such attribution was undoubtedly implicit. Only on two occasions is reference made to individuals who longed for God's 'holy spirit' to purify or guide them.[5] Nevertheless, within the same era as Je-

4. Biblical scholars have noted the difficulty in interpreting Jesus' exorcisms as *necessarily* linked with the banishment of evil powers. I leave that discussion to their expertise.
5. Ps 51 and Isa 63:10, 11. See Ju Hur, *A Dynamic Reading of Luke-Acts,*

sus, the Qumran community readily spoke of God's Holy Spirit.[6] This community sometimes invoked the Holy Spirit to cleanse them in preparation for God's coming, to sustain them in pure living, or to guide them into truth.[7] One senses in this community an awareness of divine holiness as encompassing both a state of separation and integrity of living.

With Jesus' coming, it seems that God's Spirit refers to the same God as that of the Israelite ancestors. God is once again doing new things and inviting people to a change of heart. In the Second Testament, the Holy Spirit announces God's final purposes for creation, while in the person and ministry of Jesus of Nazareth, God's Spirit is also recognised as truly active.

In order to explore the 'holiness' of God's Spirit, I will refer first to the evangelist Luke's writings. Luke uses the term 'Holy Spirit' fifty-four times within his Gospel and the Acts of the Apostles.[8] For Luke, Jesus' birth and ministry reveal the overwhelming influence of God's holy-making Spirit in unifying or reconciling creation to God. Especially within early sections of the gospel, the Holy Spirit[9] is active in bringing God and creation together—in

Journal for the Study of the New Testament, Supplement Series 211 (Sheffield: Sheffield Academic Press, 2001), 49.

6. Ju Hur, 'Excursus', in *A Dynamic Reading of Luke-Acts*, 74–86.
7. In Ju Hur, citing the Qumram *Manual of Discipline*: 'Thou hast shed thy Holy Spirit upon me that I may not stumble' (1 QH 7:6–7), 84.
8. See Ju Hur, *A Dynamic Reading of Luke-Acts*, 136. Out of the seventy-four references to God's Spirit in Luke and Acts, 'Holy' Spirit is used fifty-four times.
9. Joseph Fitzmyer states that in Luke 1:35, the Greek text has no defi-

Mary of Nazareth through whom the Holy Spirit gifts the world with Jesus, in her cousin Elizabeth who, moved by the Spirit, extols Mary's faith, and in prophetic Simeon, upon whom the Holy Spirit rests.

As Jesus begins his public ministry, God's overture to creation continues. The Holy Spirit descends on Jesus at baptism; he is led into the wilderness 'by the Spirit' (Luke 4:1); he emerges from the wilderness 'filled with the power of the Spirit' (Luke 4:14); and he proclaims to his people in Nazareth that 'the Spirit of the Lord' (Luke 4:18) is upon him. Perhaps Luke's particular description of persons 'filled with the Spirit' suggests that God's Spirit was laying claim to, or even 'taking possession of', those who would act to further God's reign.[10] For Luke, the event of Jesus' entrance into, and commitment to, history is Spirit-enabled and signals God's desire to share divine holiness with finite creation. Theologian Elizabeth Johnson captures such significance in her words: 'Through his [Jesus'] human history, the Spirit who pervades the universe becomes concretely present in a small bit of it; Sophia pitches her tent in the midst of the world'.[11] Late in the Gospel, when the risen Jesus encounters his disciples, Jesus advises them to await 'what my Father promised' (24:49)—a promise fulfilled early in Luke's *Acts*, when the

---

nite article. Hence, it is 'holy Spirit' who comes upon Mary. See J Fitzmyer, *The Gospel According to Luke I-IX*, Anchor Bible Series (New York: Doubleday, 1979), 350.

10. See Elizabeth and Zechariah as 'filled with the Spirit' (Luke 1:41 and 1:67); see also Peter and Stephen (Acts 4:8 and 7:55).
11. Elizabeth Johnson, *She Who Is: The Mystery of God in Feminist Theological Discourse* (New York: Crossroad, 1993), 150.

gift of the Holy Spirit is lavished on them and on all who are open to the gift.

Alongside Luke's writings, Paul's letters encourage early Christian communities to open themselves to God's Spirit.[12] Only with the Spirit's influence can they live the new life inaugurated by Jesus, and signal to other communities God's ultimate hopes for the world. While not naming the Spirit 'holy', Paul reminds his communities about the holiness to which God calls them—claimed as they are for Christ through baptism in his Spirit. Holiness and life in the Spirit are, for Paul, synonymous.

A further understanding of the holiness offered by Jesus relates to people being saved not only *from* evil powers and things that bind, but *for* life with God. Paul reminds the Galatians, for example, that through the gift of the Spirit, they have been freed from obligations to human-made rules concerning 'special days, and months, and seasons' (Gal 4:10) in order to experience freedom in Jesus. However, Paul warns that when they reject God's claim, they also reject true freedom. In relation to the ongoing effectiveness of Jesus' salvation, biblical scholar James Dunn writes: '"Holy Spirit" denotes supernatural power, altering, working through, directing the believer . . . [it is] the eschatological gift par excellence.'[13] But he also adds: '[This gift] is only the start of a life-long process of being saved.'[14]

12. See for example, Rom 8:1–17; 1 Cor 3: 16-17; Gal 5: 13–22.
13. James Dunn, 'Spirit and Holy Spirit in the New Testament (1978)', in *Pneumatology* (Grand Rapids: Eerdmans, 1998), 10.
14. Dunn, 'Spirit and Holy Spirit', 14.

Between events recorded in the Second Testament and the early fourth century CE, the Holy Spirit was recognised as the power behind mission, was linked with the holiness of baptism, and was included in prayers of praise to God. Yet, only gradually, was the Spirit named as equal both with Jesus and with the One whom he called *Abba*/ Father. There was reticence about naming the Spirit 'divine'. In the third century, Origen, aware of the distinction between evil spirits and God's holy-making Spirit, described the latter as 'resting in the pure of heart for the Holy Spirit cannot tolerate the partnership and company of an evil spirit'.[15] Cyril of Jerusalem, two centuries later, used graphic descriptions of the evil power of the devil in order to establish a contrast with the ennobling powers of the Holy Spirit.[16] The same contrast between God's holy-making Spirit and other spirits is acknowledged today.

Because God's Spirit, distinctly related to Jesus Christ, was a living reality in the early church, people could not deny the Spirit's presence and power. Yet, theologians struggled to declare the equality of the Holy Spirit with Jesus and with his God. The creed of 325 from the Council of Nicaea simply stated: 'We believe in the Holy Spirit'. Possibly, the word 'Holy' was included to indicate God's desire to make creation holy, as well as to distinguish God's Spirit from other spirits abroad. Only later in the

15. Origen, *De Principiis* I, iii, 8, cited in *With Bright Wings: A Book of the Spirit*, edited by Mary Grace Swift (New York: Paulist Press, 1976), 93.
16. Cyril of Jerusalem, *Catechesis XVI*, cited in Swift, *With Bright Wings*, 96.

fourth century, after a concentrated burst of theological reflection on the Holy Spirit, did the Council of Constantinople offer a fuller understanding of the Holy Spirit—as divine, Giver of Life, worthy of worship and glory. After 381, the Spirit within Christian communities was mostly addressed as 'Holy Spirit'. It is to the implications of such naming that I now turn.

The Holy Spirit or God's Spirit?

I begin this section by admitting the challenge of writing about the mysterious Spirit. Theologian Kilian McDonnell, in citing Gabriel Marcel's words, 'a mystery is something in which I myself am involved', suggests the difficulty of articulating the nature of the Spirit. McDonnell suggests that it is only in attending to the Spirit that one might venture reflection on the Spirit. He says, '[Mystery] is . . . beyond the possibility of being grasped or laid hold of . . . The Spirit is not separable from the very faith processes by which an attempt is made to 'define' who the Spirit is . . . we must use the Spirit to understand the Spirit.'[17] Even the most profound human reflection on the Spirit can only point towards the mystery, and will always require testing, as well as placing in perspective.

In the following section, I will use a variety of terms—'Holy Spirit', 'God's Spirit', and 'Spirit'—to point towards the one divine reality. I include the latter terms because, ironically, the holiness attributed to God's Spirit has some-

17. Kilian McDonnell, *The Other Hand of God: The Holy Spirit as the Universal Touch* (Collegeville: The Liturgical Press, 2003), 213–214.

times led to practices and attitudes that are diminishing of human persons and, by implication, of God as well. For example, language such as the Holy Spirit 'dwelling within' can be traced to biblical roots.[18] Such phrases, however, can be misunderstood. They may suggest that humans 'own' the Spirit, or that humans alone locate the Spirit's presence. It is not the Spirit's holiness, nor holiness per se, that present difficulties. On the contrary, holiness offered by God's Spirit can both enlarge the vision and potential of human persons, and also invite them to experience a holiness linked intrinsically to the life and death of Jesus.

In the context of this project, I will propose three ways by which to understand the Spirit's continuing role vis-à-vis human persons.[19] I will explore the gifts of freedom, power, and wholeness. I will connect these gifts with the Holy Spirit for two reasons. First, this research project was instigated with the spirit world in view. My discussion, therefore, will centre on God's 'holy' Spirit in the context of other spirits whose presence often reduces or contradicts gospel understandings of holiness—diminishing human freedom, power, and wholeness. Second, I will reflect on God's Spirit as linked with Jesus' gifting of the Spirit to his original followers.

18. See John 14:17, 'You know him [the Spirit of truth] because he abides with you, and he will be in you.'

19. Paul outlines *many* gifts and fruits of God's Spirit. See 1 Cor 12:8–11 and Gal 5:22–23.

God's creative Spirit pulsating everywhere is not diminished by the link with Jesus—unless his followers minimise the Spirit's influence. Dunn, in pondering Jesus' ongoing gift of the Spirit, states: 'The emptiness, dryness, dullness, superficiality of modern Christianity would have astonished the first Christians.'[20] The Holy Spirit is anything but dull and superficial. I will suggest that the Spirit liberates, empowers, and transforms the entire created order. My focus in this chapter is, however, on the human community because the latter—individually and collectively—have the power and responsibility to account for their treatment of earth and on all species dwelling therein. I will begin by addressing the gift of freedom.

The Holy Spirit enables Freedom

The exercise of freedom is arguably the fundamental human gift. Therefore, situations wherein persons, freely or unwillingly, become subject to a power which prevents proper human choice, are usually destructive.[21] Captivity of any person by individuals, groups, evil spirits, or addictions stifles the growth of the captive, and may ultimately lead to the reduction of that person's ability to choose—as well as to the death of potential within that person.

By contrast, most persons long to share life freely with another. Free and mutual giving between one person and

20. James Dunn, 'Rediscovering the Spirit (1972)', in *Pneumatology* (Grand Rapids: Eerdmans, 1998), 54.
21. I am considering adult functioning humans.

another creates a communion that enlivens both. Christianity esteems freely-given mutual love at the heart of its faith by reference to God who is a freely-giving communion of love—a Trinity of divine 'persons'. Christian faith also holds that both divine and human love are self-expressive, and that both are fulfilled when freely offered and received. Genuine love does not force a response. Divine love, by its nature, offers itself unconditionally. Human beings have witnessed this in the life, death, and resurrection of Jesus. Paul's statement about God's love being 'poured into our hearts through the Holy Spirit who has been given to us' (Rom 5:5) is uttered in the context of Jesus' self-offering unto death, which releases the Holy Spirit. It is the freedom of such love that is my focus. I wish to suggest, with the assistance of Karl Rahner's theological understanding of 'freedom',[22] that freedom is the gift through which the human person and the divine Spirit most closely intersect.

Rahner describes freedom as a continual choosing in life, during which persons attain both human fullness and, at the same time, consciously or unaware, the end-point of their life. Rahner depicts the goal of persons to be the achievement of human fullness through other-centred love. For Rahner, such fullness is glimpsed in divine holy Mystery, the source of true freedom. Yet, divine Mystery can interrupt individual lives when, for example, individuals encounter the intricacies of creation, or the love

22. Karl Rahner, 'On the Origins of Freedom', in *Karl Rahner: Theologian of the Graced Search for Meaning*, edited by Geoffrey Kelly (Minneapolis: Fortress Press, 1992), 118–127.

of others, or even the absence of both. Rahner suggests that persons, in responding to holy Mystery, are simultaneously drawn towards an infinite horizon—towards God. In exercising multiple choices, persons who possess a transcendent dimension to their lives choose to confirm or reject their ultimate direction. If one's ultimate hope is to experience relatedness and fulfillment at the core of oneself, then every choice, according to Rahner, either confirms or jeopardises the attainment of that goal.

Nonetheless, Rahner is aware of the human difficulty in consistently choosing what is good. He is conscious of the mix of good, evil, and indifference in a world that is also full of divine presence. Thus, he suggests that God is present to human persons through the Spirit (in Christian tradition often called God's 'Love' or 'Gift'), to enable them to choose what will lead to ultimate freedom. Rahner sometimes speaks of God's mysterious presence as grace or as the Holy Spirit. He explains the divine Spirit as assisting persons to open their human spirit to the possibility of choosing wisely. For Rahner, the human journey towards committed freedom is aided by God's Spirit working with the human spirit. Divine Spirit enables persons to choose freely so that, having tasted liberating moments in life, they might, in their own right, choose eternal freedom at death when they entrust themselves to God.

However, there are millions of people for whom choices to reach personal potential do not exist. In a context in which Johnson describes God's Spirit as moving with 'bold engagement against the principalities and powers that crush and oppress', she also speaks of 'many millions of people plagued by war, by domestic violence, by fear of the knock on the door at night, and by circumstances that send them fleeing as vulnerable refugees'.[23] Many human persons long for the freedom to choose in a significant way—whether it be choosing work that does not demean, or choosing educational possibilities for children. In such cases, a vision of God's Spirit daily working with an individual person to enable perseverance, strength, and commitment also reveals a freedom chosen many times over during many months and years.

The missionary Paul, in his letter to the Romans (8:19–23), describes the Spirit of God as groaning within creation while God's purposes wait to be fulfilled. The Spirit sometimes groans within situations, and sometimes accompanies those who groan. For Rahner, each person's freedom is realised during life's journey—whether the journey involves those with abundant human freedoms or those struggling to accept one day after the next. Ultimately, the greatest human choice is for persons to give themselves lovingly and unconditionally to the mysterious Holy One who continues inviting them into fully relational living. Johnson describes with simplicity what Rahner is suggesting. She says of God's Spirit: 'Her loving in the world is gracious and inviting, never forcing or using violence but respectfully calling to human freedom, as is befitting a gift.'[24] Johnson's words on divine Spirit and freedom also describe the link between divine Spirit and power. Within the Christian Tradition, the element of

23. Johnson, *She Who Is*, 136.
24. Johnson, *She Who Is*, 143.

power has also been attributed to the divine Spirit. It is to that gift which I now turn.

The Holy Spirit offers Power

The context of this reflection on power is that in which evil generally, or spirit as an 'evil' spirit, binds persons and prevents them, through their own resources, from breaking free. Such a situation indicates one entity exercising power over another. In such conditions, affected human persons cannot control their own lives, since they exist under the influence of a greater power. In cases where persons are physically, emotionally, or spiritually bound, any change in the situation usually depends on a third party discovering the source of captivity and working to release the bonded ones from it.

There are, however, less perceptible negative powers. Theologian Bernard Cooke, in a pertinent study of power in relationship to the Holy Spirit,[25] examines power which is linked to cultural expectations, fear-mongering, political and ecclesiastical structures, fame, wealth, media, and advertising. Such powers are not always easily noticed. Nevertheless, they often represent seductive forms of power-wielding by groups of persons who, for various reasons, consider themselves to be arbiters for others.

The power of the Spirit, by contrast, is power used in service of the gospel, and in service of one's neighbours, for the purpose of liberation. In the case of a person held

25. Bernard Cooke, *Power and the Spirit of God: Towards an Experience-Based Pneumatology* (New York: Oxford University Press, 2004).

bound by an 'evil' spirit, it is possible for someone specially gifted with ecclesial power to invoke the power of God's Holy Spirit and enable the bound person to be released. In some religious traditions, those entrusted with this task prepare for such actions with prayer, fasting, and a request for openness to God's Spirit working within them. One might say that, as with some gospel exorcisms, the power of God's Holy Spirit is invoked against the power of the evil spirit. Such manifestation of divine power is effected on greater or fewer occasions, depending on different cultural understandings of the spirit world.

As noted previously, the Spirit of God was recognised as powerful and effective in the First Testament. Similarly, in the Christian tradition, the Holy Spirit has been invoked as offering power to Jesus' followers. Again, I will focus mainly on Luke's writings. For Luke, the Holy Spirit was powerfully at work in characters of the Infancy narrative—informing and preparing them for participation in God's imminent deed of the conception and birth of God's Son. This same Spirit ushered Jesus into his ministry, empowered him as he proclaimed God's word in the synagogue, and filled him with joy as the disciples worked wonders. This Spirit also enabled disciples bereft after Jesus' death to recognise him as the risen One. The Spirit accompanied them in their awaiting 'what my [the] Father promised' (Luke 24:49), and gifted them with fearlessness and boldness as they preached the message of Jesus' life, death, and resurrection in often hostile worlds. Luke's *Acts* conjures up scenes of vitality, growth and ongoing conversion for the disciples and those to whom they went. The cause of such activity is said to be the power of the Holy Spirit.[26]

However, accompanying the marvelous depictions of power in the above instances, there is another aspect to Second Testament perceptions of the Spirit's power. In gospel depictions of Jesus and his disciples, there is also a disturbing aspect to the Spirit's power. The divine power acclaimed in Mary's song of praise early in Luke's gospel, suggests the raising up of the powerless and the downfall of the mighty. Jesus, speaking under the power of the Spirit in his hometown synagogue, is praised for fine words, and then hustled from the town. Jesus, who began teaching in the power of the Spirit, exhorts his followers, 'Blessed are you . . . when they exclude you' (Luke 6:22). The disciples are without comprehension when Jesus' testimony to truth is set aside by Pilate, and Jesus is condemned to death. If, in the Lukan account, Jesus' 'entire ministry [was] under the aegis of the Holy Spirit',[27] then being a person of the Spirit seemed to prepare him for discord and, eventually, public disgrace.

It is Paul who best attends to the significance of the Holy Spirit for Jesus' followers. In his letters, Paul exhorts different communities to rely on the Spirit and not on the Law. He recognises that dependence on the Spirit's power gives not only the assurance of faith, but simultaneously

26. Stephen, 'full of grace and power,' did great wonders and signs (Acts 6:8). While Peter speaks to the Gentiles in Cornelius' house, 'the Holy Spirit fell upon all who heard the word' and they were baptised (Acts 10:44).

27. Fitzmyer, *The Gospel According to Luke I-IX*, 230.

leads to freedom (Gal 5:4–6). Paul exhorts his followers to pray while depending on the power of the Spirit, and thus their prayer will conform to God (Rom 8:26–27). He warns his disciples to live peacefully and not to offend the Spirit whom all have received with the Spirit's differing gifts (1 Cor 12:11). Paul expects the fledgling communities, living in the power of the Spirit, to revoke competitive ambitions and earthly conceptions of power (cf 1 Cor 3:3–9).

According to gospel criteria, the power of the Spirit does not belong to those who believe themselves to be superior, or who believe that external works can justify them, or who consider themselves socially acceptable. The power of the Holy Spirit is offered to anyone willing to turn to God, prepared to discern with the Spirit, and courageous enough to depend constantly on the Spirit.

The Holy Spirit empowers people in daily life and in ministry—in listening and preaching, instructing and serving, gathering together and healing. The Spirit does not necessarily remove personal inadequacies, fears, or doubts. Rather, the Spirit invites individuals to rely on power from God and simultaneously to act in trust. The power of the Spirit works with the gifts and the personal power of the one(s) invited to receive. If welcomed, God's effective Spirit does not fail.

There is a strong connection between the Spirit who empowers and the Spirit who makes whole. It is the Spirit's link with wholeness which I will finally address.

The Holy Spirit makes Whole

In this section I wish to offer a third and foundational reason for naming God's Spirit 'Holy'. I will suggest that in relation to both individuals and communities, the holiness brought by the Spirit is also about wholeness. It is in relation to the concept of wholeness that the Holy Spirit can provide a monitor for Christian practices that sometimes destroy human wholeness. It is also alongside the wholeness associated with God's Spirit that the results of other spirit practices need to be gauged.

In one respect, the link between the Holy Spirit and the process of 'making holy' the earth, people, and places is assumed. In the early years of Christianity, Paul reminded individuals and groups of believers that they had been changed by accepting baptism. They had been washed (1 Cor 6:11). John the evangelist spoke of believers being 'born from above' (John 3: 3). In each case, the implication was that baptised believers ought to reveal a new way of living—in union with Jesus Christ. Those who had been joined to Christ in baptism had been made holy. They belonged to a new age in history, God's time of fulfillment. Through the life, death, and resurrection of Jesus—and the sending of Jesus' Spirit—the world and all within had been freed from the grip of sin and its powers. Creation and its creatures had been re-set in the direction of God who had originally created everything good.

However, holiness like freedom needs constantly to be enacted. But, should human beings refuse the gift, God's possibilities continue. The creed from the Council of Nicaea concluded with the words, 'We believe in the Holy Spirit'. These words likely derived from the community's affirmation of God's ongoing offer of the Spirit to continue 'making holy', despite individual and communal infidelities.

In respect of individual persons, the Holy Spirit has often been expressed as working in the depth of persons—transforming, renewing, making holy (sanctifying), healing, and restoring people to a state of wholeness. Examples from the Christian tradition affirm this reality.

In the first century, we hear Paul remind the community at Rome to 'be transformed by the renewing of your mind' (Rom 12:2).

In the twelfth century we hear mystic Hildegarde of Bingen pray:

> O sacred Fire! O Paraclete, Spirit! Thou art the life of every creature's life.
>
> Thou art the Holy One, vivifying all being!
>
> Thou art the Holy One, healing with thine unction those that are dangerously bruised!
>
> Thou art the Holy One, cleansing our festered wounds!
>
> O breath of holiness![28]

In the late twentieth century we hear John V Taylor state: 'To think deeply about the Holy Spirit is a bewildering,

28. Hildegarde of Bingen, 'Sequence', cited in Swift, *With Bright Wings*, 122.

tearing exercise, for whatever [the Spirit] touches [the Spirit] turns inside out.'[29]

In their distinctive way, and spanning eras of Christian history, each reflection captures the intimate role of the Spirit vis-à-vis human persons. Each reflection also suggests the profundity of the Spirit's touch. The Holy Spirit enables the inner spirit of the person to be freed, repaired, or made holy. Such action by the Spirit invites a person to become more whole, or even whole for the first time. The Spirit does not stop at freeing and liberating. The Spirit re-makes, re-gathers, re-orders, so that through the holy-making power of God, individuals with specific gifts and individual potential are opened further to attain deeper self-possession through the aid of the Spirit. Theologian Mary Grey describes the Holy Spirit as 'today's energy for connectedness',[30] working within individual bodies, spirits, and minds, while Bernard Cooke describes the Spirit as 'an eschatological invitation to fullness of life'[31]—an invitation that begins to take shape, even now.

The whole-making Holy Spirit, however, is not confined to engagement with individuals. The Spirit's effect within one human person is transferable also to communities. The Spirit, often expressed in Christian Tradition as 'love' or 'communion', acts among disparate individuals or groups to draw them into deeper relationship with one

29. John V Taylor, *The Go-Between God: The Holy Spirit and the Christian Mission* (London: SCM Press, 1972), 179.
30. Mary Grey, 'Where does the Wild Goose Fly To? Seeking a New Theology of Spirit for Feminist Theology', *New Blackfriars* 72/846 (1991): 95.
31. Cooke, *Power and the Spirit*, 82.

another. Today, it is often this element of the Holy Spirit about which theologians speak. Theologian Nancy Victorin-Vangerud describes the Spirit of God as 'the communal holy and whole-making presence of God',[32] engaging with and among human beings in their relationships with God and creation. When, at one moment in history, hostility between groups discontinues, one might fruitfully ask whether the Spirit promised by Jesus Christ might not be changing hearts today.[33] Wherever struggles towards the free and just treatment of others begins to occur, it is possible that God's Spirit has been working with human spirits to create something new.[34]

Dunn, in speaking about Paul's expectations of the Spirit at work in the community at Corinth, says, 'It was a society-creating experience, a body of Christ-creating experience, an experience of being knit into a community'.[35] Today, Cooke, also affirming the social role of the Spirit, states:

> Seen from a theological point of view, love, ultimately the out-reaching 'expression' of di-

32. Nancy Victorin-Vangerud, *The Raging Hearth: Spirit in the Household of God* (St Louis: Chalice Press, 2000,) 207.
33. In May 2007, the agreement between Northern Ireland Protestants and the Irish Republican Army to form a government together might well indicate the role of the Spirit in bringing to a further stage the Peace accord signed on Good Friday, 1998.
34. See Paul encouraging the Corinthian community to pass on the gift of reconciliation (2 Cor 5: 17–20).
35. James Dunn, 'The Spirit and the Body of Christ', in *Pneumatology* (Grand Rapids: Eerdmans, 1998), 346.

> vine love that is God's Spirit, is the most powerful of powers. It is the power that breaks the cycle of violence in Jesus' dying and rising . . . it is the prophetic power already working in history to achieve that relating of humans to one another in justice and peace that is 'the reign of God'.[36]

Possibly less easy to detect, but nonetheless as real as individual transformation, the Spirit's role in bringing opposing groups together, in opening hearts, in removing long-held fears is also a powerful sign of the whole-making power of the divine Spirit. Perhaps it is witnessed when political adversaries agree one more time to sit down and begin talking again. When the Spirit prods groups to interact anew, another part of God's broken body is made whole. It is made holy.

Conclusion

In this chapter I have suggested that the First and Second Testaments both reveal the liberating, empowering, and transformative aspects of God's Spirit. While rarely named 'Holy' in the First Testament, God's Spirit in the Second Testament attracts the name 'Holy' because of the intimate connection between the saving love of God witnessed in the person of Jesus and his disciples. Both Jesus and his followers manifested a particular sense of free-

36. Cooke, *Power and the Spirit,* 176.

dom, empowerment, and desire to live fully (ie, wholly) through the Spirit of God working with them and in them. It was the Holy Spirit, gifted most directly through Jesus' self-sacrificing love on the cross, that would make alive in his followers the ongoing gift of salvation. Wherever saving love is operative, there God's holiness is present.

The divine Spirit of the Christian Scriptures—whether termed God's Spirit, the Spirit, Spirit-Sophia, or Holy Spirit—presents alternative visions of freedom, power, and holiness to whatever is experienced by persons under the influence of evil spirits. It is the reality of God's Spirit, rather than the naming of such, that eventually matters. If use of the term 'the Holy Spirit' tends to reduce the expansiveness of the mysterious Spirit's presence and power in the world, then one needs to use that name with care. What ultimately counts is that communities who follow Jesus Christ 'in the Spirit' become, as one contemporary theologian suggests, 'force fields of faith, hope, and love'.[37]

Bibliography

Browning, WRF. 'Holiness', in *A Dictionary of the Bible* (Oxford: Oxford University Press, 1997).

Cooke, Bernard. *Power and the Spirit of God: Towards an Experience-Based Pneumatology* (New York: Oxford University Press, 2004).

37. Michael Welker, *God The Holy Spirit*, translated by JF Hoffmeyer (Minneapolis: Fortress Press, 1994), 341.

Dunn, James. 'Rediscovering the Spirit (1972)', in *Pneumatology*, vol 2 of *The Christ and the Spirit* (Grand Rapids: Eerdmans, 1998), 43–61.

Dunn, James. 'Spirit and Holy Spirit in the New Testament (1978)', in *Pneumatology*, vol 2 of *The Christ and the Spirit* (Grand Rapids: Eerdmans, 1998), 3–21.

Dunn, James. 'The Spirit and the Body of Christ (1988)', in *Pneumatology*, vol 2 of *The Christ and the Spirit* (Grand Rapids: Eerdmans, 1998), 343–357.

Fitzmyer, Joseph. *The Gospel According to Luke I-IX*. Anchor Bible Series (New York: Doubleday, 1979).

Grey, Mary. 'Where does the Wild Goose Fly To? Seeking a New Theology of Spirit for Feminist Theology', in *New Blackfriars* 72/846 (1991): 89–96.

Johnson, Andy. 'Holiness', in *The New Interpreter's Dictionary of the Bible: D-H*, edited by Katherine Doob Sakenfeld (Nashville: Abingdon Press, 2007), 2:846–847.

Johnson, Elizabeth. *She Who Is: The Mystery of God in Feminist Theological Discourse* (New York: Crossroad, 1993).

Ju, Hur. *A Dynamic Reading of Luke-Acts*. Journal for the Study of the New Testament, Supplement Series (Sheffield: Sheffield Academic Press, 2001).

McDonnell, Kilian. *The Other Hand of God: The Holy Spirit as the Universal Touch* (Collegeville: The Liturgical Press, 2003).

Rahner, Karl. 'On the Origins of Freedom', in *Karl Rahner: Theologian of the Graced Search for Meaning*, edited by Geffrey Kelly (Minneapolis: Fortress Press, 1992), 118–127.

Slee, Nicola. 'The Holy Spirit and Spirituality', in *The Cambridge Companion to Feminist Theology*, edited by

Susan Frank Parsons (Cambridge: Cambridge University Press, 2002), 171–189.

Swift, Mary G, editor. *With Bright Wings: A Book of the Spirit* (New York: Paulist Press, 1976).

Taylor, John V. *The Go-Between God: The Holy Spirit and the Christian Mission* (London: SCM Press, 1972).

Victorin-Vangerud, Nancy. *The Raging Hearth: Spirit in the Household of God* (St Louis: Chalice Press, 2000).

Welker, Michael. *God The Holy Spirit,* translated by JF Hoffmeyer (Minneapolis: Fortress Press, 1994).

'Spirit Possession' and 'Deliverance Ministry' in the Auckland Assembly of God, 1970–1983

Laurie Guy

The focus of this essay is the burgeoning, high-profile, central-Auckland congregation of the Assemblies of God (AOG) from 1970 to 1983. The church did not reflect all Pentecostalism in New Zealand, or even all the Assemblies of God congregations. But it did reflect commonly-held Pentecostal practices, and it was a 'flagship' in its huge influence on individuals and other congregations.

The Auckland Assembly of God senior pastor from 1970 to 1983 was Neville Johnson. The congregation increased from four hundred Sunday attendees at the start of his ministry to four thousand at its end.[1] By then, it had

1. Estimates of the numbers attending in 1983 vary. J. Harper ('The Church That's Taking over Auckland,' *Metro* 29, November, 1983: 129) indicates that the weekly congregation was then two thousand strong. That figure was likely for one of its services, three of which

outgrown its original buildings at 510 Queen Street and was holding its worship services in the Auckland Town Hall as it awaited completion of massive new buildings at Beaumont Street (now Victory Christian Centre).

The church's focal emphasis was strikingly spiritual and other-worldly. This included teaching about the threat of demons, and the offer of 'deliverance ministry' to expel demons from affected people. To understand this deliverance ministry, we need to note relevant trends in wider society, as well as reflecting on how deliverance ministry became prominent in the church prior to 1970.

In my focus on the Auckland Assembly of God, I had to face the problem of the lack of church records and church publications. As a consequence, I have drawn particularly on two strands of evidence. The first is the transcript of a talk Neville Johnson gave to students at the Lower Hutt AOG Bible College in August, 1971. The second strand of evidence draws on interviews with five participants in the Auckland AOG. Three participants were on the staff of the church for some of the period, 1970-1983. Another was a missionary sent out from that church to the Philippines in the late 1970s, and the fifth person was a grass-roots member who served as a church usher. The five interviewees reflect a wide spectrum of

---

were held each Sunday. Ian Clark (*Pentecost at the Ends of the Earth: The History of the Assemblies of God in New Zealand (1927–2003)*, Blenheim, NZ: Christian Road Ministries, 2007, 184) indicated morning services of around two thousand, five hundred attendees in 1983. My figure of four thousand is extrapolated from email comments of Tim Johnston (a staff member of the church in 1983) to me, dated August 16, 2007.

perspectives today, two remaining very enthusiastic about the church's deliverance ministry of that time, one more cautiously supportive, one cautiously negative, and one strongly negative. My discussion will largely be descriptive—what was taught and what was practised in relation to deliverance—not a systematic theological or psychological critique.

Societal Factors:

Societal developments likely had some bearing on the church's approach to spirit possession and deliverance. Ideas often gain prominence in church circles because they resonate with developments in society. Two films reflect societal interest in spirit possession around the time period of our focus: *Rosemary's Baby* screened in 1968 (based on a 1967 novel), and *The Exorcist* screened in 1973 (based on a 1971 novel). A sense of crisis and social ferment was then to the fore. Young people were challenging deeply held values. There was a defiant flaunting of 'sex, drugs, and rock 'n' roll.' The continuing felt threat of communist menace persisted. Churches faced the issue of appropriate response to a rapidly changing world. The outcome was a major new bifurcation in western Christianity. A more 'liberal' approach argued that Christianity must change with the changing times, exhibiting a more 'horizontal' focus on this world—focusing on people and their concerns, and stressing qualities of love, justice and peace. In contrast, a more 'conservative' approach sought to reaffirm the historic truths of Christianity and its more 'vertical' aspects—more 'other-worldly' and supernatural in focus.

The upsurge in focus on Satan and evil spirits reflected a more vertical and other-worldly response. The 'dark side' of supernatural reality gained in prominence. Mass-market authors fuelling this perspective included Hal Lindsey (*Satan Is Alive and Well on Planet Earth*, 1973), Frank Peretti (*This Present Darkness*, 1986) and Tim LaHaye and Jerry Jenkins (*Left Behind*, 1995).

Developments within Pentecostalism

Focus on evil spirits led to increased concern about people having evil spirits, particularly in Pentecostal churches. This is unsurprising, given Pentecostalism's fundamentalist, Scripture-reading stance, and its heightened emphasis on supernatural reality. The latter dimension is evidenced in the major prominence given to matters such as an experience-based 'baptism in the Spirit', other-worldly 'speaking in tongues', directly-mediated God-speech through prophecy and 'words of knowledge', and being channels of divine power in matters such as healing. This sort of approach lends itself to an awareness of evil spirits and to claims of supernatural power to expel such spirits.

Internationally, Pentecostalism as an identifiable movement began in the United States at the beginning of the twentieth century. It reached New Zealand through visits by Pentecostal evangelist Smith Wigglesworth in 1922 and 1923. Numerous Pentecostal groups emerged over subsequent decades. The largest of these, the Assemblies of God, formed in New Zealand in 1927. Pentecostalism as a whole remained numerically very small over the next generation. In 1956 the census total for all types of adherents was 2,285. However, from the 1960s, it has had dramatic growth from that small base—Pentecostals numbered 78,954 in the 2006 census. The AOG grew rapidly between 1965 and 1977 when Frank Houston was its superintendent—from twenty-six congregations to eighty.[2] In addition to the growth of Pentecostal churches, Pentecostalism influenced many other conservative Christians in more diluted form, particularly through the charismatic movement, which in turn influenced many mainline Christians in the 1970s and 1980s.

Pentecostalism has typically been very open to the reality of Satan and evil spirits.[3] Wigglesworth, for example, seems to have asserted that all sickness was the work of evil spirits.[4] On one occasion in Wellington in 1922, he claimed that after he had 'wrestled' into the night with the Devil, he was instrumental in healing a young woman dying of consumption.[5] AH Dallimore, prominent in Pentecostal-style ministry in Auckland in the 1930s, described the 'author of sickness' as 'definitely the work of Satan'.[6] Dallimore's giving prominence to evil spirits is also shown in a 1933 newspaper report indicating that, in special services in New Plymouth, he denounced min-

2. Ian G Clark, 'Assemblies of God Heritage: Tracing Our Roots', *Evangel*, October, 1987: 14.
3. Walter J Hollenweger, *The Pentecostals* (London: SCM, 1972), 377ff.
4. *NZ Truth*, June 24, 1922: 12.
5. *NZ Truth*, June 10, 1922: 5.
6. *Revival Fire Monthly* 3, no. 9 (January 1937): 6–7 (copy in Carey Baptist College archive).

isters 'on the ground that they no longer included the casting out of devils in their services'.[7] Independent New Zealand Pentecostal evangelist, Rob Wheeler, showed a similar perspective in linking sickness and evil spirits in 1962: 'Many sicknesses are caused directly by evil spirits, and can be treated by casting out these spirits'. Wheeler went on to list sicknesses caused by evil spirits: 'asthma, some cases of heart trouble, paralysis, fevers, etc.'[8]

A crucial question for Pentecostals in their increased focus on the 'dark side' since the late 1960s is whether evil spirits can control Christians. A framework which views Pentecostal Christians as both 'reborn' and 'baptised in the Spirit' suggests a negative answer. Commonly, however, this has not been the case. Pentecostal teaching could cause church attendees to ask themselves whether they are afflicted by an evil spirit, and they may have exorcisms of Christian people.

Earlier in the twentieth century, Pentecostals did not face such an emphasis. The official line of the American parent-body of the Assemblies of God was that Christians could not be demon-possessed.[9] However, denominational lines between Pentecostal groups have not been as sharp in New Zealand as they may have been in America.

---

7. *New Zealand Observer*, September 7, 1933: 5.
8. *Bible Deliverance*, Easter, 1962: 3.
9. Assemblies of God, *Where We Stand* (Springfield, MO: np, 1990), 15-23 (statement approved by the general presbytery of the Assembly of God in 1972); Derek Prince, *They Shall Expel Demons: What You Need to Know about Demons—Your Invisible Enemies* (Grand Rapids: Chosen Books, 1998), 38.

There has been a great deal of cross-over and cross-fertilisation.

In the 1950s, a 'Latter Rain' movement emerged within New Zealand Pentecostalism, bringing with it a renewed emphasis on supernatural manifestations of spiritual power.[10] One triumphalist strand of its teaching involved a 'manifestation of the sons of God', which included all evil spirits being seen 'scattered before the triumphant power of God's people'.[11] While the movement itself did not particularly focus on deliverance, it created a very intense, spiritual climate that could easily mutate to include that focus. The Latter Rain movement fuelled quite a bit of cross-fertilisation of teaching and practice amongst the various New Zealand Pentecostal groupings. While not all New Zealand AOG leaders embraced this Latter Rain emphasis, many did so, including Neville Johnson.[12] Latter Rain influence helps explain why the New Zealand AOG largely took a stance on deliverance ministry that was at odds with the position of its parent body in America.

---

10. James E Worsfold, *A History of the Charismatic Movements in New Zealand* (Bradford, MA: Puritan Press, 1974), 297.
11. Brett Knowles, *The History of a New Zealand Pentecostal Movement* (Lewiston, NY: Edwin Mellen Press, 2000), 36–37, 67.
12. Transcript of interview with Evan Squires, May 30, 2007, 2; transcript of interview with Tim Johnston, June 27, 2007, 3.

Materials Influencing Notions of Spirit Possession and Deliverance Ministry

Before examining the emphasis of the Auckland AOG, 1970–1983, I will discuss literature with a strong demonic deliverance emphasis that has been very influential in New Zealand. This sort of material deeply influenced individuals and churches, including the Auckland AOG. While some of the material is later than the period under discussion, it existed earlier in some oral or print form. This material includes:

- *Pigs in the Parlor: A Practical Guide to Deliverance*, written by Americans Frank and Ida Mae Hammond in 1973. The book has sold over one million copies internationally, and circulated extensively in New Zealand. Its authors noted several times their major reliance on the approach of Derek Prince.[13]

- *They Shall Expel Demons: What You Need to Know about Demons—Your Invisible Enemies*, written by Derek Prince in 1998. British-born Prince had earlier undertaken postgraduate study in philosophy

13. Frank and Ida Mae Hammond, *Pigs in the Parlor: A Practical Guide to Deliverance* (Kirkwood, MO: Impact Books, 1973), foreword, 93, 107. For another influential American book of that era, see Don Basham, *Deliver Us from Evil* (Washington, DC: Chosen Books, nd [c.1972]).

at Cambridge University, prior to a Pentecostal-type conversion during World War Two. In the 1960s, he embraced, and promulgated internationally, the view that demons might grip Christian believers. His first visit to New Zealand in 1968 included the conducting of public deliverance services.[14] Prior to his death in 2003, Prince visited New Zealand a number of times, teaching in the Queen Street AOG on several occasions in the 1970-1983 period. His thought clearly influenced the understanding of Neville Johnson.[15]

- *Demons Defeated*, written by New Zealand healing-evangelist Bill Subritzky in 1985.[16] Subritzky, a prominent property developer and lawyer, experienced a spiritual turn-around in 1971. An Anglican, he moved into a charismatic style of ministry shortly thereafter. A prominent strand of his Pentecostal theology and style was

14. Derek Prince, *They Shall Expel Demons: What You Need to Know about Demons—Your Invisible Enemies* (Grand Rapids: Chosen Books, 1998), 72.
15. See, by way of example, direct reference to Derek Prince in the transcript of teaching of Neville Johnson at Christian Life (AOG) Bible College, August, 1971, 14.
16. For a brief news item and accompanying video on Subritzky's healing ministry, see http://tvnz.co.nz/view/page/411419/868561 (accessed June 15, 2007).

> deliverance from evil spirits. Subritzky indicated his 'deep debt' to Derek Prince which encouraged him to become involved in deliverance ministry from the time of his spiritual turn-around.[17] Although Subritzky apparently had occasional ministry in the Queen Street AOG only from around the late 1980s (something that was still continuing in 2007), he had personal contact with Neville Johnson in the 1970s, accompanying him to Perth around 1974 to explore the purchase of property as a base for future ministry there by Neville Johnson.

A notable aspect of these books is a very literal reading of Scripture, especially regarding spirit encounter in the ministry of Jesus and the early disciples. They expect similar encounters today. There is no critical reading of the Second Testament text; hence there is commonly an appeal to Mark 16:17 ('in my name they will cast out demons'), with no reflection on the fact that the text is not found in the earliest manuscripts.[18] Often, the literalist approach is built on an isolated text or biblical example. Jesus' command to the Gerasene demon to name itself (Lk 8:30) became almost a standard technique of some of the writers—demons should be required to name themselves

17. Bill Subritzky, *Demons Defeated* (Auckland: Dove Ministries, 1985), foreword, 3, 79, 96.
18. Prince, *They Shall Expel*, 64, 76; Hammond, *Pigs in the Parlor*, 53.

and then be cast out.[19] Naïveté and lack of reflection in such literalism is exemplified in Subritzky's distinguishing angels and spirits on the basis that demons do not have wings but angels usually do.[20] Overall, there is virtually no reflective hermeneutic of interpretation in relation to the biblical material.

A second feature of the deliverance emphasis of this literature is that deliverance is based on intuitive sensing of an evil spirit or demon. How can deliverance ministers know that their intuition matches reality? There is no clear answer apart from an experiential one: 'I sensed, I saw, I know'.

Another aspect is that readers would be left with a deep sense of the prevalence of evil spirits. The books typically carry lists of symptoms of people gripped by evil spirits. The Hammonds' list includes emotional, mental, speech, and sex problems, along with addictions, physical problems, and religious error.[21] Prince has an extensive list of names of demons, including epilepsy, head pain, migraine, thrombosis, criticism, gossip, stress, disappointment, masturbation, self-pity, and witchcraft.[22]

The writers commonly dislike the term 'possessed' because of its connotation of total ownership. As the writers have a Pentecostal theology of Spirit baptism, it looks odd to speak of Holy Spirit possession and demonic possession in the same breath. They avoid this difficulty

19. Hammond, *Pigs in the Parlor*, 82–83; Subritzky, *Demons Defeated*, 87.
20. Subritzky, *Demons Defeated*, 65.
21. Hammond, *Pigs in the Parlor*, 28.
22. Prince, *They Shall Expel*, 96–97.

by having a tripartite understanding of human nature—body, soul and spirit—each part being markedly distinct from the other parts (a theology expressed also by Neville Johnson).[23] Demons thus inhabit only a part of the human person—their cellar, not their living room; their soul, not their spirit. The writers note that the Second Testament Greek term, *daimonizomai*, is better translated as 'demonised' or having demons.[24] Yet the writers present a picture of demons needing to be expelled from the bodies of people. This may suggest that their theology is a possession-type theology, even though they may avoid spirit-possession language.

Virtually anything regarded as evil may be attributed to a spirit. Subritzky attributed 'much sickness' to spirits. Prince listed demons of colitis, crippling, asthma, schizophrenia and cancer.[25] Although Prince briefly indicated that he was not negating the important role of the medical profession, the overall tenor of his book would encourage devotees to think of deliverance ministry rather than of medical help.[26] Such a perspective would lead to clashes with the medical profession, especially where the illness was psychiatric in nature. The Hammonds seemed largely to attribute schizophrenia to an evil spirit, describing it as 'the deepest, most involved and most determined deliverance that we have encountered'.[27] What would psy-

23. Neville Johnson, teaching transcript 1971, 11, 20; noted also in transcript of interview of Frank Smedley, July 21, 2007, 3.
24. Hammond, *Pigs in the Parlor*, 1; Subritzky, *Demons Defeated*, 39.
25. Prince, *They Shall Expel*, 192, 200.
26. Prince, *They Shall Expel*, 164.
27 Hammond, *Pigs in the Parlor*, 133.

chiatrists think of their patients undergoing exorcism for such problems?

Subritzky took the view that many churches had 'the spirit of sectarianism.' To him, 'feminism' was a 'great harlot spirit' and homosexuality was demonic. People with a Hindu background commonly had 'the spirit of a monkey god.' There could be demons of gluttony, anger, pride, lust, unbelief, doubt, and procrastination. Subritzky himself had been delivered from 'the spirit of alcohol'.[28] Prince had been delivered of a spirit of fear, a demon causing a feverish cold, a spirit of stiffness, and a demon of yoga. His wife, Ruth, had been freed from a spirit of humanism, acquired through her earlier university studies.[29]

Spirits could come through the curse of someone else.[30] They could also come through involvement in martial arts, rock music, hypnotism, and acupuncture.[31] They could be inherited, the consequence of sins being visited down to the third and fourth generations (Deut 5:9), especially through a family background in the occult or in false religions.[32] Even apparently minor matters, such as indiscriminate laying on of hands and idle words, could

28. Subritzky, *Demons Defeated,* 6, 22, 26, 107, 124, 124, 127, 129, 235. On the linkage between homosexuality and the demonic, see also a report wherein Neville Johnson indicates a spirit of homosexuality over Auckland in 1983, in J Harper, 'The Church that's Taking over Auckland', *Metro* 29 (November, 1983): 129.
29. Prince, *They Shall Expel,* 79, 82, 83, 84, 147.
30. Subritzky, *Demons Defeated,* 79.
31. Prince, *They Shall Expel,* 119, 132, 135.
32. Subritzky, *Demons Defeated,* 67; Prince, *They Shall Expel,* 104.

be the vehicle for a demon habitually gaining access to a person.[33] Prince, for example, narrated how his wife Ruth had hands laid on her for a common cold at a healing meeting. When she awoke the next morning, her hands were curled up, stiff, and hurting. Discerning that someone with arthritis had laid hands on her the night before, she renounced the spirit of arthritis, and within five minutes all arthritic symptoms were gone.[34]

Such teaching pointed to the majority of Christians being gripped by evil spirits. When Derek Prince first preached on deliverance in the church he pastored, he had fifty people out of his audience of one hundred seeking deliverance on the spot. He asserted, 'I have encountered comparatively few Christians who did not seem vulnerable to demonic activity'.[35] The Hammonds posed the question, 'Does everyone need deliverance?' and gave their answer, 'Personally, I have not found any exceptions'.[36] Obviously, this would foster a great deal of introspection and fear: 'Have I too got a demon?' This could encourage exaggerated fear in a sensitive person, promoting unwellness rather than wellness. Graphic descriptions of phenomena occurring during deliverance intensified the risk of imbalance: coughing, vomiting, drooling, spitting, foaming, gagging, crying, screaming, sighing, roar-

33. Prince, *They Shall Expel*, 103.
34. Prince, *They Shall Expel*, 109.
35. Prince, *They Shall Expel*, 64, 66, 101.
36. Hammond, *Pigs in the Parlor*, 12.

ing, belching, yawning, trembling, violent shaking, vile smells, barking, slithering, and feigning death.[37]

The Arrival of Deliverance Ministry at the Auckland Assembly of God

Derek Prince brought deliverance ministry into fresh prominence in New Zealand around 1968. Almost immediately, the then-pastor of the Auckland AOG, Bob Midgley, introduced deliverance ministry into his church's practice, and this was continued by his successor, Neville Johnson, from 1970 onwards. While Derek Prince himself did not have a major presence in the Auckland AOG, his influence was clearly strong. He seems to have been a Sunday preacher in the Auckland AOG on several occasions during Neville Johnson's ministry.[38] Clearly, his deliverance ministry approach was welcome, even though that may not have been his primary focus when he visited the church.

The two AOG pastors, Midgley and Johnson, differed in temperament and practice. Midgley was more of an evangelist. In Pentecostal circles, the evangelist's role commonly included calling people to come forward at an 'altar call' to be 'saved', to be 'baptised in the Spirit', to be healed, etc. The evangelist was an 'action man' whose ministry produced visible results.[39] Inviting people to

37. Hammond, *Pigs in the Parlor*, 52; Subritzky, *Demons Defeated*, 164.
38. Smedley interview, 9; Tim Johnston interview, 2, 7.
39. 'Action man' as a description for the evangelistic-type ministry was used by Frank Smedley, interview, 2.

come forward for deliverance ministry meshed well with that approach. Johnson was more of a mystically-oriented teacher, and less of an action man. While Johnson continued the earlier approach of deliverance ministry, it gradually had diminishing focus in his Auckland ministry.[40] At the same time, his evangelistically-oriented associate pastor, Geoff Lloyd, might give strong emphasis to deliverance ministry at times. According to the memory of Frank Smedley, Lloyd 'had a so-called evangelistic gift and perhaps more than any of them he would be into the old casting demons out'. So might visiting evangelists. Any excesses from them were excusable: they were transitory itinerants; they were expected to produce manifestations; and excesses were understood to be a common accompaniment of an evangelist's ministry.[41]

The 1971 Teaching of Neville Johnson on Spirits and Deliverance

Deliverance was not the centre of Johnson's teaching. Much more central was a pervasive notion of a spirit world, both good and bad. The good side included being drenched ('baptised') with the Holy Spirit. There was always more to entering into this spiritual reality. Even being baptised in the Spirit was not enough, Johnson stressing that Christians should move beyond baptism in the Spirit to having also a 'baptism of fire'.[42] Further-

40. Evan Squires interview, 2, 4; Smedley interview, 2.
41. Smedley interview, 6.
42. A sermon of Johnson's heard by the author around 1973.

more, there was esoteric teaching on entering an elite circle of Christians—the 'sons of Zadok'.[43] Johnson conveyed an atmosphere of deep spirituality. His frequent visions, dreams, and 'words of knowledge' placed him on a pedestal in the eyes of his followers. Johnson might see a demon or something from the dark side on someone's shoulder.[44] This sounds riskily subjective. However, those who experienced such subjective knowing from Johnson often felt that he was describing a reality which matched their circumstances, and which he could not otherwise have known. Bill Bartlett and his wife, recent immigrants from Canada when they first went to the Auckland AOG in 1970, had an experience of this 'word of knowledge':

> Marilyn was actually delivered from a thing that we brought from Canada. She was having all kinds of migraine headaches . . . I . . . suggested that we go and see Neville and tell him about it. And he prayed with her and God told him that 'you have in your house an image of a frog with its tongue out, a wolf with its growling and it' . . . He went through every image that was on this totem pole type stone. It was a black stone carving and it was in the bed cupboard right beside the bed. And that

43. The reference is to the priestly family that stayed loyal to David in 2 Sam 15, when there was widespread abandonment of David's rule in favour of his usurping son, Absalom. Johnston interview, 2; Smedley interview, 10–11.
44. Johnston interview, 4.

> image had an effect on Marilyn and—it was revealed by God that—to Neville—that she had to find it. And she did and I took it to the old Mangere Bridge, right about the middle, and I threw it as far south as I could. And it was fixed. She never had a migraine since.[45]

Such 'seeing' gave Johnson special standing amongst his people. In the memory of Tim Johnston, 'Neville [Johnson] was seen to be someone who had special revelation, and in the end, "Neville said" would probably have been—probably had a higher authority than "the scripture says"—although he wouldn't have said it that way.'[46] Bill Bartlett's adulation was quite unrestrained: 'We worshipped Neville and that was wrong'.[47]

Neville Johnson's teaching evoked a deep spiritual atmosphere and longing. Thus, while Frank Smedley later distanced himself markedly from the Auckland AOG-type approach, he could still speak appreciatively of its 'very spiritual environment'.[48] Bill Bartlett spoke of his deep hunger for a 'beautiful ongoing relationship with God' and his sense of being shattered when he approached an AOG woman who he thought had arrived at that plane, only to be told that she hadn't attained it either—she remained 'longing for that place'.[49] Johnson's

45. Transcript of interview with Bill Bartlett, May 30, 2007, 9–10.
46. Johnston interview, 3.
47. Bartlett interview, 6.
48. Smedley interview, 11.
49. Bartlett interview, 9.

teaching evoked perfectionist aspirations, almost an experiencing of heaven on earth now through a beautiful life in the Holy Spirit.

Johnson was conscious of both the bad and the good spirit world. A lot of evil was attributable to demons. Johnson not uncommonly described demons that he had seen. A veritable hierarchy of demons operated at many levels of reality, influencing nations, cities, places, and objects.[50] On one occasion he described the central part of the city of Auckland as having 'a spirit of homosexuality'.[51] Johnson, having seen a vision of a huge demon over Hollywood, stressed that picture theatres were dangerous places that could lead to picking up an evil spirit. It was not that all movies were wrong (Johnson did, after all, watch some television), but what was wrong was the place itself, a haunt of demons similar to a heathen place of worship also being a haunt of demons.

Living in a world teeming with dark spirits necessitated constant vigilance. How Christians were to live out this vigilance was often expressed in mystical, Scripture-connected language. They needed 'the whole armour of God' (Eph 6:11), the 'hedge' of God's protection (Job 1:10), etc. Tim Johnston explained:

> [T]here was a whole ranking of evil powers and some of these powers were over nations and some over cities and—so there was a whole kind of a concept of this culture out

50. Johnston interview, 2; Squires interview, 9.
51. Harper, 'The Church That's Taking over Auckland', 129.

> there of various evil entities and we would come against them in prayer meetings—constantly in prayer meetings we would be praying against evil powers.[52]

Neville Johnson's teaching on deliverance from evil spirits emerged from this worldview of spiritual reality.

Johnson's Teaching at the Christian Life (AOG) Bible College, August, 1971

Johnson saw God as progressively restoring full gospel truth, progressively restoring the church as it was known in the Acts of the Apostles. His comments on the demonic realm came in the context of that teaching. Johnson took seven parables from Matthew 13, treating them not in terms of their apparent meaning, but as markers of future stages of the church, from its beginnings to the present time. The third Matthean parable—that of the mustard seed—displayed the church, from about 100 AD, expanding markedly, yet going into qualitative decline after the heyday of the apostles. The church grew with many branches (a picture of Roman Catholicism), but the birds of the air made nests in its branches. The earlier parable of the sower (Matt 13:4, 18) indicated that birds represented evil. Thus, the parable of the mustard seed indicated a future age with a church full of demonic spirits. The present restoring phase of the Holy Spirit included the 'getting of

52. Johnston interview, 2.

those spirits out of the church once again'.[53] This interpretation provided a justification for deliverance ministry in Johnson's time.

How did Johnson know that God was undertaking restoration in his time? Johnson's argument was mixed up with astrology. Astonishingly, Johnson taught this, while rejecting astrology:

> In 1962 a significant thing happened. Now astrology is wrong, it is forbidden in the Word of God. In Genesis 1, God said that he set the stars, the moon, and the planets for signs and for seasons. The scriptures tell us that the plan of salvation is written in the stars. In 1962, the predominant sign of the Southern Hemisphere particularly was Pisces, the sign of the Fish. We had just come through a tremendous age of world-wide evangelism [referring to Jesus' language of becoming fishers of people]. But in 1962, February 26, it changed to Aquarius. Sign = the Man with the water pot, pouring out water. It is particularly dominant over the Southern Hemisphere. From then on, God has poured out His Spirit across New Zealand on the denominational people . . . So we find a new phase of what God is doing, the pouring out of the Spirit of God.[54]

53. Johnson, teaching transcript 1971, 2.
54. Johnson, teaching transcript 1971, 4.

Johnson recognised that restoration included 'a cleansing of the church.' He linked that cleansing with the development of deliverance ministry in and from America in 1968. Any early excesses were to be expected, as God initially overemphasises new teachings and practices in order to get them established: 'You have to take the train past the station in order to get the carriages to the platform'.

Johnson did not attribute all evil behaviour to demons. There was also human responsibility, 'the flesh' (Gal 5:19). However, the 'flesh' was a doorway to Satan, and persisting 'in the flesh' allowed a spirit to come in—something beyond human control:

> This began as a work of the flesh, and for every work of the flesh there is a spirit just waiting for you to keep manifesting desires and works of the flesh, the hedge is being broken down and he can get in. You now have a double problem; you have the flesh and a demon on the inside. You continually yield to it; it will drive you out into a place you never intended to go. Sometimes we can enjoy our anger, we can enjoy a certain amount of criticism, or other things, saying we can contain this, it is my flesh, but I can contain it. You know, I enjoy a little of it, but if you continue in it, you will open the door for a spirit to come in. It began as flesh, but Satan was baiting that flesh. He was drawing that flesh out,

> and as soon as the door was opened he began to get in.[55]

Johnson warned that even Christian spiritual practice could lead to witchcraft, if it was wrongly expressed. Thus, using the Holy Spirit to dominate another through, say, prophecy, could lead to a wrong spirit, a spirit of witchcraft. Women prophets were particularly at risk of going off into error in using God's gifts to dominate others and being at risk of picking up this kind of spirit.[56]

Linkage between spirit possession and the flesh meant that, for Johnson, there was no single solution. Both aspects must be dealt with. First, get rid of temptations (eg, magazines) that are feeding the demon-problem: 'The first thing to do is to starve him out . . . God expects you to work on this first for deliverance . . . Cut it off . . . Learn to starve him out.' Only then could an expelling of the spirit successfully occur. Even that was not the final solution. Delivered Christians must thereafter 'build the walls' by resisting the temptation. They must continue to 'cut off the food'. Johnson instanced praying for a woman who was delivered from an evil spirit. Although she began thanking and praising God for her deliverance, she was not taught to 'build the walls'. Two weeks later she was again in a bad state. Johnson began to pray for her, questioning a spirit that surfaced, and finding that it had brought in seven other spirits (cf Luke 11:26). Why? The

55. Johnson, teaching transcript 1971, 9.
56. Johnson, teaching transcript 1971, 10.

woman had exposed herself to spiritual peril because she had not learnt the 'principles of building the walls'.[57]

Johnson sensed evil spirits indwelling in people because the owners had objects to which spirits were attached. This he attributed to 'the law of association'. Anything with wrong spiritual links was dangerous: 'the association will attract a spirit'. Missionaries were at risk if they brought pagan artefacts home. In his August, 1971 address, Johnson's concern about artefacts focused especially on Māori artefacts. He instanced an owner's need to get rid of a souvenir Māori canoe on the basis that paua-shell eyes 'represent[ing] guardian spirits of the water' were embedded in it. Tiki were another threat:

> If you have a tiki in your possession, you will have a problem with unclean thoughts. Why? The major tiki is a foetus of an unborn child—the one twisted up. It is a symbol of immorality. That thing will attract an evil influence; I know this from experience, over and over again. They must be destroyed.[58]

While aspects of Johnson's talk indicated that his concern was with objects that were connected with non-Christian religious beliefs (not only Māori objects but also a picture

57. Johnson, teaching transcript 1971, 10–12. The reference to 'building the walls' stems from Prov 25:28, where a person without self-discipline is compared to a broken-down city.
58. Johnson, teaching transcript 1971, 17.

of a Buddha and the poster of a Hindu god), his language seemed at times to attack Māori culture itself:

> There is a tremendous increase in our country of Māori culture—it is everywhere like it never was before. All this Māori culture and carving is of spiritual significance and has a spiritual background. God is preparing this country for what he wants to do, but it works both ways. When it rains, it is a type of the Holy Spirit; not only does the wheat come up, but it softens the earth and the weeds can get through, and both come up under the same rain. So there is an increase in demonic activity. The Māori side will have to be broken in New Zealand before there is any breakthrough—the revival itself may break through, but there are tremendous strongholds in this realm in our country. Whether that is connected with that culture and that form of worship, whether it be a tiki or carving—be very careful about that thing—my advice to you is to get rid of it, out of your home.[59]

Despite Johnson's more targeted attack on things related to Māori spirit-beliefs, the overall effect of his teaching would leave a follower inclined to believe that all things Māori (*taha Māori*) must be avoided as dangerous.

---

59. Johnson, teaching transcript 1971, 17.

The Practice of Deliverance Ministry at the Auckland AOG

The last years of Bob Midgley's ministry and the first years of Neville Johnson's were a heady time. The practice of deliverance was new. Crowds of people were starting to pour into the church and there was a remarkable sense of the Holy Spirit at work. Those seeking deliverance after a main church meeting would be ushered into an adjacent hall to be prayed over by teams of volunteers. There could be thirty people seeking deliverance on any one occasion, with several being prayed over at the same time in different parts of the hall. Sometimes there was a hubbub of noise, including weeping and, occasionally, gnashing of teeth or screaming.[60] Enthusiastic 'deliverers' might shout commands to spirits inside people to name themselves—names such as 'spirit of lust', 'spirit of anger', and 'spirit of witchcraft'. Naming enabled deliverers to take control over spirits prior to their expulsion.[61] Occasionally, disturbed people would race outside.[62] Others might become so caught up in the supercharged atmosphere of the meeting that they could do backward flips into the air.[63] Teaching might create an expectation of manifestation as demons left through the mouth—coughing, spitting, or vomiting.[64] In the heady early days, there

60. Bartlett interview, 5, 6, 8.
61. Smedley interview, 5; Squires interview, 9; Johnston interview, 9.
62. Bartlett interview, 2.
63. Smedley interview, 2, 12.
64. Squires interview, 1; Smedley interview, 5.

was even a mop-up crew with a plastic bucket to catch the vomit or to clean up afterwards.[65]

How did the deliverers know that there was a demon? Much of this was based on subjective impressions. In addition, anything outside the person's control—for example, the inability to give up drinking—could have demonic causation.[66] Neville Johnson saw most out-of-control behaviour as spirit-caused:

> You say, I have progressed in something all of my life, even before conversion, and I have progressed in it even after being a Christian—a particular work of the flesh and I can't control it, so maybe it's a spirit. What shall I do? If you have progressed in it, there is every probability that it is a spirit.[67]

Johnson's teaching raised the issue of identifying boundaries between physically-caused problems and spiritually-caused problems. There was some acknowledgement of a place for medicine, but boundaries were often blurred.[68] On the whole, the tendency was to look for spiritual causes of physical or mental problems.[69] Even a common cold might stem from a demon.[70] Evan Squires' concussion in a rugby game led to his having migraine

65. Bartlett interview, 4.
66. Squires interview, 4.
67. Johnson, teaching transcript 1971, 11.
68. Smedley interview, 4.
69. Johnston interview, 5.
70. Smedley interview, 4.

headaches over the following fifteen years. When he went to Neville Johnson for prayer about this condition, Johnson articulated the view that a demonic spirit got in while Squires was unconscious. He then simply prayed, 'Spirit of migraine, come out'. Squires has had headaches since that time, but he has never had another *migraine* headache.[71]

The causation boundary between mental unwellness and spiritual deliverance was particularly problematic. Into the early 1970s, out-of-control mental unwellness tended to be regularly diagnosed as demonic activity, with other possibilities initially being given lesser consideration.[72] Such an approach risked greater confusion and disturbance for the sufferer. Colin Hayes interviewed fifteen Pentecostals at the end of the 1990s who had been treated for mental depression in the previous five years, and who considered themselves 'substantially recovered' or 'recovered' from depression. All attended Pentecostal churches at the time of their depression, and thirteen still did so (the other two moving on to other churches). In general, the interviewees found their personal beliefs helpful and sustaining, but found their churches' involvement in their conditions unhelpful and condemnatory.[73]

---

71. Squires interview, 8.
72. Squires interview, 4.
73. Colin Hayes, 'Responses to Depression within Pentecostal Churches: An Examination of Pastoral and Clinical Perspectives on the Experience of Depression amongst Pentecostal Christians' (PhD dissertation, New Covenant International University, Lake Worth, Florida, 2000), 216, 217, 227, 327.

The Auckland AOG teaching created a sense that demons were everywhere ('so maybe my problem is demonic'). This world-view engendered a mood of fear.[74] At the same time it could lead to quick-fix optimism—'my (out-of-control) problem is caused by a demon that can be exorcised'.[75] Deliverance could also become an avoidance mechanism, an abdication of personal responsibility: 'I'm not responsible for the way I live; it's all caused by a demon.'[76] Having a demon cast out was often a more attractive option than assuming moral responsibility and a personally disciplined life.

The Auckland AOG mutated markedly during the period under study, partly, at least, through social lift as the church became more middle class. Dramatic semi-public deliverances largely disappeared in the later 1970s. Increasingly, there was recognition that significant counselling must accompany deliverance. Some, at least, of the Auckland AOG pastors came to realise that only a minority of those seeking deliverance required deliverance; others needed a mixture of counselling and self-discipline. Although less emphasis was placed on a deliverance approach, a demon-deliverance diagnosis remained a significant possibility.

74. Johnston interview, 1.
75. Evan Squires interview, 5; Frank Smedley interview, 13.
76. Frank Smedley interview, 5.

Conclusion:

The heyday of deliverance emphasis in the Auckland AOG coincided with an exuberant atmosphere of Holy Spirit activity at a time of social crisis. While the deliverance emphasis had its roots in America, especially in the ministry of Derek Prince, it was also part of a widespread Pentecostal trend in New Zealand. Deliverance ministry emerged from a very other-worldly, spiritually-focused theology. It was based on a narrow reading of 'patchwork quilt' proof-texts sewn together from all parts of the Bible.[77] It relied on subjective, intuitive revelation which could easily see demons lurking behind all sorts of character flaws, behaviours, and illnesses. Early major excesses later subsided. Deliverance ministry may have done some good. It certainly also did a great deal of harm. Was its theology really Christian in nature, or was it grounded in a more animistic understanding of reality?

Bibliography

Assemblies of God. *Where We Stand*. (Springfield, MO: np, 1990).

Clark, Ian G, 'Assemblies of God Heritage: Tracing Our Roots', *Evangel*, October, 1987: 8–16.

Clark, Ian G, *Pentecost at the Ends of the Earth: The History of the Assemblies of God in New Zealand (1927–2003)* (Blenheim, NZ: Christian Road Ministries, 2007).

77. Frank Smedley interview, 3.

Hammond, Frank and Ida Mae, *Pigs in the Parlor: A Practical Guide to Deliverance* (Kirkwood, MO: Impact Books, 1973).

Harper, J, 'The Church that's Taking over Auckland', *Metro* 29, November, 1983:122–35.

Hayes, Colin, 'Responses to Depression within Pentecostal Churches: An Examination of Pastoral and Clinical Perspectives on the Experience of Depression amongst Pentecostal Christians'. PhD diss., New Covenant International University, Lake Worth, Florida, 2000.

Hollenweger, Walter J, *The Pentecostals* (London: SCM, 1972).

Knowles, Brett, *The History of a New Zealand Pentecostal* Movement (Lewiston, NY: Edwin Mellen Press, 2000).

Prince, Derek, *They Shall Expel Demons: What You Need to Know about Demons—Your Invisible Enemies* (Grand Rapids: Chosen Books, 1998).

Subritzky, Bill, *Demons Defeated* (Auckland: Dove Ministries, 1985).

Worsfold, James E, *A History of the Charismatic Movements in New Zealand* (Bradford, MA: Puritan Press, 1974).

Transcripts:

Bartlett, Bill. Interview by L Guy, June 23, 2007, Auckland, New Zealand.

Bhana, Tak. Interview by L Guy, July 19, 2007, Auckland, New Zealand.

Johnson, Neville. Transcript of teaching at Christian Life (AOG) Bible College, August, 1971, Wellington, New Zealand.

Johnston, Tim. Interview by L Guy, June 27, 2007, Auckland, New Zealand.
Smedley, Frank. Interview by L Guy, July 21, 2007, Auckland, New Zealand.
Squires, Evan. Interview by L Guy, May 30, 2007, Auckland, New Zealand.

Spirit and Spirits: The Shape of a Catholic Pneumatology of Healing

Susan Smith

For centuries in many parts of the world, people have believed, and many still believe, that they live in a spirit-inhabited world. The eighteenth, nineteenth and twentieth century emissaries of western civilisation—colonial officials, the military, medical and educational personnel, and missionaries—were convinced that such beliefs would vanish once people were exposed to the benefits of western civilisation. This has meant that today, many Catholics appear reluctant to address the question of demonic possession. Yet demonology and the healing of people suffering from mental and physical illness are real issues for countless millions of people, irrespective of their denominational affiliation, particularly in the Majority world.[1]

1. In this paper, I am using the term 'Majority' world as a descrip-

I have never been part of a Catholic Charismatic community where people have experienced, first- or second-hand, the phenomenon reality of spirit possession, and the subsequent need for healing. Nevertheless, I have been involved on four occasions with people who appeared to have been possessed by spirits, or who feared the possibility of spirits seeking to hurt them.

Let me recall these experiences. The first occurred while I was living in Bangladesh in the 1970s. A young Christian girl was brought to our convent in Chittagong. She was apparently being pressured into marrying a young Muslim man and because she did not want this, the young man's family has supposedly been responsible for a sudden and inexplicable illness that had overtaken her. In vain, the girl's family had sought medical support from the local Catholic dispensary and Catholic doctor, and so the Catholic priest was invited in to exorcise her; again, nothing was achieved. In desperation the family took her to a local Muslim mullah, who succeeded in restoring the girl to health.

Something similar occurred while I was working in Papua New Guinea in the 1980s. Another young Catholic girl was brought to the mission station, apparently possessed by evil spirits, and again this possession supposedly had its origins in a proposed, arranged marriage relationship that she did not want. Her distress was obvi-

---

tor of the countries of Asia, Africa, Latin America, Melanesia and Polynesia. 'Minority' world refers to those who live in what are described as the 'first-world', 'developed', or 'northern' countries of Europe, North America, and Oceania.

ous, and there were material aspects that were strange. For example, her clothes were disintegrating before our eyes. In this instance, I drove her to the small, local dispensary hospital staffed by German sisters who provided her with some security and medication, and the next day she seemed to have recovered.

In the late 1980s, I while I was living in Ruatoria, I was asked on two occasions to bless homes whose owners believed were inhabited by evil spirits. They referred to this as *mākutu,* which means 'accursed'. I took along some holy water and candles, and we prayed together, after which I blessed the house and then sprinkled holy water in those rooms considered the most at risk. The inhabitants were happy with what I had done and spoke of feeling more at peace.

I was more than happy to be present in a ministering capacity in such situations, but I must admit to feeling a certain detachment from these events, as demonic possession was never something about which I consciously thought. My particular understanding and practice of Catholicism could best be described as liberal, which meant a certain scepticism about spirit possession, and its corollary, miraculous healings.

In 2005, I watched *The Exorcism of Emily Rose,* a film based on the true story of Annaliese Michel, a young German Catholic woman who died in 1976 after unsuccessful attempts to cure her, through medication and exorcism, from an alleged state of demonic possession. Neither the medication nor the exorcism 'worked', and the priest exorcist was subsequently charged with medical neglect by a German court. Emily Rose's story provided the basis for the 2005 American film. The film's media publicity and box-office takings pointed to the interest that spirit possession generates in contemporary society.

Finally, my personal involvement with missiologists, missionaries, and ministers from the Majority world has alerted me to the many healing ministries that seek to free people from demonic possession, from sickness and disease. Such involvement, coupled with my own recent reading of Pentecostal literature,[2] has convinced me that Catholics should not ignore the reality of spirit possession, even if their liberal Catholicism owes much to Enlightenment values.

Therefore, the invitation to be part of the School of Theology's research on spirit possession has led me to reflect a little more on the reality of this phenomenon, and now to explore, in a more structured way, what Catholic tradition and teaching suggest to us about spirit possession, and how this may be of value in Aotearoa New Zealand. In this essay, I wish to explore spirit possession in the Catholic tradition, the official responses to such possession, contemporary popular responses, and the implications of such research for the Catholic Church today.

---

2. See, for example, Julie C Ma, *When the Spirit Meets the Spirits: Pentecostal Ministry among the Kankana-Ey Tribe in the Philippines*, edited by Richard Friedli, revised edition, Studies in the Intercultural History of Christianity (Frankfurt-am-Main: Peter Lang, 2001); *Asian and Pentecostal: The Charismatic Face of Christianity in Asia*, Asian Journal of Pentecostal Studies Series 3, edited by Allan Anderson and Edmond Tang (Oxford: Regnum Books International, 2005).

Spirit Possession in the Catholic Tradition

In the ancient world, demonic possession[3] was frequent among the pagan peoples, who believed that many sicknesses had their origins in the activities of evil spirits that could be driven out by sorcerers as distinct from physicians. Surprisingly, demonic possession did not figure so prominently in the First Testament, although Saul was said to have been troubled by an evil spirit (cf 1 Sam 16:14). Josephus further elaborates on this when he writes some one thousand years later:

> But as for Saul, some strange and demoniacal disorders came upon him, and brought upon him such suffocations as were ready to choke him; for which the physicians could find no other remedy but this, that if any person could charm those passions by singing, and playing upon the harp, they advised them to inquire for such a one, and to observe when these demons came upon him and disturbed him, and to take care that such a person might stand over him, and play upon the harp, and recite hymns to him.[4]

3. 'Demonic possession' may be defined as the presence of an evil and exterior entity that directly controls a person, that is, exercises control over the person's body and mind. While demonic possession has not been scientifically proven, some instances of it may be consistent with the possessed person's religious and/or cultural tradition. This explains why religious persons within that culture may be suited to exorcising the affected individual.
4. Josephus, Jewish Antiquities VI.8.2, in *Josephus*, edited by H St J

In the Second Testament, however, particularly in the synoptic gospels, there are numerous references to people possessed by evil spirits. Jesus is portrayed as the one who heals them from possession. These spirits testify to Jesus as the Son of God, and therefore as one who can exercise power over them (cf Mark 1:24; Matt 8:29; Mark 3:12; Luke 4:33–34), a testimony that continues after the resurrection of Jesus (cf Acts 16:16–18). The technical term for this driving out of the demonic spirit is exorcism, and the Christian tradition holds that Jesus passed on this power to his disciples (cf Mark 6:7; 16:17). As this collection contains a paper specifically dedicated to Jesus the healer in the New Testament, I will not develop this point any further.

There are also many references to exorcisms throughout the Christian story. Thus, Justin Martyr, writing in the early second century, states:

> For every demon, when exorcised in the name of this very Son of God—who is the First-born of every creature, who became man by the Virgin, who suffered, and was crucified under Pontius Pilate by your nation, who died, who rose from the dead, and ascended into heaven—is overcome and subdued.[5]

Thackeray, The Loeb Classical Library (London: Heinemann, 1928), 2.250–51.

5. Justin Martyr, *Dialogue with Trypho*, Chapter LXXXV, http://www.earlychristianwritings.com/text/justinmartyr-dialoguetrypho.html (accessed May 4, 2008).

Origen was an early 'Father of the Church' who initially taught in Alexandria, and then relocated to Caesarea after a dispute with his bishop. In his *Contra Celsus,* written to refute the writings of Celsus the Platonist, he claimed that:

> After this, through the influence of some motive which is unknown to me, Celsus asserts that it is by the names of certain demons, and by the use of incantations, that the Christians appear to be possessed of (miraculous) power; hinting, I suppose, at the practices of those who expel evil spirits by incantations. And here he manifestly appears to malign the Gospel. For it is not by incantations that Christians seem to prevail [over evil spirits], but by the name of Jesus, accompanied by the announcement of the narratives which relate to Him; for the repetition of these has frequently been the means of driving demons out of men, especially when those who repeated them did so in a sound and genuinely believing spirit.[6]

Two centuries later, the famous philosopher, theologian, and Bishop of Hippo, Saint Augustine wrote:

6. Origen, *Contra Celsus*, Book 1, Chapter 6, http://www.newadvent.org/fathers/04161.htm (accessed May 4, 2008).

> It is by true piety that men of God cast out the hostile power of the air which opposes godliness; it is by exorcising it, not by propitiating it; and they overcome all the temptations the adversary by praying not to him, but to their own God against him. For the devil cannot conquer or subdue any but those who are in league with sin; and therefore he is conquered in the name of Him who assumed humanity, and that without sin, that Himself being both Priest and Sacrifice, He might bring about the remission of sins, that is to say, might bring it about through the Mediator between God and men, the man Christ Jesus, by whom we are reconciled to God, cleansing from sin being accomplished.[7]

Such attestations in patristic literature point to the ongoing importance of exorcism in the early church, a practice that continued throughout the Middle Ages. Church councils passed laws, and papal bulls were promulgated.[8] Priests had the power of exorcism conferred upon them, which was important in an age when diabolical possession and witchcraft figured prominently in the life of the Church, and lay exorcisms disappeared. The Council of

---

7. Saint Augustine, *The City of God*, Book X, Chapter 22, http://www.newadvent.org/fathers/120110.htm (accessed May 4, 2008).
8. See, for example, the papal bulls of Innocent VIII (1484), Julius II (1504), Adrian VI (1523).

Trent (1545–1563) sought to control all activities that dealt with the miraculous and the divine. This reform meant a thorough-going 'clericalisation of exorcism'.[9] Baptismal exorcisms became an integral part of the early church's baptismal ritual. This was not meant to suggest that catechumens were possessed, but rather that as a consequence of original and personal sin, they were more likely to succumb to the power of Satan whom they were called upon to renounce. It is important to distinguish between baptismal exorcisms and those exorcisms which have as their purpose freeing a person from demonic possession.

In 1614, Pope Paul V authorised the promulgation of the *Rituale Romanum* which contained the formal rite to be used by priests in exorcisms. The *Rituale* included only twenty-nine benedictions, and local synods and dioceses immediately hurried to issue hundreds of 'additional conjurations and adjurations that dealt with specific needs that the Roman rite ignored'.[10] The *Rituale* was insistent that a priest verify whether or not a person was actually possessed before carrying out an exorcism, and generally speaking, priests were cautioned against carrying out ex-

9. Moshe Sluhovsky, *Believe Not Every Spirit: Possession, Mysticism, and Discernment in Early Modern Catholicism* (Chicago: The University of Chicago Press, 2007), 62.
10. Sluhovsky, *Believe Not Every Spirit*, 64. 'The basic formula went something like the following late fifteenth century short conjuration: "I exorcise you, unclean spirit, in the name of God the Almighty Father + [making the sing of the Cross] and in the name of Jesus Christ his Son + and by the power of the Holy Spirit + that you should recede from this Servant of God, [name of the afflicted person]".'

orcisms. After the Enlightenment, advances in medical science meant that diagnoses of possession became rare. Furthermore, in the twentieth century, Catholic belief in the devil as a person seemed somewhat diminished. Many Catholics probably would agree with Bultmann's oft-quoted comment:

> It is impossible to use electric lights and the wireless and to avail ourselves of modern medical and surgical discoveries, and at the same time to believe in the New Testament world of demons and spirits.[11]

The *Rituale* remained virtually untouched until 1954, when Pope Pius XII (1876–1958) wrote into it two minor revisions that reflected an awareness of contemporary psychological insights. Although the first reference to "exorcist" as an official church office had occurred in a letter of Pope Cornelius in 253, as the twentieth century drew to a close, the significance of such an office had faded for many Catholics, leading Pope Paul VI to suppress the order of exorcist in 1972 (*Ministeria Quaedam*). In 1992, Pope John Paul II authorised the publication of the *Catechism of the Catholic Church*, the official exposition of church teaching, which included the church's teaching on exorcism. Pope John Paul II, aware that belief in spirits, healings, and exorcisms were beginning to impact more significantly on mainstream Catholicism, particularly in

11. R Bultmann, 'The New Testament and Mythology', in *Kerygma and Myth*, edited by HW Bartsch (London: SPCK, 1953), 2:5.

the Majority world, recognised that exorcism was once again emerging as an important ministry. The *Catechism of the Catholic Church* teaches:

> When the Church asks publicly and authoritatively in the name of Jesus Christ that a person or object be protected against the power of the Evil One and withdrawn from his dominion, it is called exorcism. Jesus performed exorcisms (Mark l:25f.) and from him the Church has received the power and office of exorcising (Mark 3:15; 6:7, 13; 16:17). In a simple form, exorcism is performed at the celebration of Baptism. The solemn exorcism, called 'a major exorcism,' can be performed only by a priest and with the permission of the Bishop. The priest must proceed with prudence, strictly observing the rules established by the Church. 'Exorcism is directed at the expulsion of demons or to the liberation from demonic possession through the spiritual authority which Jesus entrusted to his Church. Illness, especially psychological illness, is a very different matter: treating this is the concern of medical science. Therefore, before an exorcism is performed, it is important to ascertain that one is dealing with the presence

> of the Evil One, and not an illness (cf *Code of Canon Law,* can. 1172).'[12]

Early in 1999, Cardinal Jorge Arturo, prefect of the Congregation for Divine Worship and the Discipline of the Sacraments, introduced an updated exorcism ritual, *De Exorcismis et Supplicationibus Quibusdam* ('Of Exorcisms and Certain Supplications'), which local episcopal conferences were to translate into the language/s of their local church. The guidelines accompanying the updated ritual emphasised the importance for the priest-exorcist in correctly diagnosing the true nature of illness too easily attributed to demonic possession. It warns that exorcists 'first of all, must not consider people to be vexed by demons who are suffering above all from some psychic illness'.[13]

A *New York Times'* comment probably captured well the reaction of liberal Catholics:

> Issuing the revised text could 'provide some incentive for the appointment of more official exorcists', said Michael W Cuneo, a Fordham University sociologist who is writing a book on exorcism in American culture. But Mr. Cuneo said that despite a 'flourishing market for exorcisms,' most Catholic bishops in the

12. *Catechism of the Catholic Church* (Homebush, NSW: St Paul's/Liberia Editrice Vaticana, 1994), no 1673.
13. Jorge Arturo Medina, *De Exorcismis Et Supplicationibus Quibusdam* (Vatican City: Vatican Libreria Editrice, 2003), #47.

> United States considered exorcism 'to be antiquated, to be an embarrassment, to be a survival of medieval superstition.'[14]

Scepticism about Spirits or Acknowledgement of Spirits?

As the twentieth century drew to a close, important changes were occurring in the wider Christian community. First, since the late 1960s, numbers of people in mainline churches became part of what came to be known as 'the Charismatic movement'. Mainline churches tend to attribute this development to the reclaiming of pneumatology in theological discourse, while Pentecostal scholars argue that it has its roots in the pervasive influence of Pentecostalism on both Protestantism and Catholicism.[15] Initially mainline churches were somewhat suspicious of this development, but by 1975, the US Catholic Bishops' Conference appeared more positively disposed toward the charismatic renewal movement in the American Catholic Church, and all that implied in respect of spirit possession and healing. In the wider Catholic community, the support and patronage of the bishop of Malines, Belgium, Jo-

---

14. John Tagliabue, 'Vatican's Revised Exorcism Rite Affirms Existence of Devil', http://query.nytimes.com/gst/fullpage.html?sec=health&res=9F05E0D81339F934A15752C0A96F958260 (accessed October 14, 2007).
15. Allan Anderson, 'Introduction', in *Asian and Pentecostal: The Charismatic Face of Christianity in Asia,* edited by Allan Anderson and Edmund Tang, Asian Journal of Pentecostal Studies Series 3 (Oxford: Regnum Books International, 2005), 1–12.

seph Cardinal Leon Suenens, also significantly advanced the Charismatic movement in the Minority world.

Second, the demographic reality of the church was fast changing. The Catholic population worldwide was strongest in the Majority world, where many had not had the same exposure to Enlightenment values, or to educational methodologies that concentrated more on the development of the student's critical faculties. Furthermore, the often lower socio-economic status of peoples of the Majority world means that the expensive medical procedures open to Minority world groups are not possible for them, and so there is a tendency to understand healing as a spiritual reality that relies on the powers of certain individuals in the community who are recognised as being healers. These healers may be women or men, Christian or traditional, but are people who have seldom been exposed to years of medical training in tertiary institutions.

In an informative 1980 article, priest/anthropologist Aylward Shorter[16] traced the changing relationship of the Tanzanian Catholic Church toward healing, a relationship which was characteristic of the Catholic Church elsewhere. In the 1960s, he became aware of a local spirit-medium who was exercising a healing ministry in a rural Catholic community, despite opposition from Catholic foreign missionaries. Those healed were 'burdened with different forms of anxiety, medical, moral and social'.[17] Despite missionary opposition, the very success of the

16. See Aylward Shorter, 'Spirit Possession and Christian Healing in Tanzania', in *African Affairs* 79/314 (1980).
17. Shorter, 'Spirit Possession and Christian Healing in Tanzania', 48.

traditional healer's ministry meant that many were attracted to what Shorter defines as 'an exercise in social medicine and inward healing. It identified with the concerns of disoriented people and gave them new hope. No doubt also it encouraged and even accelerated physical healing in some cases.'[18] From the mid 1970s onwards, the Tanzanian Catholic Church actively encouraged a ministry of healing, regarding it as integral to community building at a local level. This decision was influenced by both the Charismatic movement, with its emphasis on the importance of community prayer for the sick, and by the indigenous healing and diviner-traditions of Africa.

To some extent, the more positive response of official Catholicism to spirits and healing was driven by the growing impact of Pentecostalism in the Majority world. Catholic commentator John R Allen, writing on Pope Benedict's visit to Brazil in May 2007, directs attention to the remarkably swift break-up of 'Catholicism's 500-year religious monopoly in Latin America'.[19] He notes that

> the number of conversions from Catholicism to Protestantism in Latin America during the 20th century actually surpassed the Protestant Reformation in Europe in the 16th century. In 1930, Protestants amounted to one percent of the Latin American population; today

18. Shorter, 'Spirit Possession and Christian Healing in Tanzania', 49.
19. John R Allen, 'Facing Dramatic Losses, Benedict Says: "It's Worth It to Stay Catholic! "', in *The National Catholic Reporter Cafe*, http://ncrcafe.org/node/1098 (accessed May 14, 2007).

> it's between 12 and 15 percent. A study commissioned in the late 1990s by CELAM found that 8,000 Latin Americans were deserting the Catholic Church for Evangelical Protestantism every day.[20]

It has been suggested that the success of such churches in predominantly Catholic Latin America is 'because Evangelical and Pentecostal religions are better able organizationally, doctrinally, and ritually to deal with the 'pathogens of poverty'.[21] The claims of Pentecostal, Catholic Charismatic, and African Independent Churches to an unmediated access to the Holy Spirit to solve problems of illness points to the centrality of healing in their doctrine and practice. For the millions of poor Catholics in Africa, Asia, and Latin America, this emphasis assumes increasing importance given the accelerating costs of professional medical care. The possibility of such healing is particularly important for women, who are always the primary health carers. As Chestnut observes, these religions appeal because 'they are firmly rooted in the crises and afflictions that result from the inability of women to realize their practical interests, such as health and family, in the face of grinding poverty'.[22]

Most people in Majority Christian communities have little difficulty in acknowledging the reality of supernatu-

---

20. Allen, 'Facing Dramatic Losses'.
21. R Andrew Chestnut, *Competitive Spirits: Latin America's New Religious Economy* (Oxford: Oxford University Press, 2003), 14.
22. Chestnut, *Competitive Spirits*, 129.

ral powers, of 'the power of darkness' (Col 1:13), believing that 'misfortune, sickness, and death were attributed to the workings of mischievous spirits, commonly directed by ill-meaning neighbours'.[23] Jenkins argues that 'the one single key area of faith and practice that divides Northern and Southern Christians . . . is this matter of spiritual forces and their effects on the everyday human world.'[24] Or, as missiologist Andrew Walls suggests, witchcraft is an important reality for African Christians. 'Academic theologians in the West may not put witchcraft high on the agenda, but it's the issue that hits ordinary Africans full in the face.'[25]

A particular problem that may confront Catholics of a more liberal persuasion emerges in the writings of American Mennonite missiologist and anthropologist, Paul Hiebert. Hiebert, who worked as a missionary in India and the academic world in the US, has written extensively on what he calls the 'excluded middle'. Hiebert holds that many in the Majority world believe in the on-going interaction between the physical and spiritual worlds.[26] In this respect, they differ from many Minority world Christians, who tend to compartmentalise the material and spiritual. As Chinese theologian and Methodist Bishop Hwa Yung notes: 'This effectively fuses the different components of

---

23. Philip Jenkins, *The Next Christendom: The Coming of Global Christianity* (New York: Oxford University Press, 2002), 123.
24. Jenkins, *The Next Christendom*, 123.
25. Andrew Walls, cited by Jenkins, *The Next Christendom*, 124. No further information given.
26. See Paul Hiebert, *Anthropological Reflections on Missiological Issues* (Grand Rapids: Baker Books, 1994).

the world-views into an integrated whole. This contrasts sharply with the more dualistic western view shaped by the Enlightenment, which tends to dichotomize the spiritual and the physical.'[27] In effect, authors such as Hiebert and Hwa Yung argue that many in the Minority world are so imbued by a certain dualism that they cannot envisage a type of middle world in which the spiritual and physical interact.

Given the current resurgence of belief in the presence of demonic possession and the subsequent healing required through the intervention of the Holy Spirit, it seems important to tease out the implications of this for the Catholic Church in Aotearoa today. Statistics New Zealand states that in 2001, 240,000 people were of Asian ethnicity, 526,281 were of Māori ethnicity, and 231,801 were of Pacific Islands ethnicity, while the count of people of European ethnicity had declined from eighty–three per cent to eighty per cent.[28] Obviously, the ethnic composition of the Catholic church is changing too, and today over fifty per cent of all Sunday mass-goers in the Auckland urban area are of Pacific Islands ethnicity, while there are also increasing numbers of Indian, Korean, Filipino, Vietnamese, and Chinese Catholics. In other words, Catholics whose origins lie in the Majority world are as-

27 Hwa Yung, *Mangoes or Bananas? The Quest for an Authentic Asian Christian Theology*, Regnum Studies in Mission (Oxford: Regnum Books International, 1997), 78.

28 Government Statistician, *Census Snapshot: Cultural Diversity* (Statistics New Zealand, Tatauranga Aotearoa, 2001), http://www.stats.govt.nz/products-and-services/Articles/census-snpsht-cult-diversity-Mar02.htm (accessed May 14, 2007).

suming a numerical significance that was previously not there. For example, I recall getting petrol recently, and the Indian service station attendant asked me if I was going to the big healing mass. I replied that I did not know there was one on, and so he filled me in on the details regarding the visiting Indian priest who was healing 'hundreds' of people. In view of the growing importance of healing ministries, such conversations become an invitation to reassess the prevailing minimalist position characteristic of some liberal Christians regarding spirit possession.

Responses to the Growing Importance of Spirit Possession in the Exercise of Ministry

Pastoral Responses:

First, liberal Christians need to come to terms with the fact that spirit-talk and healing-talk is alive and well, not only in Africa, Asia, and Latin America, but also in Europe, North America, Australia, and New Zealand. John R. Allen reports that the growing interest in exorcisms is fuelled by two broad trends. 'The first is a rebirth of traditional forms of belief and devotion within Catholicism, and inspired by John Paul's papacy. The other is the Catholic Charismatic movement.'[29] In the modern era, spirit-possession and the subsequent need for healing were rarely addressed, or if they were, then the topic was tackled by religious groups considered marginal by mainline churches. 'This left a vacuum prone to be filled by

29. John L Allen, 'Exorcism: Ancient Ministry Attracts New Practitioners', in *National Catholic Reporter*, September 1, 2000: 5–6.

whatever anyone pleased. Though missionaries always recognised the pivotal religious importance of spirits in the respective cultures in which they were working, they generally tended to view such spirits negatively and opposed them outright.'[30] Or as Catholic missionary Frank Hoare, who worked in Fiji, writes: 'A foreign missionary should be aware of ethnocentrism and the reductionism that dismisses the local idiom and traditional cosmology. Instead crises of evil offer an opportunity for deeper dialogue between the Christian gospel and traditional beliefs and practice.'[31] Though Hoare is writing about Fiji, the reality of large migrant communities within the Minority world makes it imperative that local ministers recognise that such groups bring their local culture and idioms with them to their new homes. These still impact significantly on their lives.

Second, the often marginal nature of spirit possession in the mainline churches can foster an unhealthy curiosity among many. The success of films such as *The Exorcist* (1973), and *The Exorcism of Emily Rose* (2005), or articles about demonic possession in the popular press, testify to the fascination such stories have for people. In 2005, *The Tablet*, the London-published Catholic journal, warned that the proposal to screen exorcisms on Channel 4 television 'could be dangerous and lead to an increase in the

30. Christoffer H Grundmann, 'Inviting the Spirit to Fight the Spirits? Pneumatological Challenges for Missions in Healing and Exorcism', in *International Review of Mission* XCIV / 372 (2005): 52.
31. Frank Hoare, 'A Pastoral Approach to Spirit Possession and Witchcraft Manifestations among the Fijian People', in *Mission Studies* 21/1 (2004): 113.

number of people who believe that they are possessed by evil spirits'.[32]

Third, Catholics preparing for ministry should be educated about the reality of spirit possession. One Vatican-licensed university in Rome is offering a two month course on the theoretical and practical aspects of exorcism. The course is taught by 'an anthropologist, a professor of psychiatry, a senior police psychologist, and two licensed [priest] exorcists'.[33] This is not to suggest that there are significantly more people possessed, and as Willey points out in the same article, 'perhaps only 2 per cent to 5 per cent of the people who come to the priest for help, because they feel possessed, turn out to be genuine cases of possession'.[34] Indeed, a recurring theme in Catholic statements on possession is the need for the exorcist to discern carefully whether the sick person is in fact possessed, or suffering from mental or physical illness. For the Catholic, exorcism is always to be a last resort used after the failure of professional medical help to bring about change in a person.

Theological Responses

First, in addressing the question of demonic possession and healing, the theologian must recognise that misfor-

32. Isabel de Bertodana, 'Exorcism to Be Televised', *The Tablet* 259/8576 (2005): 42.
33. David Willey, 'Depart from Me, Satan', *The Tablet* 259/8576 (2005): 9.
34. Willey, 'Depart from Me, Satan', 9.

tune—poverty, marital conflict, unemployment or childlessness—can induce physical and/or mental illness. The problem is that though 'mainline churches have institutionalised mechanisms to address these needs it is usually done in a compartmentalised way which leaves certain aspects of the needs unmet'.[35] This suggests that theology, and the teaching of theology, have to be contextualised and inculturated to a greater extent, so that future ministers are well aware of the cultural and religious realities that will impact on their ministries.

Second, there is a greater need for the Catholic Church to engage in dialogue with indigenous traditions on the one hand, and on the other hand, with Pentecostal and charismatic churches, as spirit possession and healing constitute a more integral part of their faith life and practice. Catholics have much to contribute to such conversations, as they tend to have a more positive view of culture. As Pentecostal scholar Allan Anderson writes: 'The Pentecostal tendency, inherited from western missionaries, to demonise God's revelation in ancient [indigenous] religions is not helpful and creates unnecessary conflict.'[36] Generally speaking, Catholicism has been better disposed toward indigenous traditions, and this presents one important area for dialogue. But dialogue with 'the traditional cosmologies of a people'[37] will generate understanding to the extent that the Christian is capable of sustained and

35. Philomena Njeri Mwaura, 'Response', in *International Review of Mission* XC/356-357 (2002): 66.
36. Anderson, 'Introduction', 10.
37. Hoare, 'A Pastoral Approach to Spirit Possession', 133.

respectful listening. Hoare continues that this can be difficult, as the missionary may offer 'a ready-made leadership role without [any] knowledge of and sensitivity to the people'[38] among whom they minister.

Third, Catholic theologians need to further expand the parameters of their pneumatologies. Feminist theologians such as Elizabeth Johnson have pushed the boundaries of pneumatology in their works on the Trinity.[39] Johnson builds her trinitarian theology from below by emphasising that often the human person's first experiences of the Trinity occur through their awareness of the presence of the Spirit in creation. Johnson writes: 'To this movement of the living God that can be traced in and through experience of the world, Christian speech traditionally gives the name Spirit.'[40] That is, belief in the presence of the Spirit in creation is often experienced, rather than acquired through a learning process. Catholic theologians Jacques Dupuis and Stephen Bevans have re-examined and re-envisioned trinitarian theologies in an attempt to find new theological foundations for interreligious dialogue.[41] The

38. Hoare, 'A Pastoral Approach to Spirit Possession', 133.
39. See Elizabeth A Johnson, *She Who Is: The Mystery of God in Feminist Theological Discourse* (New York: Crossroad, 1992); Catherine Mowry LaCugna, *God for Us: The Trinity and Christian Life* (San Francisco: HarperCollins, 1991).
40. Johnson, *She Who Is*, 124.
41. See Stephen Bevans, 'The Church as Creation of the Spirit: Unpacking a Missionary Image' (paper presented at the Presidential Address, American Society of Missiology, 2006); Stephen B Bevans and Roger P Schroeder, 'We Were Gentle among You: Christian Mission as Dialogue', in *Australian EJournal of Theology*, Pentecost Special Edition (2006); Stephen B Bevans, 'God Inside Out: Toward

world-wide growth of healing ministries and the actions of the Holy Spirit in peoples' lives suggest that Catholic theologians now need to articulate pneumatologies that highlight the healing mission of the Spirit in our midst. Pentecostal scholarship is already pursuing this today, and some of their contemporary literature merits careful reading by Catholics.[42]

Conclusion

Belief in spirit-possession and the subsequent need for healing through exorcisms have long been part of the Christian story, beginning with the synoptic gospel accounts of Jesus curing those possessed by evil spirits.

---

a Missionary Theology of the Holy Spirit', in *International Bulletin of Missionary Research* 22/3 (1998); Jacques Dupuis, 'Religious Plurality and the Christological Debate', *Focus* 15/2–3 (1995); Jacques Dupuis, 'The Spirit, Basis for Interreligious Dialogue', in *Theology Digest* 46/1 (1999); Jacques Dupuis, 'Christianity and Other Religions: From Confrontation to Encounter: 1. The Storm of the Spirit', *The Tablet*, October 20, 2001; Jacques Dupuis, *Toward a Christian Theology of Religious Pluralism* (Maryknoll: Orbis Books, 1997); Jacques Dupuis, 'From Religious Confrontation to Encounter', in *Theology Digest* 49/ 2 (2002).

42. See Allan Anderson, 'Toward a Pentecostal Missiology for the Majority World', in *International Symposium on Pentecostal Missiology* (Baguio City, Philippines: 2003); Allan Anderson, 'Pentecostals, Healing and Ecumenism', *International Review of Mission* 93/370-371 (2004); Allan Anderson, 'The Holy Spirit, Healing and Reconciliation: Pentecostal/Charismatic Issues at Athens 2005', in *International Review of Mission* 94/374 (2005); Anderson and Tang, editors, *Asian and Pentecostal: The Charismatic Face of Christianity in Asia*.

Church tradition has likewise affirmed this as an authentic dimension of the Christian life. The Enlightenment, the subsequent professionalisation of care of the sick, and the shift from healing to medical care, have marginalised this important ministry. At the same time, the advances of medical science in improving the quality of care offered to the sick should not be minimised, and neither should contemporary medical science's diagnostic capacity be by-passed in identifying both the causes and possible remedies for a particular illness. The Catholic Church rightly points out that exorcism should not precede such diagnoses and the remedies that they may advance.

On the other hand, the reclamation of healing, particularly in cases of spirit possession, its holistic quality, its appeal to the economically marginalised, and its social quality which sees illness as more than biologically-induced, means it would be foolish to ignore this growing phenomenon. But such recognition requires a better articulation of pneumatologies that reflect the role of the Spirit for those engaged in such ministry. This is a challenge for important sectors of the mainline churches, given their tendency to dismiss spirit possession as superstition. Many people, particularly in Majority communities, aware of an intimate relationship between religion and healing, have little difficulty in seeing that medical care and faith-healing can be in partnership. When medical methods fail, people can resort to spiritual healing, and vice versa. The tendency is for most people to supplement conventional responses to disease with religious ones.

Finally, it is important for the Catholic Church is to engage in a 'wider ecumenism' with indigenous traditions, and with Pentecostals and Evangelicals for whom spirit possession and healing have had a much greater significance. A particular Catholic contribution could be to direct attention to the causal nature of illness which often has its root in poverty, and in the inability of poor people to access appropriate medical care. Healing ministries need to be complemented by the practice of Catholic social teaching, reinforcing the notion that the two are not either/or options.

Bibliography

Allen, John L. 'Exorcism: Ancient Ministry Attracts New Practitioners', in *National Catholic Reporter*, September 1, 2000, 5–6.

Allen, John R. 'Facing Dramatic Losses, Benedict Says: "It's Worth It to Stay Catholic!"', in *The National Catholic Reporter Cafe*, http://ncrcafe.org/node/1098 (accessed May 14, 2007).

Anderson, Allan. 'The Holy Spirit, Healing and Reconciliation: Pentecostal/Charismatic Issues at Athens 2005', in *International Review of Mission* 94/374 (2005): 332–336.

———. 'Introduction', In *Asian and Pentecostal: The Charismatic Face of Christianity in Asia*, edited by Allan Anderson and Edmund Tang (Oxford: Regnum Books International, 2005), 1–12.

———. 'Pentecostals, Healing and Ecumenism'. *International Review of Mission* 93/370-371 (2004): 486–496.

———. 'Toward a Pentecostal Missiology for the Majority World', in *International Symposium on Pentecostal Mis-*

siology (Baguio City, Philippines, 2003), 1–18. In the author's possession.

Anderson, Allan, and Edmond Tang, editors. *Asian and Pentecostal: The Charismatic Face of Christianity in Asia*, Asian Journal of Pentecostal Studies Series 3 (Oxford: Regnum Books International, 2005).

Saint Augustine, *The City of God*, Book X, Chapter 22, http://www.newadvent.org/fathers/120110.htm (accessed May 4, 2008).

Bertodana, Isabel de. 'Exorcism to Be Televised', in *The Tablet* 259/8576 (2005): 42.

Bevans, Stephen. 'The Church as Creation of the Spirit: Unpacking a Missionary Image', Presidential Address, American Society of Missiology Annual Conference, 2006.

Bevans, Stephen B. 'God Inside Out: Toward a Missionary Theology of the Holy Spirit', *International Bulletin of Missionary Research* 22/3 (1998): 102–105.

Bevans, Stephen, and Roger P Schroeder. 'We Were Gentle among You: Christian Mission as Dialogue', in *Australian EJournal of Theology* 7, 2006.

Bultmann, R. 'The New Testament and Mythology', in *Kerygma and Myth*, edited by HW Bartsch (London: SPCK, 1953), 2:1–12.

Chestnut, R Andrew. *Competitive Spirits: Latin America's New Religious Economy* (Oxford: Oxford University Press, 2003).

Dupuis, Jacques. 'Christianity and Other Religions: From Confrontation to Encounter: 1. The Storm of the Spirit', in *The Tablet*, October 20, 2001: 1481–1485.

———. 'From Religious Confrontation to Encounter', in *Theology Digest* 49/2 (2002): 103–108.

———. 'Religious Plurality and the Christological Debate', in *Focus* 15/2–3 (1995): 1–8.

———. 'The Spirit, Basis for Interreligious Dialogue', in *Theology Digest* 46/1 (1999): 27–31.

———. *Toward a Christian Theology of Religious Pluralism* (Maryknoll: Orbis Books, 1997).

Government Statistician. 'Census Snapshot: Cultural Diversity', Statistics New Zealand, Tatauranga Aotearoa, http://www.stats.govt.nz/products-and-services/Articles/census-snpsht-cult-diversity-Mar02.htm (accessed May 14, 2007).

Grundmann, Christoffer H. 'Inviting the Spirit to Fight the Spirits? Pneumatological Challenges for Missions in Healing and Exorcism', in *International Review of Mission* XCIV/372 (2005): 51–73.

Hiebert, Paul. *Anthropological Reflections on Missiological Issues* (Grand Rapids: Baker Books, 1994).

Hoare, Frank. 'A Pastoral Approach to Spirit Possession and Witchcraft Manifestations among the Fijian People', in *Mission Studies* 21/1 (2004): 113–137.

Hwa Yung. *Mangoes or Bananas? The Quest for an Authentic Asian Christian Theology*, Regnum Studies in Mission (Oxford: Regnum Books International, 1997).

Jenkins, Philip. *The Next Christendom: The Coming of Global Christianity* (New York: Oxford University Press, 2002).

Johnson, Elizabeth A. *She Who Is: The Mystery of God in Feminist Theological Discourse* (New York: Crossroad, 1992).

Josephus. 'Jewish Antiquities', In *Josephus*, edited by H St J Thackeray (London: Heinemann, 1928), 250–251.

Justin Martyr, *Dialogue with Trypho*, Chapter LXXXV, http://www.earlychristianwritings.com/text/justinmartyr-dialoguetrypho.html (accessed May 4, 2008).

LaCugna, Catherine Mowry. *God for Us: The Trinity and Christian Life* (San Francisco: HarperCollins, 1991).

Ma, Julie C. *When the Spirit Meets the Spirits: Pentecostal Ministry among the Kankana-Ey Tribe in the Philippines*, edited by Richard Friedli, revised edition, Studies in the Intercultural History of Christianity (Frankfurt-am-Main: Peter Lang, 2001).

Medina, Jorge Arturo. *De Exorcismis et Supplicationibus Quibusdam* (Vatican City: Libreria Editrice Vaticana, 2003).

Mwaura, Philomena Njeri. 'Response', in *International Review of Mission* XC/356–357 (2002): 65–69.

Origen, *Contra Celsus*, Book 1, Chapter 6, http://www.newadvent.org/fathers/04161.htm (accessed May 4, 2008).

Shorter, Aylward. 'Spirit Possession and Christian Healing in Tanzania', in *African Affairs* 79/314 (1980): 45–53.

Tagliabue, John. 'Vatican's Revised Exorcism Rite Affirms Existence of Devil', http://query.nytimes.com/gst/fullpage.html?sec=health&res=9F05E0D81339F934A15752C0A96F958260 (accessed October 14, 2007).

Willey, David. 'Depart from Me, Satan', in *The Tablet* 259/8576 (2005): 9.

Conclusion: Opening Up Conversations

Philip Culbertson and Susan Smith

'God is dead', proclaimed the German philosopher, Friedrich Nietzsche, in 1882. The widely-quoted statement entered into popular conversation when the April 8, 1966 cover of *Time* magazine asked, 'Is God dead?' A number of liberal Christian theologians in the 1960s and 70s, including Paul van Buren, William Hamilton, Thomas Altizer, and the Jewish rabbi, Richard Rubenstein, believed the answer was 'yes'. Rubenstein could not reconcile the idea of an all-powerful and all-loving God with the Jewish experience of the Holocaust. Liberal Christian theologians argued that secularism and secularisation had rendered obsolete the Christian foundations that were woven into European culture, and had also become a part of those societies where European settlers had subsequently dominated indigenous cultures, including North America, Australia, New Zealand, and the islands of the

Pacific. These and other like-minded theologians began to identify western culture not only as post-modern, but also as post-Christian.

By extension, if God were dead, then so also were the spirits and angels whom God created and who are with God. The 'death of God' phenomenon engendered a certain reductionist approach to traditional Christian faith, and it was readily assumed that Christian faith, as it was usually understood, would diminish in significance over time.

As the new millennium dawned, this was not happening. The extraordinary growth of Christian communities in Asia (particularly in China, where the Christian population is rapidly approaching one hundred million), Africa, and Latin America means that neither Christianity nor God is dead for millions of people. Nor does the experience of Christian churches in the United States suggest that God is dead, as today religion vitally informs the American political scene. Although it is common to regard Western Europe, Australia, and New Zealand as thoroughly secularised, nevertheless, in New Zealand the increasingly significant Polynesian and migrant churches, the phenomenon of the emergence of the Destiny Church, and the growth of intentional Christian communities of a more orthodox orientation, suggest that Christianity is far from dead in our country. Therefore, to uncritically describe New Zealand as secularised is inappropriate.

What seems apparent is that Christianity, at least in the near future, will be more traditionalist and conservative, and even more fundamentalist, than liberal Christians have experienced in the past five decades. God is not dead, but well and truly alive, and so are spirits and angels.[1] It is also apparent that the Christians of Asia, Africa, Latin America, and the migrant churches are dissatisfied with those western theologies that are heirs to the Enlightenment. In 1989, anthropologist and 'Christian warrior' Charles Kraft argued that the western worldview had largely dispensed with the supernatural, was driven by materialistic values, had allowed the horizontal dimension of religion to dominate or render unnecessary the vertical dimension, was rationalistic, and valued individualism above community.[2] Given that it was the Enlightenment mindset which shaped much missionary activity in the modern era, this effectively precluded the development of theologies that adequately addressed the concerns of cultures other than its own. The missionary mindset neglected the fact that African, Asian, Latin American, and Pacific cultures were more holistic, more community-focussed, and less inclined to radically separate the natural from the supernatural. On the other hand, these cultures not only tolerated, but indeed encouraged, an emphasis on the spirit world. Such people move more easily between the spiritual and material world than do their 'enlightened' western colleagues.

And yet, the reluctance of liberal Christians to acknowledge the reality of the realm of spirits is a relatively

---

1. See, for example, Philip Jenkins, *The Next Christendom: The Coming of Global Christianity* (New York: Oxford University Press, 2002).
2. See Charles H Kraft, *Christianity With Power: Your Worldview and Your Experience of the Supernatural* (Ann Arbor, MI: Servant Publications, 1989), 27–34.

recent phenomenon, even in the western world. Traditionally, western theologians have been more concerned with what might be called 'high theology'—questions of ultimate truth and meaning, in which conclusions are arrived at rationally—rather than with 'folk' or 'popular' religion, which allows people to engage easily with the spirit world. However, western literature demonstrates historically that ghosts and spirits were part of the western mindset. We need only to think of such Shakespearian tragedies as *Hamlet* or *Macbeth*, Christopher Marlowe's *Faust*, or the fiction of Edgar Allen Poe, Stephen King, and Anne Rice, while a biographical novel such as Carlo Levi's *Christ Stopped at Eboli* suggests that, in the first part of the twentieth century at least, peasants of southern Italy were far more attuned to the popular religion of gnomes and spells than to the high theology of the Catholic Church.[3] Furthermore, the popularity of films such *The Exorcist* (1973), *The Witches of Eastwick* (1986), *Angel Heart* (1987), *Ghost* (1989), *Stigmata* (1999), or *The Exorcism of Emily Rose* (2005) likewise attest to the ongoing enthusiasm of contemporary westerners for entering, even if only in a voyeuristic fashion, into the spirit world.

Demons and spirit possession also figure in the lyrics of jazz and country and western tunes, as well as the work of other pop music artists such as Charlie Daniels, Ma-

3. Carlo Levi, *Christ Stopped at Eboli: The Story of a Year* (New York: Time Life Education, 1982). Levi was exiled by Italy's Fascist government in 1935 to a remote village in Calabria. *Christ Stopped at Eboli* evokes the pre-Christian mentality of the region's peasant population.

donna, The Rolling Stones, Van Halen, Fatboy Slim, Beth Orton, The Allman Brothers, Macy Gray, various contemporary Christian rock groups, and any number of heavy metal bands. While some might dismiss these examples as expressions of profit-driven popular culture, they have also made indelible marks on people of all ages, in many countries around the world. Those lasting impressions would not have been possible were there not some residue of ancient beliefs in the world of spirits, even among the most rational voyeurs.

The growing contemporary interest in spirit possession prompted eleven past and present faculty members of The University of Auckland's School of Theology, along with two of the School's recent post-graduate students, to offer essays that in some way explored the reality of spirit possession in Oceania today. Authors were chosen because of their particular research, teaching, or ministry competencies, and this explains the division of the book into three sections. The first section draws on the experiences of those engaged in pastoral ministry with people who believe they are possessed, or those whose particular research interests are the relationship of faith, culture, and praxis. In the second section, the function and place of spirit language in the biblical texts is examined, while the last section's focus is somewhat broader, addressing some of the historical responses to spirit possession, as well as emerging pneumatologies of good and bad spirits and their impact on the human condition.

The Spirit World in a Pacific Context

Following the introduction by Elaine Wainwright, Head of the School of Theology, the first essay in the body of this collection was chosen not only because of its emphasis on personal experiences with spirit possession, but also because it is written by a highly respected *kaumatua* (elder) from Aotearoa's indigenous community. This placement reflects the commitment of the School of Theology to biculturalism and contextual theology, and the 'pride of place' given to those whose forebears were already living in this land before the European sailors and Christian missionaries arrived.

Henare 'Pa' Tate writes with passion about the mysteries of dealing with the spirit world when it manifests itself, particularly among Māori. He discusses some of the ways that spirits make their presence known, the ways in which their departure can be measured, and how they should be approached in-between. His focus is not on 'fixing things'; rather he adopts a relational stance, in which the desires of the present spirit/s can be known. Tate is neither narcissistic nor overly-confident about his abilities to deal with the spirit world. He relies on his deep faith as a Roman Catholic priest, combined with his lifelong knowledge of the rich and complex variety and expectations of Māori culture. What is striking about this opening essay, as well as the ones which immediately follow it, is that Tate finds no inherent conflict between the world of indigenous spirituality and mental health, and the Catholic faith in which he was carefully trained. This ability to hold two worlds in dialogue with each other is a significant marker of contextual theology.[4]

Philip Culbertson and Mary Caygill, both practical theologians within the School of Theology, do what practical theologians are expected to do: enter into dialogue with other disciplines—in this case, Pasifika anthropology. But as well, their contribution to this volume is unique in that it employs a qualitative research methodology, wherein Samoans and Tongans with direct experience of the world of Pacific spirits have been interviewed and then quoted in the essay in their own words. While this type of research methodology is presumed within Practical Theology, it tends to be less common in the other theological disciplines.

Culbertson and Caygill's article makes it clear that the indigenous world of spirits is very alive and well among the older generations of island-born Tongans and Samoans. Sadly, the younger, New Zealand-born generations are losing touch with this traditional world. Older generations hold this ancient world in tension with the teachings of the church about both the Holy Spirit and 'evil' spirits, and the essay, in places, illustrates the ambiguity which causes the interviewees to sometimes confuse the two. Older Pacific Islanders, on the whole, are appreciative of what the missionaries brought to them, and have been able to establish a devout and syncretic faith. This is one of the major challenges of contextual theology in the Pacific, to be able to find ways not to 'hide' their indige-

4. See Stephen Bevans, *Models of Contextual Theology* (Maryknoll: Orbis, 2002).

nous, pre-contact spirituality from the eyes of the Church, but rather to let both traditions affirm each other. Because Christ and Culture have been so interwoven with each other in some areas, but not in others, one of the tasks of Pacific contextual theology is how to unravel the relationship between the two. On the whole, addressing these two sometimes-complementary, sometimes-antagonistic traditions is a task only recently begun among theologians who are themselves Pacific-born.

Ann Nolan's essay addresses the tension between the Cartesian-informed scientism of modern psychiatry, and the holistic belief systems of Pacific Islanders. Those who are in touch with the indigenous spirit world of Oceania are often diagnosed by western psychiatrists as 'delusional', and treatment plans rarely take notice of the holism of mind, spirit, body, and relationships that informs Pacific identity.

But certain Christian approaches to healing can be equally ignorant. Churches often do not treat people holistically either, splitting the troubled spirit from the mind, body, and relation systems. From a holistic point of view, broken relationships, ill health, and the experiencing of visions all may signal the inbreaking of the spirit world into everyday lives, but for the spirits' needs and message to be recognised, relationships must be investigated, the physical body diagnosed, mental processes unravelled, and spiritual health assessed. None can be treated apart from the others.

Repeated recent calls for as more holistic approach to be taken seem to have little impact on the medical and psychiatric communities of New Zealand. As Nolan points out, such calls have come from many quarters, including a number of documents sponsored by New Zealand governmental departments, and yet the holistic treatment that Pacific people so desire is too rarely available. As one research participant stated:

> It is not that the hospital is of no use. The work of the hospital with regards to the treatment of physical illnesses is important. The problem arises where there is a need for holistic treatment, and this is not undertaken . . . This is true of the treatment for mental unwellness where doctors have separated the whole into three parts, treating only the physical. You cannot divide a Samoan person because if my mind is unwell, everything else becomes unwell.[5]

Theology, and both medicine and psychiatry, have a long history of complicated struggles for power and authority over each other. In the interests of a well-being that extends across a variety of individualistic and communal cultures, a conversation among these disciplines about the spirit world and holism is long overdue.

Winston Halapua, a Tongan clergyperson with long working experience in Fiji, brings a voice to this collec-

5. Kiwi Tamasese and others, '*Ole Taeao Afua,* the New Morning: A Qualitative Investigation into Samoan Perspectives on Mental Health and Culturally Appropriate Services', in *Australian and New Zealand Journal of Psychiatry* 39 (2005): 305.

tion of essays that is deeply informed by cultures of both Polynesia and Melanesia. In keeping with these cultures and their communal nature, Halapua offers an analysis of spirit possession that is embedded in relationality: the relationships of family, kinship, village, class, culture, and environment. Echoing some of the themes highlighted by Culbertson and Caygill, Halapua understands that spirit possession affects, and is treated by, whole groups of people whose identity is interwoven. And these relationships are in turn embedded in land, ocean, and all creation. His exploration of a 'lens' which is both theologically and psychologically sound is a significant contribution to the scope of this volume. His moana hermeneutic of well-being speaks to both international and oceanic contexts, and in that sense, his work too is an expression of the foci of Practical Theology. His holistic 'creationism', emphasising how interdependent God, humanity, earth, and ocean are, is in many ways reminiscent of the work of American theologian Matthew Fox, in that Halapua explores the expansive creativity in which God and humanity meet.

Each of these four essays reflects the important role of culture in determining what we see, how we think, and where and how we find God at work. Yet, even writing about culture in Aotearoa New Zealand, with its multicultural make-up, means that great care must be taken. Who has the right and authority to define what Māori culture is and is not? 'Who, for and/or against whom, defines *fa'a Samoa* and *vaka-i-taukei*? What non-native values and concerns have assimilated into, and co-opted, those definitions? What native cultural differences are silenced, ignored, and/or homogenised in order for those definitions to delimit? In whose interests?'[6] These are significant issues, already familiar to anthropologists of the Pacific, which must be taken into account when discussing the spirit world of Oceania. The differences between the many cultures present in 'our sea of islands'[7] must not be glossed over. Nor must the differences between the many religious cultures among the writers and readers of this volume—Catholic, Anglican, Baptist, Methodist, and otherwise—be glossed over. To do so would be to do a disservice to the spirits themselves.

As Susan Smith points out later in the book, much of the growing edge of Christianity in Aotearoa New Zealand is among the indigenous populations of the Pacific Ocean, as well as migrants from the Pacific Rim. These new Christians bring with them a very different sense of the spirit world than is traditional to western theology, or what Musa Dube calls 'The Theology of the Empire'.[8] For much of the past two millennia, Christian theology, intentional colonisation, and western imperialism have been 'joined at the hip'. Māori, Tongan, Samoan, and other Oceanic theologians are beginning to challenge the traditionally colonial forms of Christian theology, calling instead for new theologians to arise among the Pacific

6. Jione Havea, 'Would the Real Native Please Sit Down!' In *Faith in a Hyphen: Cross-Cultural Theologies Down Under*, edited by Clive Pearson (Adelaide: Openbook Publishers, 2004), 201.
7. Epeli Hau'ofa, 'Our Sea of Islands', in *A New Oceania: Rediscovering Our Sea of Islands*, edited by E Waddell, V Naidu, and E Hau'ofa (Suva: University of the South Pacific, 1993), 2–16.
8. Musa W Dube, *Postcolonial Feminist Interpretation of the Bible* (St Louis: Chalice Press, 2000), especially chapter 8.

populations to articulate theologies which are more contextual and more informed about the centuries-old traditions indigenous to the 'sea of islands', traditions which long pre-date the arrival of the Christian missionaries. These emerging theologians are asking for theologies which respect Pacific ancestors, cultural values, holistic wisdom, and the ancient 'baskets of knowledge'[9] or 'the languages of life'.[10] African critic Achille Mbembe points out how difficult it seems to be for the western political and philosophical [and theological] worlds to grant credibility to indigenous wisdom, experience, and the right to self-determination:

> . . . as a general rule, the experience of the Other, of the *problem of the 'I' of others and of human beings we perceive as foreign to us*, has almost always posed virtually insurmountable difficulties to the Western philosophical and political tradition. Whether dealing with Africa or with other non-European worlds, this tradition long denied the existence of any 'self' but its own.[11]

9. Rāwiri Taonui, 'Ranginui—The Sky', *Te Ara: The Encyclopedia of New Zealand,* updated 21-Sep-2007, http://www.TeAra.govt.nz/EarthSeaAndSky/Astronomy/RanginuiTheSky/en (accessed May 27, 2008).
10. Achille Mbembe, *On the Postcolony* (Berkeley: University of California Press, 2001), 15.
11. Mbembe, *Postcolony*, 2.

The challenge to Practical Theology, of which these four essays are a splendid representation, is to craft non-colonising Christian theological statements in a way that is respectful of the experience and wisdom that is and has been resident in the Pacific, since long before the missionaries and other outsiders arrived.

The Spirit World of the Bible

A pair of First Testament scholars, Keith Stuart and Alice Sinnott, offer contrasting interpretations of the *Book of Tobit* in their examination of a spirit-inhabited world. Sinnott explores the reality of empowerment by good spirits, symbolised by Raphael. She then demonstrates how the English author Salley Vickers' 2000 novel, *Miss Garnet's Angel*, focuses attention not only on the presence of evil or demonic spirits in the world, but more noticeably on the presence of good spirits or angels, who like Raphael, are there to accompany human persons on their often difficult life journeys. This approach is very Catholic, given that tradition's belief in the presence of angels and of guardian angels who are there to protect us, and offers an alternative perspective from the more usual depiction of the presence of evil spirits out to possess and dominate human beings. Her paper signals that spirits can be helpful, rather than overpowering or diminishing human dignity.

Like the *Book of Tobit, Miss Garnet's Angel* opens with a description of a diminished character. Miss Garnet, a retired school teacher, is diminished by the death of her friend with whom she has shared a home for some thirty years, and implicitly by her enthusiasm for communism, an ideology which is no longer life-giving, and which denies the individual her dignity and freedom. Vickers attributes a parabolic quality to *Tobit,* as the choices open to Tobit and Tobias are analogous to the choices that face all of us. *Tobit* and *Miss Garnet's Angel* allow contemporary readers to examine their own life choices in respect of good or evil, life or death. Thus, when Miss Garnet arrives in Venice to re-start her shattered life, she is drawn to the Guardi panels in the Chiesa dell' Angelo Raffaele which graphically portray both the interior journey of Tobit, and the geographical journey of his son Tobias which also takes on the character of an inner journey. Tobit and Tobias' movement from diminishment of life to fullness of life occurs through the active agency of the good spirit, the angel Raphael. Sinnott succeeds in focussing attention on the links between an ancient text and a twenty-first century novel, so that both can speak to the contemporary reader. Her intertextual approach to a pre-Christian and post-Christian text is indeed rewarding.

Keith Stuart, on the other hand, offers an interpretation of the Book of Tobit which highlights the role of evil spirits in the ancient world, as well as in the contemporary world. In the latter instance, the spirits are less understood as an extra-terrestrial reality, and more understood as the collective spirit of a group which seems to diminish human freedom in some way. In making this assertion, Stuart draws on his experience in a Catholic charismatic youth group, wondering whether he was the victim of a group process which sought to control his life.

Although Stuart states that his purpose is to use a sociological approach to the text, he has complemented this with a historical-critical approach, as his bibliography makes clear. He rightly argues that the literary form of *Tobit* is that of a novella which explores how diasporic Jews living in the Hellenistic world should respond to the debilitating effects of the constant assaults on their culture and religion. In *Tobit,* negative responses to this impact manifest themselves as illness in the case of Tobit, death in the case of Sarah's seven husbands, and powerlessness in the case of Sarah. He argues that the powerlessness of Sarah to overcome the death-dealing activities of Asmodeus is linked to her low social status. This insight warrants further development through considering Sarah's social status as a woman without a husband, and as a colonised person, given that implicit in Tate's paper and explicit in Wainwright's is the linking of spirit possession to marginalisation.

Both Sinnott and Stuart's bad and good spirits are personalised and given names in the biblical text. Given the predilection of Christian fundamentalists to attribute historicity to such biblical characters, it would seem that the historicity or non-historicity of such biblical characters could emerge as a subject for conversation and further exploration among liberal and evangelical Christians and First Testament scholars.

Elaine Wainwright's essay, like Stuart's, emphasises the marginalised character of persons judged by society as being possessed by an evil spirit. She locates a philosophical foundation for her approach in the Algerian Franz Fanon's 1963 publication, *The Wretched of the Earth,* and its analysis of the psycho-social dynamics of the colonisation process. Wainwright argues that the oppression experienced by the colonised is symbolised in Mark's gospel by the demonic possession of the oppressed and marginalised in Palestinian society. In her interpretation of the possessed man in the country of the Gerasenes (Mark 5:1–20), Wainwright suggests that the man's conflicted state points to the conflicted nature of first century colonised Palestine, a society in which some of the groups that made up Israelite society, such as the priestly class, were happy enough to be co-opted by the Roman authorities to assist in the governance of the people, while others, such as the Zealots, actively resisted such a line of action. But most of the citizenry, as Mark's narrative makes clear, simply suffered.

Disturbances in mental health continue to be characteristic of many colonised peoples today. In Aotearoa New Zealand, the co-leader of the Māori Party, and former Associate Minister of Health in the Labour Government, Tariana Turia, addressing the New Zealand Psychological Society Conference in 2000, argued that the violence of colonisation had traumatised Māori to such an extent that it contributed significantly to what Pākehā referred to as dysfunctional behaviour, and which the latter mistakenly believed had its genesis in personal inadequacies.[12] Turia claimed that

---

12. Tariana Turia, 'Speech Notes', Speech to New Zealand Psychological Society Conference 2000, Waikato University, Hamilton, August 29, 2000, http://www.converge.org.nz/pma/tspeech.htm (accessed May 26, 2008).

> . . . [w]ith personal identity inextricably tied to whanau, hapu and iwi identity, indigenous people still have to counter the problems of the conspiracy of alienation, assimilation and deculturation launched against them well over a century ago. I have been accused in Parliament in the past week of indulging in 'sociological clap trap' when linking colonisation to family violence.

Wainwright's sociological analysis and post-colonial hermeneutic need to be read alongside the contributions of Tate, Halapua, Caygill, and Culbertson, all of whom examine the reality of a spirit-inhabited world in marginalised groups in Oceania. Again, the different authors are pointing to a correlation between socio-economic, cultural, and religious status, confirming the need for continuing exploration along these lines.

Spirits through the Lens of Theology and History

Systematic theologian Helen Bergin argues that all human persons have an innate yearning to achieve freedom, defined not so much as the self-fulfilment of one's personal goals in life, but as an openness and receptivity to the grace of God or God's Spirit in one's life. This receptivity also invests the search for freedom with a transcendent goal—the quest for divine mystery. Although Bergin does not quote from Augustine, she would undoubtedly resonate with Augustine's words: 'Thou hast formed us for Thyself, and our hearts are restless till they find rest in Thee'.[13] Drawing on the trinitarian theologies of Karl Rahner and Elizabeth Johnson, Bergin argues that, for a variety of reasons, peoples' capacity to search for such freedom is limited by psychological and socio-economic factors beyond their control.

From a consideration of freedom, Bergin moves to examining the meaning of the power that comes from the Spirit. Spirit-gifted power is not 'power over', but rather empowerment of the individual to strive for goodness and wholeness—in her own life and the lives of others. In fact, the human person becomes a microcosm of the cosmic struggle between the forces of good and evil. Christians would not dispute Bergin's analysis, but the challenge for theologians is how a 'high' theology can engage with other disciplines such as psychology or sociology. Medical science and psychology normally approach the problem of mental illness unaccompanied by conversations with theology. Unfortunately, such avoidance does not augur well, either for the afflicted person or for those attempting to cure or heal the illness. Many of those affected by what the theologian might name as spirit possession, and the mental health worker might name as mental illness, often are religious people, and the religious dimension characteristic of such conditions needs to be acknowledged more readily than is the case in contemporary Aotearoa New Zealand. The bi-cultural character of New Zealand government institutions means that Māori social workers

13. Augustine of Hippo. *The Confessions*, Book 1, Chapter 1.1, http://www.leaderu.com/cyber/books/augconfessions/bk1.html (accessed May 27, 2008).

and mental health workers are now more inclined to cooperate in the healing process, but this union of two different approaches needs to be expanded.

Church historian Laurie Guy offers an interesting insight into the assumed reality of evil spirits and their exorcism in his account of the central Auckland Assembly of God Church between 1970–1989, a time of social unrest in the wake of the 1960s social revolutions that had rocked much of the western world. Guy is right to emphasise that churches with a narrow agenda of spiritual healing and glossalia are likely to surface in such times. Because he writes as an historian rather than a psychologist, he does not attempt to demonstrate why the 1970s saw such a significant increase in the number of New Zealanders whose religious lives were dominated by a fear of spirit possession and who sought healing through exorcism. In times of social turmoil, some people seek a return to a simpler, more orthodox, vertical type of Christian belief, which understands the world in black and white, good and bad categories. These binary oppositions suggest that the adherents of such faith positions are locked into the lower stages of faith and moral development identified by the theologian James Fowler and psychologist Eric Kohlberg, who both drew on the cognitive development schema of Swiss theorist Jean Piaget. That this phenomenon occurred at the same time that the mainline churches—Anglican, Catholic, Methodist and Presbyterian for example—were increasingly seeking to involve their membership in gospel-driven social action programmes merits future exploration.

In wrapping up the main body of this collection, Susan Smith's essay echoes some of the themes touched upon earlier, particularly by the four writers in the first section of the book, 'The Spirit World in a Pacific Context'. As in the case of Henare Tate's essay, Smith too has had some direct personal experience with spirit possession, in the Pacific as well as internationally. While anchoring her remarks in an a careful critique of Scripture, and the patristic and Vatican traditions, she points out, via the writings of American theologian Paul Hiebert and Chinese theologian Hwa Yung, that many Christians outside the western church believe in the on-going interaction between the physical and spiritual worlds.

Smith's essay ends with a bold challenge, for the Catholic Church to engage in a 'wider ecumenism' with indigenous traditions, and with Pentecostals and Evangelicals for whom spirit possession and healing have had a much greater significance. The spiritual hunger of 'majority world Christians' is not easily met by classical historical or systematic theologies. Often, the insistence on shaping indigenous Christians to meet the pre-determined needs of these classical disciplines produces a form of cultural and contextual schizophrenia, in which the world of the Church and the world of the spirits are held apart, or hidden, from each other, or the various Christians theologies become barriers to each other, denying Christ's own wish that 'all may be one' (John 17:21). In addition to learning to dialogue about these issues with sociologists, anthropologists, psychiatrists and psychologists, medical and mental health professionals, the artists of popular culture, and the people of the many and varied indigenous cultures throughout the world, Christians need to learn, again, to dialogue with each other.

As the different papers in this book make apparent, the phenomenon of the spirit world is impinging more and more on popular consciousness. This volume represents an attempt to understand more of this reality from a theological perspective, given theology's traditional interest in good and bad spirits. But other disciplines also need to engage in conversations about the diverse human beliefs in spirits. In supposedly secular societies like that of Aotearoa New Zealand, disciplines such as psychology or anthropology may in fact be somewhat dismissive of theology as a dialogue partner, but such a conversation is imperative, particularly given the impact of new migrant congregants on the older Pākehā churches, or the increasing number of people from non-white cultures who are seeking counselling. Similarly, sociology also has something important to contribute, as little work has been done in identifying how gender, ethnic, and socio-economic status correlate with spirit possession. Nor has there been any significant examination as to the incidence of spirit possession among different religious groupings—for example, is demonic possession more or less likely to occur among Catholics and Anglicans than in Pentecostal communities?

There are good pastoral and theological reasons for pursuing these conversations within the Church, but it is also important that theologians and ministers engage with their colleagues from other disciplines, as it would seem that the reality of belief in a spirit world is going to impact increasingly on peoples' lives into the future.

Bibliography

Augustine of Hippo. *The Confessions,* Book 1, Chapter 1.1, http://www.leaderu.com/cyber/books/augconfessions/bk1.html (accessed May 13, 2008).

Bevans, Stephen. *Models of Contextual Theology* (Maryknoll: Orbis, 2002).

Dube, Musa W. *Postcolonial Feminist Interpretation of the Bible* (St Louis: Chalice Press, 2000).

Hau'ofa, Epeli. 'Our Sea of Islands', in *A New Oceania: Rediscovering Our Sea of Islands,* edited by E Waddell, V Naidu, and E Hau'ofa (Suva: University of the South Pacific, 1993), 2–16.

Havea, Jione. 'Would the Real Native Please Sit Down!', in *Faith in a Hyphen: Cross-Cultural Theologies Down Under,* edited by Clive Pearson (Adelaide: Openbook Publishers, 2004), 199–210..

Jenkins, Philip. *The Next Christendom: The Coming of Global Christianity* (New York: Oxford University Press, 2002).

Kraft, Charles H. *Christianity with Power: Your Worldview and Your Experience of the Supernatural* (Ann Arbor, MI: Servant Publications, 1989).

Levi, Carlo. *Christ Stopped at Eboli: The Story of a Year* (New York: Time Life Education, 1982).

Mbembe, Achille. *On the Postcolony* (Berkeley: University of California Press, 2001).

Nietzsche, Friedrich Wilhelm. *The Gay Science,* Book 4, 1882. In *The Encarta Book of Quotations,* edited by Bill Swainson (New York: St. Martin's Press, 2000).

Tamasese, Kiwi, Carmel Peteru, Charles Waldegrave, and Allister Bush. 'Ole Taeao Afua, the New Morning: A Qualitative Investigation into Samoan Perspectives on

Mental Health and Culturally Appropriate Services', in *Australian and New Zealand Journal of Psychiatry* 39 (2005): 300–309.

Taonui, Rāwiri. 'Ranginui—The Sky', *Te Ara: Encyclopedia of New Zealand*, updated 21-Sep-2007, http://www.TeAra.govt.nz/EarthSeaAndSky/Astronomy/RanginuiTheSky/en (accessed May 12, 2008).

Turia, Tariana. 'Speech Notes', Speech to New Zealand Psychological Society Conference 2000, Waikato University, Hamilton, August 29, 2000, http://www.converge.org.nz/pma/tspeech.htm (accessed May 13, 2008).

List of Contributors

Helen Bergin is a Dominican woman religious who teaches adult education within the Catholic Institute of Theology in Auckland, as well as courses in systematic theology within the School of Theology at the University of Auckland. Her areas of research include the Holy Spirit and the writings of Edward Schillebeeckx.

Mary Caygill is an ordained Methodist minister currently living and working in Auckland in the dual positions of being Principal of Trinity Methodist Theological College and Lecturer in Theology at the University of Auckland. She has a background in nursing, health, social work, and community development. Her research interests include the Theology of Embodiment, the interface between Critical Disability Studies and Disability Theology, along with the relationship between spirituality and well-being.

Philip Culbertson is an ordained Episcopal priest who recently semi-retired after fifteen years of teaching theology in Auckland. At present, he is Adjunct Lecturer in Theology at the University of Auckland, and a copy-editor for a major US religious publishing house. He resides now in Palm Springs, California. His research interests include contextual theology, practical theology, gender and sexuality studies, Pasifika cultures, and the relationship between psychotherapy and spirituality.

Laurie Guy is vice-principal (academic) of Carey Baptist College in Auckland, and lectures there and in the Tyndale-Carey Graduate School in church history. His research specialises in church and society interactions in New Zealand.

Winston Halapua is Principal of the College of the Diocese of Polynesia at St John's Theological College in Auckland, a lecturer in the School of Theology at the University of Auckland, and the Anglican Bishop for the Diocese of Polynesia in Aotearoa New Zealand. His research interests include poverty, marginalisation, militarism, leadership, theology, and social ecology.

Ann M Nolan has been employed as a medical social worker in the Auckland District Health Board for twenty-six years. Over the past twelve years, she has been engaged in completing higher degrees in theology and philosophy. Her philosophical interests include the philosophy of mysticism, phenomenology of religion, and ethics. Her theological interests and research include medieval mysticism, the history of dialogue, the writings of Martin Buber, Edith Stein, the Second Vatican Council 1962–65, and theological ethics.

Alice M Sinnott, a Sister of Mercy, is currently lecturing in Biblical Studies at the School of Theology at the University of Auckland, and at the Catholic Institute of Theology. Her research interests include Colin McCahon's Biblical Interpretations, The Book of Ruth in Art, God as Creator in the Bible, and Speaking about God Today.

Susan Smith is a Sister of Our Lady of the Missions, who retired from lecturing at the University of Auckland in 2006, although she is still involved with the School of Theology as a supervisor, author, and editor. Her current research interests include Missiology and the New Testament, and she is involved in teaching in the Asian provinces of her religious congregation.

Keith Stuart is currently an Archivist in the central North Island. His research interest in Second Temple Jewish literature began when he was a member of the Franciscan order. He has worked as a counsellor in the fields of HIV/AIDS and drug abuse. Prior to training as an archivist, Keith worked as an adult educator in the health sector. He returned to study at Auckland University and completed a Masters in Biblical Literature in 2002.

Henare Tate is an ordained Catholic Māori priest who has recently retired from the Auckland School of Theology after eighteen years of involvement in teaching Māori Theology and Spirituality. He is retiring to Motuti in Hokianga, but will continue some form of teaching of Māori Theology. He is a member of the Catholic Institute of Theology in Auckland. He will continue to facilitate the Continuing Faith Education programmes in Māori Theology and Spirituality. He is about to present his PhD thesis to the Melbourne College of Divinity, entitled 'Towards some foundations of a Systematic Māori Theology'. He regularly presents an iwi-based programme called 'The Dynamics of Whanaungatanga'.

Elaine M Wainwright is Professor of Theology and Head of the School of Theology at the University of Auckland. She is a New Testament scholar with research interests in hermeneutics and healing, and is currently engaged in an ecological reading of the Gospel of Matthew.

CPSIA information can be obtained
at www.ICGtesting.com
Printed in the USA
BVHW070013220920
589338BV00001B/76

9 781921 511639